CASE STUDIES ON
EDUCATIONAL
ADMINISTRATION

CASE STUDIES ON EDUCATIONAL ADMINISTRATION

SECOND EDITION

Theodore J. Kowalski

Ball State University

 **Longman** *Publishers USA*

**Case Studies on Educational Administration,
Second Edition**

Longman, 10 Bank Street, White Plains, N.Y. 10606

Associated companies:
Longman Group Ltd., London
Longman Cheshire Pty., Melbourne
Longman Paul Pty., Auckland
Copp Clark Longman Ltd., Toronto

Acquisitions editor: Virginia L. Blanford
Development editor: Virginia L. Blanford
Production editor: Linda Moser/Books By Design
Cover design: Pompeo Design
Production supervisor: Richard Bretan

Library of Congress Cataloging-in-Publication Data
Kowalski, Theodore J.
    Case studies on educational administration / by Theodore J.
Kowalski. — 2nd ed.
        p.   cm.
    Includes bibliographical references and index.
    ISBN 0-8013-1422-4
    1. School management and organization—United States—Case
studies.
LB2805.K63   1994
371.2'00973—dc20

94-1359
CIP

BK
$ 4|40

1 2 3 4 5 6 7 8 9 10-CRS-9897969594

Contents

Preface

Initiatives to restructure schools have produced an array of weighty questions about the future practice of school administrators. To what extent will administrators be expected to be leaders rather than managers? How will decentralization affect the duties of principals and superintendents? How will the work lives of administrators change if teachers finally achieve the status of true professionals? Such queries are central to current efforts to revise both the instructional process and the curricula of professional preparation programs.

Case Studies on Educational Administration, Second Edition is a tool that can play a meaningful role in helping to prepare the next generation of educational leaders. Case studies provide an excellent vehicle for bridging theory with practice; but beyond this attribute, they also create opportunities for developing skills in critical thinking, problem solving, decision making, and reflective practice. All of these elements have assumed added importance in a world where each year change occurs more rapidly.

The cases in this book present a range of problems encountered by contemporary practitioners in the school and school district. On page vii there is a matrix that links the cases to these important educational issues. None of the cases is taken to its conclusion so that you can assume the role of decision maker. This format has many advantages with respect to critical thinking and problem solving. Decisions can be interfaced with your professional knowledge and previous experiences. In essence, as you use this book, you will be practicing reflection as well as honing your leadership skills.

My thanks go to the many administrators who provided information regarding the cases, to my colleagues in the Department of Educational Leadership at Ball State University for their insights, and to the students in my doctoral seminars who offered suggestions for improving the book.

My thanks, too, to the many professors of educational leadership who shared their experiences using case studies and offered comments about the structure of the book. I am especially grateful to the following individuals, who reviewed the manuscript and provided constructive criticisms and insightful recommendations:

Fred Carver, University of Georgia
Edward Chance, University of Oklahoma
Gene Gallegos, California State University at Bakersfield
Sandra Gray, Southwest Missouri State University
James Guthrie, University of California at Berkeley
Richard Hatley, University of Missouri at Columbia
Larry Hughes, University of Houston
Ned Lovell, Mississippi State University
Marcelle Lovett, University of North Florida
Ulysses Spiva, Old Dominion University
Kenneth Washington, University of Massachusetts
Kathryn Whitaker, University of North Colorado

Matrix of Topics by Case Number

Topics	1	2	3	4	5	6	7	8	9	10	11	12	13	14	15	16	17	18	19	20	21	22	23
Administrator-Teacher Relationships	•	•		•		•	•		•	•		•				•	•	•		•			•
Business Management						•											•						•
Careers (Career Development)			•		•		•													•		•	
Central Office Administration	•	•		•	•		•	•	•							•	•	•	•	•			•
Change	•		•	•		•	•	•	•	•			•			•			•	•	•	•	•
Communication	•	•		•	•	•	•	•	•		•			•	•		•	•	•	•	•	•	•
Conflict and Conflict Resolution	•	•		•	•	•	•	•	•		•					•	•			•	•	•	•
Culture and Climate of Schools		•		•	•		•	•					•									•	•
Decentralized Governance								•	•							•						•	•
Decision Making				•	•	•	•	•	•	•	•			•	•		•	•		•	•		•
Ethical/Moral Issues	•			•	•			•		•	•	•		•				•		•	•	•	•
Gender Issues in Administration	•			•						•				•						•	•		•
Instruction/Curriculum Issues	•			•	•	•	•			•						•	•	•				•	•
Interpersonal Relations		•		•	•	•	•	•	•	•	•		•	•		•			•				•
Leadership Style		•		•	•		•	•	•	•			•	•	•	•					•	•	•
Leadership Theory		•		•	•	•		•	•	•						•							•
Legal Issues				•			•	•	•	•	•	•	•					•	•		•		•
Organizational Theory	•	•																					•
Outcomes of Education						•	•					•	•							•	•	•	•
Philosophy		•	•		•	•	•	•	•	•	•					•		•					•
Policy Development/Analysis	•	•	•	•			•				•		•	•	•		•	•	•	•	•	•	•
Politics and Political Behavior	•	•	•				•	•			•		•	•		•	•	•	•	•	•	•	•
Power, Use by Administrators		•		•	•		•	•						•									•
Principalship	•			•	•					•	•	•		•				•					•
Public Relations (Community Relations)	•		•						•	•								•		•	•	•	•
Role Theory	•																		•	•	•		
School Boards	•		•																•	•		•	•
School Reform	•		•			•		•	•							•	•						•
Shared Governance (Group Decisions)								•	•	•													•
Site-Based Management							•									•							•
Socialization			•		•														•	•	•		
Student Discipline (Student Services)										•		•						•	•	•			•
Superintendency	•									•		•		•	•	•				•			
Teacher Professionalization		•		•	•	•				•							•	•				•	•
Teacher Unions (Collective Bargaining)		•		•					•	•						•							
Work Conditions (Job Satisfaction, Stress)			•										•	•	•					•	•		•

Introduction

In the varied topography of professional practice, there is a high hard ground overlooking the swamp. On the high ground, manageable problems lend themselves to solutions through the application of research-based theory and technique. In the swampy lowland, messy, confusing problems defy technical solution.

(Donald Schon, 1990, p. 3)

In the late 1980s, the National Policy Board on Educational Administration (1989) called for sweeping changes in the professional preparation of school administration. In part, such recommendations came in response to several earlier reform documents that criticized principals and superintendents for lacking vision, planning skills, and leadership qualities. But those who attempt to raise the quality of professional preparation face several unique conditions. For example, there is no standardized national curriculum in school administration that universities follow; practitioners and professors do not always agree on the types of improvements that are needed (Kowalski & Reitzug, 1993).

Nevertheless, two glaring realities direct the study of school administration. First, most degree candidates in this specialization aspire to become principals or school-district administrators. In their courses, they often are joined by practitioners who periodically return to the university to update their knowledge and skills. As a result, most of the individuals enrolled in organized academic programs aspire to become practitioners of this specialization in elementary and secondary schools.

Second, there has been a long-standing myth that school administrators are divided into two camps: those who see the profession dominated by theory and those who see the profession dominated by practical management issues. Few administrators today do not accept the premise that both theoretical constructs (especially those focusing on organizational behavior and leadership) and technical skills (especially those focusing on managerial responsibilities) are essential. The real challenges of professional education are (1) to meld theory and practice and (2) to prepare practitioners to effectively use the process of *reflection* (a process of integrating professional knowledge with experience to create a modified knowledge base).

Schon (1983) aptly noted that practitioners in virtually all professions in contemporary society often become bewildered because the technical skills they acquired in academic preparation are no longer sufficient to assure effectiveness. This is true because effectiveness entails the ability to apply professional knowledge in the context of changing environmental and organizational conditions. Imagine a physician who graduated from medical school 25 years ago but who has failed to keep current with advances in technology, prescription drugs, or surgical procedures. This person's knowledge and skills, although accurate, are severely limited by the contexts of modern medicine and modern surgical procedures. Hence, the physician has accurate knowledge of anatomy and body chemistry but does not know about contemporary tools such as laser surgery.

School administrators face similar conditions. Just over the past 10 to 15 years, changes in demographics, the economy, and the political structure have altered the nature of many communities. In that same period, advances in learning theory, technology, and planning procedures have changed schools. Just consider how modern information systems create a whole new world for technologically advanced schools. Can one truly expect that a principal will remain effective without engaging in lifelong learning? As with other professionals, the decision-making processes of administrators are affected by existing conditions in which they work (Estler, 1988).

THE USE OF REFLECTION

If educational administration is to exist as a profession, its practitioners must possess (1) a theoretical base for practice, (2) technical skills required to perform managerial responsibilities, and (3) the ability to engage in reflective practice—the process by which the practitioner integrates knowledge, skills, and experience. Schon (1990) differentiated between "knowing-in-action" and "reflection-in-action." The former is embedded in the socially and institutionally structured context shared by members of a given profession. The latter represents a form of artistry that is especially critical when conditions are less than rational. If needs, motivations, and behaviors in schools were completely predictable, the application of professional knowledge would suffice. But in the real world of practice, artistry (a quality developed by refining professional knowledge on the basis of experience) often separates effective administrators from their peers.

Reflection is not a process one acquires naturally. It can and should be learned in professional preparation. In teacher education, clinical experiences have long been an integral part of the curriculum, but only in the past few years has there been an emphasis on using these opportunities to apply acquired knowledge to teach students how to reflect as professionals. Doyle (1985) observed the following:

> For clinical experience to be fruitful in developing appropriate knowledge structures, however, beginning teachers must receive descriptive, analytical feedback about performance. In other words, the clinical program must include experience and an opportunity to reflect upon the meaning of the experience. (p. 33)

The degree holder in educational administration should be thoroughly practiced in theoretical reflection, philosophical inquiry, research, and history, as well as prepared in the areas of administrative and technical practice. The graduate experience should emphasize the theoretical dimensions of practice, the historical roots of school administration practice, and research instead of the simple transmission of techniques. One of the most essential tasks for professors of educational leadership is the effective bridging of theories with established craft knowledge. To do this, professors must devote more attention to the application of knowledge. Students must be prepared to incorporate reflection into their leadership practices.

Case Studies on Educational Administration, Second Edition focuses on one proven method of associating academic study with the real world of school administration—the case study. Reports on educational reform in the 1980s accurately cited the need for the infusion of reality into preparation programs for educators (e.g., Task Force on Teaching as a Profession, 1986). As noted, these recommendations are not novel; they reinforce what studies of practitioners already indicated. In an interview regarding needed improvements in the preparation of professional educators, noted researcher Lee Shulman stated it this way:

> I'd like to see much greater use of cases, much like what is done in law and business education. That might reorient the teaching of teachers from the current model, which is either entirely field based, where you have little control over what goes on, or entirely classroom based, where everything is artificial. We have to create a middle ground, where problems of theory and practice can intersect in a realistic way. The genius of the case method, especially in business, is that you use realistic problems, but you can still deal with both the theoretical and the tactical aspects. (Brandt, 1988, p. 43)

Hence, one asset of the case study is that it provides a vehicle for honing the process of reflection.

DEFINING CASE STUDIES

A case is a description of an administrative situation, commonly involving a decision or problem (Erskine, Leenders, & Mauffette-Leenders, 1981). Frequently, the terms *case study* and *case method* are used interchangeably. This is an error. A case study is the general description of a situation and may have several purposes: (1) as a method of research, (2) as a method of evaluation, (3) as a method of policy studies, and (4) as a teaching method. Thus, case study refers to the narrative description of the incident, not its intended purpose. Case method, on the other hand, has specific reference to using the case studies as a teaching paradigm. More specifically, the case method entails a technique whereby the major ingredients of a case study are presented to students for the purpose of studying behaviors or problem-solving techniques.

Several other related terms may cause confusion and, thus, deserve explanation. One of these is *case work*. This term is commonly used in psychology, sociology, social work, and medicine. It connotes the development, adjustment, remedial, or corrective procedures that appropriately follow diagnosis of the causes of maladjustment. Another term is *case history*. This has reference to tracing a person, group, or organization's past (Merriam, 1988).

Unfortunately, there is no universal definition of or style for a case study; some case studies may be only a few paragraphs, while others are hundreds of pages (Immegart, 1971). As Lincoln and Guba (1985) wrote:

> . . . while the literature is replete with references to case studies and with examples of case study reports, there seems to be little agreement about what a case is. (p. 360)

Variance in case length and style is often related to their intended purpose. Cases commonly fall into one of three categories: true cases (no alterations to names, dates, organizations), disguised cases, or fictitious cases (hypothetical examples to illustrate a principle, concept, or specific set of conditions) (Matejka & Cosse, 1981).

THE CASE METHOD AS AN INSTRUCTIONAL PARADIGM

The case method technique has gained acceptance in business administration, law, and medicine. The best-known successes belong to Harvard University. There the continued emphasis on the case method in the Harvard Business School is evidenced by publications such as *Teaching and the Case Method* (Christensen, 1987). In business courses, case studies use real incidents to hone student skills with regard to problem solving, formulating and weighing alternative decisions, and assessing leadership behaviors. The acclaim surrounding the effectiveness of the Harvard Business School approach has influenced the teaching methods at a number of prominent business schools.

Essentially, case studies can serve two purposes when used as a teaching model. First, they can be employed to teach students new information, concepts, and theories. For example, the professor may attempt to teach that conflict in organizations is inevitable. When this is done, the student will deal with new knowledge through the process of induction. That is, by reading a case that exemplifies the concept, the student will note associations between certain factors. When these associations are repeated (e.g., in other cases), the student is expected to master the concept through induction. It is through this process that reflection can be taught.

Second, cases can serve as a vehicle for applying acquired knowledge and skills in specific situations. Application can serve several goals such as teaching reasoning, critical thinking, and problem-solving skills. In this respect, application also can be used to teach concepts (e.g., general problem solving), as well as skills, but the concepts are related to processes associated with leadership and management. It is through this process that reflection is reinforced.

There are two universal aspects of the case method. One is the Socratic method and the other is the presentation of selected information included in the case study (e.g., facts about individuals, facts about school districts). This information is referred to as *situational knowledge*. Each person who reads a case is exposed to the same situational knowledge. Why, then, do individuals often develop varying interpretations from the situational knowledge? The answer to this question relates to the ways that individuals process the information they obtain from reading the case. This processing is called *abstraction*. Each reader essentially filters situational knowledge through his or her own values, beliefs, experiences, and acquired knowledge. Since we do not share identical philosophies, experiences, and education, and since we do not possess equal levels of ability with regard to processing information, we tend to arrive at varying conclusions.

In studying the ways in which teachers make decisions, Shavelson and Stern (1981) observed the following:

> . . . people selectively perceive and interpret portions of available information with respect to their goals, and construct a simplified model of reality. Using certain heuristics, attributions and other psychological mechanisms, people then make judgments and decisions that carry them out on the basis of their psychological model of reality. (p. 461)

These outputs become critical to one's experiences with the case method. They explain why individuals, even experienced practitioners, do not always select the same courses of action. These outputs in the case method are referred to as *specific knowledge*.

THE USE OF CASES IN EDUCATION

Within schools of education, case studies have been used most frequently as a diagnostic tool in counseling and as a research tool. Psychologists commonly employ case histories and case work in their practices. The growing acceptance of qualitative methodology in the social sciences has magnified the value of case studies in this arena. Ethnographic research is perhaps the best known of the qualitative techniques, and the work of Yin (1984) is particularly enlightening for individuals wanting to explore case-based research. His writings describe this methodology in varying contexts, including policy analysis, public administration, community psychology and sociology, organization and management studies, and public service agencies. Both terms, *ethnography* and *case studies,* have become synonyms for qualitative research (Lancy, 1993). In the past few decades, case-based research has provided richer descriptions of the work environments of professional educators (e.g., Erickson, 1986).

However, beyond its use in psychology and research, the case study has not been a conspicuous component of graduate work in education. In school administration, similar techniques have aimed at bridging theory and practice. These have included simulations and "in-basket" programs. Even back in the mid-1950s, texts were published on case studies for educators (e.g., Hamburg, 1955; Sargent & Belisle, 1955), and some leaders in the University Council for Educational Administration (UCEA) have advocated the use of case studies and simulations for over three decades (e.g., Culbertson & Coffield, 1960; Griffiths, 1963). But the procedure never really became an integral part of professional preparation. Recent research verifies that practitioners continue to identify the lecture method of teaching as the most common instructional technique they encountered in graduate school (Witters-Churchill, 1988). Clark (1986) contended that because of the complexity of educational administration, multiple approaches ought to be used in preservice and inservice education. She noted that the traditional management approach is suitable for teaching specific tasks, but that an emphasis on information gathering, observation skills, and analytical skills is best served by other teaching paradigms designed to engage the learner more fully in the classroom activities.

USING SIMULATION AND CASES

Professional schools rely on several methods to expose students to the real world of practice. The internship is one of the most common. This segment of the curriculum is typically structured as a capstone experience, but although valuable, it does not provide early and continuous experiences permitting the graduate student to associate theory with practice and develop reflection. Recognizing this limitation, many professors are expressing an interest in alternative teaching strategies that will permit a greater infusion of reality into all coursework. *Simulation* is one such process.

Simulation is designed to create vicarious experiences for students—an approximation of the practitioner's challenges, problems, opportunities, and so forth. It is a form of teaching that can be used at all stages of professional preparation. There are two general approaches: (1) providing complete data about a given situation before requiring the student to address the problem, and (2) providing basic information sufficient to permit the student to address the problem. The former is best characterized by in-basket techniques. In this process, the student receives detailed information about a position, problem, and so forth. Often this approach requires the student to spend a great deal of time studying the documents (e.g., budgets, memoranda), and it is considered most effective when specific problem-solving skills are being addressed.

The other approach focuses on using only essential information related to a given situation. This situational knowledge can be effectively transmitted through a case study. This option is usually employed when general problem-solving skills are addressed, and it is advantageous when time parameters do not permit students to review mounds of data.

Some professionals have argued that simulation is most effective when all supporting data are used to provide an information base. This notion, however, is not universally accepted. Simulations using what Cunningham (1971) called a *nonmaterial based approach* (i.e., using only basic situational information) were proven to be successful when used with educators at the University of Chicago in the mid-1960s. In fact, Cunningham noted that he changed his own views about the necessity of detailed information after viewing the successes with simulation under these conditions. Hence, simulations and cases such as those presented here provide a powerful combination for integrating theory and practice, teaching critical thinking, developing problem-solving skills, and refining the process of reflection.

USING THEORY AS A GUIDE

There are many misconceptions about theory. Some view it as a dream representing the wishes of an individual or group. Others perceive theory to be a supposition or speculation or a philosophy (Owens, 1991). In reality theories are used to synthesize, organize, and classify facts that emerge from observations and data collections in varying situations (e.g., research studies). They are developed by interfacing data collected on the same variables as they exist in different situations and/or environments. Hoy and Miskel (1987) characterized theories in educational administration as interrelated concepts, assumptions, and generalizations that systematically describe and explain regularities in behavior.

Educational leaders have the same decision-making options available to all other types of administrators and managers. When confronted with circumstances demanding action, the individual may choose one of several behaviors (Kowalski, 1988):

1. Ignore the situation and refuse to make a decision.
2. Make a decision on the basis of instinct.
3. Get someone else to make the decision.
4. Imitate the perceived successful behavior of other practitioners.
5. Make a decision on the basis of accumulated information, which creates the likelihood that the response you choose will be effective.

Any of the first four alternatives may provide a short-term solution, but continual reliance on these options is apt to eventually create problems. The final option exhibits the choice of an educated leader. It entails the utilization of information, as well as academic and craft knowledge, to create alternative decisions (contingencies), the weighing of these alternatives, and the selection of the most suitable option given the prevailing conditions. Often theory alone is insufficient. The practitioner needs to develop problem-solving skills that permit the appropriate application of knowledge.

Among the numerous decision-making models used in administration, the best known and most widely used is probably the *rational-analytical model*. This paradigm consists of four steps: (1) defining the problem, (2) diagnosing the problem, (3) searching for alternative solutions, and (4) evaluating alternative solutions (Romm & Mahler, 1986). The case method is an excellent format for applying this and similar decision-making models. Students can complete all four stages of the rational-analytical model by reading and reacting to cases.

The cases presented in this book may be addressed using any of the decision alternatives cited here. The expectation, however, is that you will apply accumulated knowledge and theory to the situations being analyzed. This processing results in specific knowledge that provides a framework for your administrative behavior.

Is decision making a science or is it an art? Clearly, leaders who master the use of decision-making models are less prone to errors than those who try to make key decisions solely on the basis of instinct. The advantage of the rational-analytical approach is that it permits you to apply general problem-solving skills to specific situations.

Each case provides a novel set of variables affecting the choices available to you. The community, the school district, the challenge, and the individual personalities are examples of variables that must be considered in reaching decisions. When you employ theoretical constructs and technical skills to analyze the existing conditions under which a choice must be made, you are using a scientific approach to decision making. This technique is strengthened through practice as you learn to blend theoretical and craft knowledge. As you grow toward becoming a seasoned practitioner, you should become increasingly skillful in applying general problem-solving abilities to specific situations.

The evolution of literature on the topic of decision making exhibits the movement of graduate study in educational leadership from a narrow training focus on technical skills to one where behavioral studies now play a critical role. In concluding that accumulated information about decision processes was eradicating the comfort of simple solutions, Estler (1988) wrote the following:

> . . . we might replace recipes with skills in analysis of organizational dynamics and contexts. Though the ambiguities of educational decision making cannot be eliminated, they can be made more understandable and less threatening. By understanding a variety of approaches to decision making and the range of organizational conditions under which they may be applicable, the administrator can be better prepared to respond to, and even enjoy, organizational ambiguity and complexity. (p. 316)

More than any other element of graduate study in educational administration, it is the knowledge base relative to decision making that illuminates the value of infusing case studies into graduate education. Those who still contend that there are tried-and-true recipes for leadership behavior that work in all situations under all sorts of conditions are either misguided or uninformed.

THE CONTENT OF THE BOOK

This book contains 23 cases selected to exemplify the diversity of challenges in contemporary educational leadership. You should not look at any case as having a single dimension even though the title or primary focus of the material may lead you to that conclusion. The cases actually are quite intricate, with multiple foci—exactly the way problems exist in the real world of practice. For example, a case may involve conflict resolution, effective communication, power, participatory decision making, and leadership style.

The narrative format used in the cases is not uniform. Some cases are divided into sections with information about the community, school district, school, and the incident presented under subheadings. Other cases contain a great deal of dialogue. Information in the real world of practice is often neither predictable nor uniform. Variance in the way information is presented in the cases reflects the unevenness of communication that exists in school districts and schools. Although the narratives vary, the format for presenting the material that follows the description of each case is uniform. Following each case there are three components:

1. The Challenge
2. Key Issues/Questions
3. Suggested Readings

In a classroom setting, the instructor determines how these supplemental components will be utilized in conjunction with the case.

One of the goals of the case method is to help you become proficient at filtering information. The practitioner needs to learn to separate important and relevant facts from those that have little or no bearing on the problem(s). Remember, you must determine what information is most crucial to your decisions.

EFFECTIVELY PARTICIPATING IN THE CASE METHOD

Two extremely important factors already have been mentioned regarding the effective use of cases. First, information filtering permits you to isolate pertinent data needed for making a decision. Second, using accumulated information and knowledge in a systematic fashion (i.e., utilizing a decision-making model) produces more enlightened decisions. With regard to this latter point, it is important to recognize the difference between education and training. Educated persons rely on past experiences and knowledge to make behavioral choices. Training, by contrast, focuses on a prescribed response given specific conditions (e.g., repairing a television). The concept of reflective thinking is essential for professional development and constitutes one of the distinguishing features of professional practice.

Beyond information filtering and the recognition of what constitutes an educated response, it is critical to note that the case method does not seek the "one right answer." Romm and Mahler (1986) noted that this is particularly true when the cases are used in conjunction with the rational-analytical model for making decisions:

> Basing the analysis of the case on the rational-analytical decision-making model, implicitly carries the message that there are no "right" or "wrong" solutions to the case. By applying the model to cases, students realize that a case always has many problems, and the definition of one of these problems as the "main" problem is often subjective and arbitrary. They also realize that once a problem has been defined, it can have different reasons and be solved in different ways, depending on whose interests are being served or being given priority. (p. 695)

One of the valuable experiences of working with case studies entails the analysis of a multitude of potential behaviors. Cases provide an open invitation to generalize (Biddle & Anderson, 1986). Thus, creativity and imagination are encouraged. When cases are discussed in group settings (e.g., the classroom), the individual can benefit from both self-analysis and the analysis of peer behavior.

Although the educated person is expected to rely on accumulated experiences and knowledge to formulate decisions, a person's behavior is never void of values and beliefs. This reality makes the case method even more challenging and exciting. Two graduate students sharing common educational experiences may arrive at two divergent positions for a given case. Why? As noted earlier, each person develops specific knowledge through a process of abstraction. The process of abstraction can be influenced by values and beliefs, as well as one's skill level in decision making, critical thinking, and problem solving.

There is one additional dimension of the case method that is undervalued. You will work with these cases in a social context. The presence of others approximates the real world of practice. Superintendents and principals rarely make decisions in isolation. Their behavior is constantly influenced and evaluated by those in their work and community environments. In this respect, the social context of learning provided by the case method is especially relevant to school administration. Your experiences with cases permit you to grow in both the affective and cognitive domains.

FINAL WORDS OF ADVICE

Engaging in case studies requires several caveats regarding your personal behavior. First, the process is an active one. Case analysis in a classroom environment is a form of cooperative learning. To achieve maximum benefits, you need to be an active participant. Second, you should not be afraid to be candid or to take risks. You can learn from positive as well as negative decisions. Third, you should respect your classmates and try to understand their behavior. The purpose is not to judge their behavior as right or wrong; the intention is to identify professional (constructs and skills) and personal (needs and motivations) influences related to their decisions.

The observations made of experiences with the case method provide a useful resource for practice. Thus, the development of a notebook in conjunction with classroom experiences is highly advised. Although no two situations are ever identical, the general principles that are addressed in the 23 cases are likely to recur throughout your career as an educational leader.

REFERENCES

Biddle, B., & Anderson, D. (1986). Theory, methods, knowledge, and research on teaching. In M. Wittrock (Ed.), *Handbook of research on teaching* (3rd ed., pp. 230–252). New York: Macmillan.

Brandt, R. (1988). An assessment of teaching: A conversation with Lee Shulman. *Educational Leadership, 46*(3), 42–47.

Christensen, C. (1987). *Teaching and the case method.* Boston: Harvard Business School Press.

Clark, V. (1986). The effectiveness of case studies in training principals: Using the deliberative orientation. *Peabody Journal of Education, 63*(1), 187–195.

Culbertson, J., & Coffield, W. (Eds.) (1960). *Simulation in administration training.* Columbus, OH: The University Council for Educational Administration.

Cunningham, L. (1971). A powerful but underdeveloped educational tool. In D. Bolton (Ed.), *The use of simulation in educational administration* (pp. 1–29). Columbus, OH: Charles E. Merrill.

Doyle, W. (1985). Recent research on classroom management: Implications for teacher preparation. *Journal of Teacher Education, 36*(3), 31–35.

Erickson, F. (1986). Qualitative methods in research on teaching. In M. Wittrock (Ed.), *Handbook of research on teaching* (3rd ed., pp. 119–161). New York: Macmillan.

Erskine, J., Leenders, M., & Mauffette-Leenders, L. (1981). *Teaching with cases.* London, Ontario: School of Business Administration, University of Western Ontario.

Estler, S. (1988). *Decision making.* In N. Boyan (Ed.), *Handbook of research on educational administration* (pp. 305–350). New York: Longman.

Griffiths, D. (1963). The case method of teaching educational administration. *Journal of Educational Administration, 2,* 81–82.

Hamburg, M. (1955). *Case studies in elementary school administration.* New York: Bureau of Publications, Teachers College, Columbia University.

Hoy, C., & Miskel, C. (1987). *Education administration* (3rd ed.). New York: Random House.

Immegart, G. (1971). The use of cases. In D. Bolton (Ed.), *The use of simulation in educational administration* (pp. 30–64). Columbus, OH: Charles E. Merrill.

Kowalski, T. (1988). *The organization and planning of adult education.* Albany, NY: State University of New York Press.

Kowalski, T., & Reitzug, U. (1993). *Contemporary school administration: An introduction.* New York: Longman.

Lancy, D. (1993). *Qualitative research in education.* New York: Longman.

Lincoln, Y., & Guba, E. (1985). *Naturalistic inquiry.* Newbury Park, CA: Sage.

Matejka, J., & Cosse, T. (1981). *The business case method: An introduction.* Richmond, VA: Robert F. Dame.

Merriam, S. (1988). *Case research in education.* San Francisco: Jossey-Bass.

Owens, R. (1991). *Organizational behavior in education* (4th ed.). Boston: Allyn & Bacon.

Romm, T., & Mahler, S. (1986). A three-dimensional model for using case studies in the academic classroom. *Higher Education, 15*(6), 677–696.

Sargent, C., & Belisle, E. (1955). *Educational administration: Cases and concepts.* Boston: Houghton Mifflin.

Schon, D. (1990). *Educating the reflective practitioner.* San Francisco: Jossey-Bass.

Schon, D. (1983). *The reflective practitioner.* New York: Basic Books.

Shavelson, R., & Stern, P. (1981). Research on teachers' pedagogical thoughts, judgments, decisions, and behavior. *Review of Educational Research, 51*(4), 455–498.

Task Force on Teaching as a Profession (1986). *A nation prepared: Teachers for the 21st century.* New York: Carnegie Forum.

Witters-Churchill, L. (1988). *University preparation of the school administrator: Evaluations by Texas principals.* Unpublished Ph.D. thesis, Texas A & M University.

Yin, R. (1984). *Case study research.* Beverly Hills, CA: Sage.

Fear of Outcome-Based Education

BACKGROUND INFORMATION

Efforts to restructure American elementary and secondary education have illuminated the public's conflicting values and beliefs. Philosophical differences exist with regard to curricular content, as well as instructional methodology, and competing expectations often are strengthened through the voices of larger groups that are both formal (e.g., national associations) and informal (e.g., the religious right).

Historically, rigorous efforts have been made to protect public education from partisan politics, and essentially this goal has been accomplished in many parts of the country. However, education and administration are not void of political activity. Whenever individuals and groups compete for scarce resources, politically driven behavior is inevitable. For this reason, contemporary practitioners must understand (1) the dynamics of political behavior and (2) the political nature of policy development.

Perceptions that school reform is most likely at the local level—that is, at the level of the school district or school—have raised expectations that educational leaders are skilled in the process of identifying alternative solutions, evaluating those solutions, and selecting the most appropriate course of action given the unique variables of the community and school district. The importance of policy development is also linked to the ascending expectations that school districts will engage in long-range planning (Kowalski & Reitzug, 1993).

Frequently, policy decisions in elementary and secondary education relate directly to community values and beliefs. Sex education is an excellent example. School districts have frequently encountered political opposition when such programs have been recommended or implemented because parents often differ markedly in their beliefs about sex and how it should be presented to their children. This case revolves around a school reform initiative that has created a great deal of controversy—outcome-based education. In its most basic form, *outcome-based education* is a process of setting goals students are expected to achieve and teaching and reteaching until everyone meets those goals (Evans & King, 1994).

Opposition to outcome-based education has taken several forms. Some outcome-based plans have been criticized for having ambiguous and unmeasurable goals; others have been judged to have goals so broad that they water down education; others are condemned because they are seen as reducing local control; and still others are attacked because they are viewed as an attempt to have schools control student attitudes and values. This last category has raised the ire of fundamentalist groups who contend that outcome-based education is a ploy to control America's youth through political and moral indoctrination.

In this case, a superintendent attempts to implement outcome-based education in a suburban community. The negative reactions of parents become solidified when a local minister provides leadership to fight the proposed program. The minister distributes literature from national groups opposed to outcome-based education, and he and his followers attempt to dissuade individual board members from backing the superintendent's initiatives. These efforts take their toll, resulting in an erosion of support.

KEY AREAS FOR REFLECTION

1. Political dimensions of educational administration
2. School reform and implications for local policy development
3. Public criticism and its effect on educational policy
4. Procedures for implementing major policy decisions
5. Outcome-based education
6. Leadership style

THE CASE

The Community

Eagan Heights is a suburb of a major city in a mid-Atlantic state. With approximately 45,000 residents, the local government consists of a mayor and a nine-member town board. The community started to develop in the mid-1950s, and currently about 100 new homes are built each year. Even though the community initially grew in response to a need for relatively low-cost housing for workers at a local truck factory, homes built since the mid-1970s have been targeted more toward middle- and upper-middle-class families.

Housing patterns in Eagan Heights have resulted in a rather diverse community. Approximately 17 percent of the residents identify themselves as African Americans and another 4 percent as Hispanics; most of these residents have middle- or upper-middle-class incomes. About 15 percent of the families in the community reported annual incomes below $20,000, and virtually all of these were nonminority families.

The School District

Eagan Heights Community School District serves approximately 8,000 students. There are two high schools, two middle schools, and ten elementary schools. Nearly two-thirds of the schools are housed in facilities that have been either built or renovated in the past 15 years.

The district's boundaries are contiguous with the city limits of Eagan Heights. The five school board members are selected via nonpartisan elections; each serves a four-year term. Current members are as follows:

Annette Small, a social worker

Reggie Prescott, owner of a local restaurant

Sheila Evercott, a housewife

Dr. Anthony Rodriquez, a podiatrist

Peter Meckava, production-line worker at the truck factory

Board members Small, Evercott, and Meckava are serving second terms, and Prescott and Rodriquez are serving first terms. Annette Small is president of the school board.

Programming in the school district has remained rather traditional. Most residents have been satisfied with the local schools, especially when they were compared with those of the large, urban school district that lies just ten miles away. The Eagan Heights schools were seen as having fewer problems with illegal drugs, teenage pregnancies, and crime. Prior to an accreditation report three years ago, which included rather negative evaluations of the two high schools, residents rarely raised questions about the quality of education in the district. Among the major concerns emerging from this report were (1) a lack of technology being integrated into the curriculum, (2) less than rigorous graduation requirements, (3) a lack of program evaluation, and (4) below average student performance on statewide achievement tests. These assessments played a major role in the dismissal of long-term superintendent Nicholas Luman.

Rather than accept a teaching assignment, Mr. Luman opted to take an early retirement and left the the school district. After a two-month search, the board selected Dr. Ebert Jackson to be the new superintendent. He had been serving as superintendent of a 4,000-student district in New Jersey. An aggressive administrator in his mid-40s, Dr. Jackson had established a reputation as an expert in the concept of outcome-based education.

Central-Office Administration

Within two years of assuming the superintendency of Eagan Heights, Dr. Jackson had replaced all three assistant superintendents. The assistant superintendent for instruction who had served with Mr. Luman had applied for the superintendency, but when the board did not select him for an interview, he too opted for early retirement. Dr. Jackson had notified the school board that he wanted to employ Dr. Donna Price for that position. She and Dr. Jackson had worked together in New Jersey for the previous four years. The board unanimously supported his request.

The other two recently employed assistant superintendents are Walter Bridgeman, business services, and Tony Mori, administrative services. Dr. Jackson selected them after he had recommended the dismissal of their predecessors during his first year in Eagan Heights. Mr. Bridgeman had been a controller for a small construction company, and Mr. Mori had been an elementary school principal in the school district.

While serving as a superintendent in New Jersey, Dr. Jackson was viewed as a bold, innovative leader who was not afraid to take risks. Administrators in Eagan Heights quickly learned of his reputation, and they were especially mindful of stories indicating that Dr. Jackson was not very tolerant of staff members who opposed his ideas.

Dr. Jackson had come to Eagan Heights confident that he could replicate the successes he had achieved in his previous position. During his first year, he appeared before numerous civic groups to outline his goals. He consistently told the community that improvement was needed and that the first step in that direction was to determine what students really accomplished in school. His message was never challenged.

Leadership Style

Superintendent Jackson held meetings with his administrative staff once every two weeks. The three assistant superintendents and the building principals were expected to be in attendance. These meetings were structured; they started and ended at specified times; and agendas were always distributed in advance. But this somewhat rigid framework did not mean that the superintendent dominated the discussions. A good portion of every meeting was devoted to discussions of relevant issues. Dr. Jackson told his staff, "We can always read reports in advance of these meetings. Rather than consume our time listening to one person talk, these meetings offer an opportunity for open dialogue. If we can't level with each other, we can't function as a leadership team."

Administrators in Eagan Heights quickly discovered that Ebert Jackson was a good listener. This was particularly evident whenever the superintendent would ask one of them a probing question about the district or about individual schools or programs. The superintendent always gave the appearance of being a very serious person—it was rare for him to engage in idle conversation. When he asked a question, he expected an answer.

During their first year in Eagan Heights, both the superintendent and his associate, Dr. Price, visited the schools often. These visits served two purposes: (1) they provided an opportunity to become familiar with the physical facilities, and (2) they provided an opportunity to talk with principals privately. During the visits, principals were usually asked about specific school goals, programs, and problems. Some principals were intimidated by these encounters. They were not accustomed to having the superintendent visit their schools, and the presence of Dr. Price at Dr. Jackson's side made them feel it was a "two on one" situation.

Over two years, principals developed varying perceptions of their new leader. Those who had supported the previous superintendent were likely to have a negative perception of Dr. Jackson. Mr. Luman did not spend much time away from the administration building during the workday; he kept a low profile in the community; and he treated administrative staff as personal friends (and many were his personal friends). The new superintendent was almost the direct opposite.

However, some principals felt positively about Dr. Jackson's leadership. These administrators found his aggressive, no-nonsense demeanor refreshing; they appreciated that he was willing to take risks; and they supported his intentions to focus more directly on instructional programming and learning outcomes.

Moving Toward Outcome-Based Education

About seven months after Dr. Jackson arrived in Eagan Heights, he presented his administrative staff with a tentative schedule for implementing outcome-based education. The schedule indicated that the next 16 months would be devoted to preparing curriculum, staff, and evaluation programs. Implementation would occur at the start of the subsequent school year.

Dr. Jackson told his staff, "I expect each of you to be ambassadors for this program. I want you to help me sell it to the community. To do this, you must understand what we are trying to accomplish and you should believe that we are moving in the right direction. Philosophical unity is extremely important if we are to achieve success."

During the following summer and school year, all administrators played a role in the planning process, as did a group of select teachers who were appointed to the planning committee by Dr. Price. Although Dr. Jackson intended to use the same program he had successfully erected in his previous job, he realized that some modifications might be necessary.

Following the completion of the planning document, open meetings were held at each school to explain outcome-based education. Dr. Price, who coordinated all planning efforts, outlined the philosophy, procedures, and goals of the program. Central to her presentation were the following objectives, which are stated as expectations for students (she referred to them as "exit outcomes"):

1. Ability to engage in independent learning
2. Appreciation of cultural diversity and individual differences
3. Ability to think critically
4. Ability to identify and solve problems
5. Ability to work with others
6. Positive self-images and positive attitudes toward school

The meetings were not very well attended, especially at the secondary schools. In most instances, more teachers were in the audience than either parents or students. Teachers were especially inquisitive about the measurement of exit outcomes. They wanted to know how these objectives would be measured. In response, Dr. Price usually provided vague answers suggesting that methods and criteria for evaluation would evolve as teachers and administrators had the opportunity to weigh alternatives.

Dr. Jackson attended all but three of the meetings held in the schools (his schedule prevented him from attending all). He always sat in the back of the room, allowing Dr. Price to conduct the meetings. The principals exhibited different behaviors in these sessions. One or two openly stated enthusiasm for the program, and several expressed optimism that outcome-based education could be beneficial; but most remained passive, giving no indication of support.

In pursuing outcome-based education, Dr. Jackson believed that he had the full support of the school board and his three assistant superintendents. He recognized, however, that some principals might be less committed.

Community Opposition

About four weeks after the public meetings were held in each of the schools, Dr. Jackson received his first indication that there could be opposition to his plan. A local minister, Reverend Arnold Morgan, wrote a letter to Mrs. Evercott, a member of the school board and his church. In this letter, he voiced concerns about outcome-based education and urged her to examine the issue in depth. She showed the letter to Dr. Jackson and asked him if he knew what might be bothering the minister. The superintendent said he had no knowledge of Reverend Morgan's concern, but explained that the intentions of outcome-based education had often been misinterpreted.

"Some conservative religious groups have been suspicious of outcome-based education. They think it is a scheme to teach values in public education," he told her. "But our program is focused on instructional outcomes. I think Reverend Morgan would be less inclined to raise concerns if he took the time to examine our plan."

Mrs. Evercott telephoned her minister and suggested that he make an appointment with the superintendent to discuss his concerns. She told him that although she was looking carefully at the program, he would be better informed if Dr. Jackson explained the objectives to him. Reverend Morgan said he would think about her suggestion.

Several weeks later, Reverend Morgan, who had not met with Dr. Jackson, and 12 supporters appeared at a regularly scheduled school board meeting. He asked to read a prepared statement to the board. Mrs. Small, the board president, said that his request could not be granted since he failed to notify the superintendent that he wanted to speak at the meeting. (All persons wanting to speak at board meetings are required by school board policy to present their request in writing to the superintendent at least three calendar days prior to the meeting.)

Dr. Jackson intervened, "Madam president, I respectfully request that you grant an exception and allow Reverend Morgan to speak. Mrs. Evercott shared with me a letter he wrote to her several weeks ago about our plans to move to outcome-based education. I think he feels very strongly about the matter, and I think it would be to everyone's benefit if he had an opportunity to share his apprehensions."

Mrs. Small nodded approval and said, "Reverend Morgan, you may proceed with your statement."

Reverend Morgan read his statement, and as Dr. Jackson expected, his opposition centered on the issue of values. He concluded by expressing hope that each school board member would look at Dr. Jackson's program carefully.

Mrs. Evercott, the first school board member to respond, said, "When we talked several weeks ago, I suggested that you sit down with Dr. Jackson and discuss what we are attempting in this school district. I think it is a mistake to assume that we will be doing something that occurred in another school district. I would feel a lot better if you examined the program personally."

"I'm afraid, Mrs. Evercott," the minister responded, "that Dr. Jackson does not have an open mind about outcome-based education. He came to Eagan Heights with the intention of pushing his ideas on us. I know you want to be a good school board member, and I know you want to support your superintendent, but it is the public and their representatives who must examine this program. This outcome-based education is being pushed all over the country, and I already know that one of the intentions is to control the values we teach our young boys and girls. I'm here to warn every one of you board members to open your eyes before it is too late."

Then Reverend Morgan's supporters distributed material obtained from a national group opposing outcome-based education. The contents included contentions that outcome-based education was a devious ploy to control the minds of young children by teaching them the values and beliefs of secular humanism.

Within days following his appearance at the school board meeting, Reverend Morgan took his campaign against outcome-based education to the general public. He wrote letters to the local newspapers; he made appearances on talk-radio programs; and he enlisted six other local ministers as his allies. By the time the school year ended in late May, Dr. Jackson and the board realized that

Reverend Morgan had been able to garner significant support for his position on outcome-based education.

Dr. Jackson and Mrs. Small tried to counteract the negative statements being made about outcome-based education by making themselves available to the media and community groups. At first, they were treated respectfully at public meetings. But as their appearances became more frequent, Reverend Morgan and his followers began to create confrontational situations. Opponents to outcome-based education carried picket signs outside the meetings; some audience members frequently interrupted the superintendent and board president as they tried to speak.

By mid-June, Mrs. Evercott withdrew her support for implementing outcome-based education as scheduled. She announced this decision at a regular school board meeting without giving prior notice to either Dr. Jackson or Mrs. Small. Her reversal, predicated largely on the notion that more time was needed to study the program before it was actually implemented, was cheered by Reverend Morgan and his supporters, who were present at the meeting. A week later, Peter Meckava announced that he too had changed his mind and, like Mrs. Evercott, stated that the reason related to inadequate time to study the program more fully.

For the first time since arriving in Eagan Heights, Dr. Jackson was doubting whether he could succeed in this environment. After Mr. Meckava's change of heart, he asked Annette Small to meet him for lunch the next day. During their meeting, the superintendent shared his concerns about the eroding support for his program. Although Mrs. Small remained totally committed to the proposal, she too had become apprehensive about Reverend Morgan's ability to influence public opinion.

"Reggie Prescott is the next target," she told Dr. Jackson. "He told me that he is getting calls and letters from patrons asking him to change his position. Since he has to consider his business, I think there is a good chance that he will reverse his position."

"I guess it is easier to opt for delay in the face of public criticism," Dr. Jackson told his school board president as they finished their meeting.

Dr. Jackson also discussed his growing concerns with Dr. Price. She made it clear that she favored staying with the plan to implement the program at the start of the coming school year.

"Look, if Prescott changes, we won't be able to move forward anyway," she told the superintendent. "So why back down at this point? I think we have to take these people to task for putting out misinformation. If we say we are going to delay for a semester or a year to do further study, you can bet that we will never be able to move to the outcome-based program. And besides, do we really want to stay here if people are unwilling to move forward with their schools?"

THE CHALLENGE

Place yourself in Dr. Jackson's position. Would you follow Dr. Price's suggestion?

KEY ISSUES/QUESTIONS

1. Why has outcome-based education become such an emotionally charged issue?

2. Assess Dr. Jackson's approach to trying to put this program in place. Would you have done anything differently?

3. Assess Dr. Jackson's relationship with his administrative staff. To what extent is this relationship cogent to the problem he faces?

4. Dr. Jackson and Mrs. Small decided to make themselves available to the media and community groups. Was this a good idea? Why or why not?

5. Analyze the behavior of board members Evercott and Meckava. What do you think caused them to change their position?

6. To what extent could this issue change Dr. Jackson's relationship with his school board?

7. What are the advantages and disadvantages of deciding to delay implementation of the program for another year?

8. Do you think there is any hope of changing Reverend Morgan's position? If so, how would you attempt to do this?

9. Is it common for parents to object to school programs that appear to teach values? What evidence do you have to support your response?

10. Are there different goals for outcome-based education? If so, what are they?

11. How might you determine the extent to which community opposition stems from general resistance to change as opposed to the specific program in this case?

12. Assess the behavior of the principals at the meetings held in each school to inform the parents about the outcome-based program.

13. Assess the leadership style of Dr. Jackson. What do you consider to be the positive and negative aspects of his behavior?

14. To what extent do you think that Dr. Jackson has created an open climate in the school district (i.e., a climate that encourages interaction with the community)?

SUGGESTED READINGS

Arocha, Z. (1993). The religious right's march into public school governance. *The School Administrator, 50*(9), 8-15.

Backes, J. (1993-1994). Outcome-based education: Total inclusion or functional exclusion. *National Forum of Applied Educational Research Journal, 7*(1), 50-53.

Berreth, D., & Scherer, M. (1993). On transmitting values: A conversation with Amitai Etzioni. *Educational Leadership, 51*(3), 12-15.

Capper, C., & Jamison, M. (1992). *Outcomes based education re-examined: From structural functionalism to poststructuralism.* (ERIC Document Reproduction Service No. ED 346 555).

Cohen, A. (1993). A new educational paradigm. *Phi Delta Kappan, 74*(10), 791-795.

Criteria for outcome-based education. (1991). *Outcomes, 10*(1), 5.

Davis, E. D. (1984). Should the public schools teach values? *Phi Delta Kappan, 65*(5), 358-360.

Doyle, M. (1993). Public education: A fertile field for religious educators. *Momentum, 24*(1), 14-16.

Education Commission of the States. (1993). *How to deal with community criticism of school change*. Denver, CO: Author.

Eisner, E. (1993). Why standards may not improve schools. *Educational Leadership, 50*(5), 22-23.

Evans K., & King, J. (1994). Research on OBE: What we know and don't know. *Educational Leadership, 51*(6), 12-17.

Glatthorn, A. (1993). Outcome-based education: Reform and the curriculum process. *Journal of Curriculum and Supervision, 8*(4), 354-362.

Graves, B. (1992). The pressure group cooker. *School Administrator, 49*(4), 8-13.

Haas, J. (1992). Issues in outcome-based education. *NASSP Bulletin, 76*(551), 97-100.

Harmin, M. (1988). Value clarity, high morality: Let's go for both. *Educational Leadership, 45*(8), 24-27.

Huffman, H. (1993). Character education without turmoil. *Educational Leadership, 51*(3), 24-27.

Jones, J. L. (1993). Targets of the right. *American School Board Journal, 180*(4), 22-29.

King, J. A., & Evans, K. M. (1991). Can we achieve outcome-based education? *Educational Leadership, 49*(2), 73-75.

Kowalski, T. J., & Reitzug, U. C. (1993). *Contemporary school administration: An introduction*. New York: Longman (see chapters 8, 13).

Lickona, T. (1993). The return of character education. *Educational Leadership, 51*(3), 8-11.

McKernan, J. (1993). Some limitations of outcome-based education. *Journal of Curriculum and Supervision, 8*(4), 343-353.

Nyland, L. (1991). One district's journey to success with outcome-based education. *School Administrator, 48*(9), 29, 31-32, 34-35.

O'Neil, J. (1993). Making sense of outcome-based education. *Instructor, 102*(5), 46-47.

Outcome-based education: The religious right's latest bogeyman. (1993). *Church and State, 46*(5), 8-9.

Paul, R. (1988). Ethics without indoctrination. *Educational Leadership, 45*(8), 10-12.

Reed, R., & Simonds, R. (1993). The agenda of the religious right. *The School Administrator, 50*(9), 16-23.

Scheuerer, D., & Parkay, F. (1992). The new Christian right and the public school curriculum: A Florida report. *School Library Media Manual, 10,* 112-118.

Sizer, T., & Rogers, B. (1993). Designing standards: Achieving the delicate balance. *Educational Leadership, 50*(5), 24-25.

Spady, W., & Marshall, K. (1991). Beyond traditional outcome-based education. *Educational Leadership, 49*(2), 67-72.

Ternasky, P. (1992). Moral realism revisited: On achievable morality. *Educational Theory, 42*(2), 201-216.

Towers, J. (1992a). Outcome-based education: Another educational bandwagon? *Educational Forum, 56*(3), 291-305.

Towers, J. (1992b). Some concerns about outcome-based education. *Journal of Research and Development in Education, 25*(2), 89-95.

Townsend, R. (1993). Coping with controversy. *The School Administrator, 50*(9), 24-27.

case 2

Protecting the Organization: Legitimate Power or Compromise?

BACKGROUND INFORMATION

Historically, the development of theories and practices used in business administration has influenced educational administration. Especially during the quarter-century following the Industrial Revolution, school boards and administrators were prone to emulate the behaviors of successful managers who led their corporations to ever-increasing profits. Over the years, however, scholars recognized that there were weighty differences between profit-seeking industries and public service organizations, and this awareness helped to shape today's academic preparation of school administrators. However, despite the realization by educators that schools are unique organizations, many critics outside the profession see schools as just another organization; for them, schools are ineffective, at least in part, because they are inefficient.

This case entails different perspectives of balancing organizational needs with individual and group needs. Managers who believe that the organization's integrity must be protected above all else are disturbed by processes that cause inefficiency and diminish the legitimate authority of the organization (and its managers). By contrast, those who view organizations as sociopolitical entities are more willing to seek compromises that meld organizational and personal (or group) interests. Central to this case is the question of whether the school district's interests are best served by political compromises or by protecting the legitimate authority of administrators and the school board.

In large measure, the problem faced by the young administrator here also relates to differences between private, industrial, profit-seeking organizations and public, professionally dominated organizations such as schools. How are employees treated? To what degree are there areas of shared decision making between administrators and employees? Can and should administrators ever share their responsibilities? Questions such as these exemplify concerns related to authority and responsibility that emerge when private and public organizations are compared.

In this case, a personnel director for a private industry provides advice to a friend and neighbor who is personnel director in the local public schools. This advice is in conflict with the direction provided to the school official by his superintendent. In this regard, the case also involves issues of personal power. That is, the case sparks questions related to how individuals influence the behavior of others.

KEY AREAS FOR REFLECTION

1. Differences between private and public organizations
2. The exercise of legitimate power by organizational managers
3. Referent and expert power and their ability to influence individual behavior
4. Conflict resolution in professionally dominated organizations
5. The use of compromise and the interests of a school system

THE CASE

The Shoreline School District is located on the banks of one of the great lakes in an industrial section of an upper midwest state. It is a large school system enrolling 19,400 pupils; but as is true with many larger cities of this type in the "rust belt," enrollment declines have been rather substantial in the past two decades. For the last ten years, the reduction in students has averaged about 1 percent per year.

Despite the steady decline in enrollments, the school board and administrative team in Shoreline have attempted to place a positive spin on the demographic condition. Rather than immediately seeking reductions in staffing and budgets, school officials contended that the loss of students presented an opportunity to improve and expand programming. Through a vigorous public relations campaign, enthusiastically supported by the teachers' union, school officials held neighborhood meetings and published newsletters outlining reasons why program expansion was necessary. Their efforts were extremely successful, and taxpayers approved two referenda to raise additional local revenues in the past 12 years.

Tim Anderson, a former middle school science teacher and middle school principal, came to Shoreline just 11 months ago largely because of the school system's reputation. Tim accepted the position of personnel director in the Shoreline School District after receiving his Ph.D. degree in school administration. His youth, 33 years of age, and his enthusiasm provided a degree of balance to a much older and experienced administrative staff.

When Tim arrived in Shoreline, Superintendent Alex Pryor saw to it that he had ample exposure in the community. Having lived in Shoreline for nearly 22 years, the superintendent believed that there was a symbolic dimension to gaining community support. In this respect, he thought Tim's youth and enthusiasm would be linked to the district's progressive posture. Dr. Pryor sponsored Tim for membership in the Rotary Club; he saw to it that his new staff member would be invited to speak before a variety of civic groups.

Tim's wife, Margie, and their two children readily adapted to Shoreline, a modest-sized city consisting of established neighborhoods. Although still an industrial community, it is one of those rare cities able to attract middle-class and upper-middle-class residents. This is largely because of the beaches and water recreation opportunities. The Andersons purchased a home just two blocks from the waterfront and became friends with most of their new neighbors.

Over the first few months in Shoreline, Tim developed a particularly close friendship with Bill Stanton, his next-door neighbor. Bill is personnel director of Shoreline Metal Products, one of the major industries in town. Since they are approximately the same age, Tim and Bill share many common interests.

Although their jobs are quite similar, Bill and Tim entered personnel administration with very different backgrounds. Bill graduated from a small, liberal arts college in Pennsylvania with a major in business and subsequently received a law degree in Washington, D.C. After working in a large law firm in the nation's capital for six years, Bill decided to seek new challenges. The position with Shoreline Metal Products, a company racked by union-related problems over the past 12 years, provided an attractive salary and an opportunity to become directly involved in labor relations. Tim, on the other hand, earned three degrees at a large state university. He was a classroom teacher for six years and principal for two years. After earning a master's degree during the summers, he resigned his teaching position to pursue a doctoral program in school administration.

One sunny October day while the two were out on the lake sailing, Tim mentioned that it seemed likely the school district would have to reduce its teaching force by about 25 before the next school year. The continuing decline in enrollments coupled with expanding programming had finally taken its toll. There simply was no more money.

"That shouldn't be all that difficult," Bill commented. "You have a master contract. Doesn't it contain a provision for making reduction-in-force decisions?"

"Yes," answered Tim. "However, our contract calls for us to form a joint committee between representatives of the teachers' union and the administration to determine if reductions are necessary. Further, this committee has the authority to determine the process for the reductions."

Bill looked astonished. "You have to be pulling my leg! Who in their right mind would ever agree to something like that? Establishing a committee and letting them decide which reductions are necessary takes away management's ability to make personnel decisions. How do you know, for example, that the union won't make these decisions solely on the basis of loyalty to their organization? How can you be assured that they won't get rid of some of the best teachers simply because they don't belong to the union?"

"I don't know," Tim replied. "This provision bothers me too. But it has been in our contract for a long time. Nobody has paid a lot of attention to it."

"Well, I think you ought to try to do something about it—and I mean right away," Bill told him. "This could cause the district a real problem with some of your big community supporters. People who fought to get tax increases in the past may be awfully disappointed if some of the best teachers are released just because they don't belong to the union."

For the next several days, Tim could not quit thinking about Bill's comments. He had a great deal of respect for his friend, and he especially admired Bill's knowledge about labor relations. The following week while Tim was having a regular meeting with the superintendent, he brought up the matter of the reduction-in-force provision.

"Dr. Pryor, I've been thinking about our last administrative meeting where we discussed the likelihood that we were going to have to eliminate about 25 teaching positions in our district before the next school year. If that forecast proves to be accurate, I'm bothered by the language in our master contract regarding how these decisions will be made. It seems to me that we would want to make reduction decisions based on teacher performance, and I'm not sure that will be possible if we have to reach compromises with union representatives. How did this provision calling for a joint committee get into the contract anyway?" Tim asked.

Dr. Pryor walked over and picked up his copy of the contract and slowly turned to the page that contained the language about reductions. He read it silently, and when he finished, he looked up at Tim. "What's the problem? This is the same language that we have had for the past seven years. What is it about the language that bothers you?"

Tim responded, "I'm troubled by the fact that this committee would review the necessity for reductions. What happens if the committee does not agree that the reductions are needed? Can we trust the teachers on this committee to make objective decisions?"

Superintendent Pryor's reading glasses were on the tip of his nose, and his eyes focused above the rims at Tim as he spoke. "That's never happened here. We had to reduce some teachers four of the last seven years and it's never happened. We always find a way to compromise—to work it out. If we have good data indicating our need to reduce staff, the teachers have worked with us."

"But Dr. Pryor, in those years we only reduced staff by one to four teachers. We've never experienced anything like 25 teacher dismissals," Tim noted.

"Tim, stop worrying. We've had big problems before, and we always find a way to work things out. Besides, we have an obligation to live up to the agreement we have with the teachers. So even if we wanted to change things, we couldn't do that until we negotiate a new contract."

Tim left the superintendent's office feeling better about the matter. He had a great deal of respect for Dr. Pryor. Maybe Bill just did not understand teachers and union issues in public education. After all, the prominent supporters of the school district had not been riled when previous reductions occurred. And as Dr. Pryor told him, the union representatives to this committee had been cooperative in the past. Tim concluded that Bill's assessment was made without his friend knowing all the facts.

That evening Tim saw Bill barbecuing in his back yard and walked over to talk with him.

"Bill, the other day you commented about the school system's reduction-in-force policy. You were pretty critical. Your comments led me to give this matter a great deal of thought. Could you be more specific about why you think our policy will not work?" Tim requested.

"Sure. For one thing, you can't do anything unless the other side agrees. That's bad management. What if they decide that you don't need to release any teachers. Are you going to go along with that? Are the union bosses willing to share the blame if you go bankrupt because you didn't reduce your teaching staff? It's as simple as that."

"Here in Shoreline, the administrators have been able to compromise with the union in the past. Alex Pryor assured me that the teachers who have represented the union on this ad hoc committee have been objective and that they were willing to look at facts and figures. If we can prove our need to reduce staff, they have cooperated in the past. So the policy has worked," Tim explained.

"Have you ever had to dismiss this many teachers in the past? I remember some dismissals two years ago. Who was targeted? Two first-year teachers. Nobody asked whether they were good or bad teachers. Cutting 25 teachers is a different matter—one you haven't faced in the past. You are probably looking at many of these 25 being loyal union members. Tim, unions look out for their own. You are supposed to look out for the organization. These are two different responsibilities. Compromising doesn't lead to the best decisions. Do you really want union leaders deciding what is best for our children? Somebody's got to be in charge—to make difficult decisions that assure that the organization's goals and purposes are protected. Compromise, my friend, is a dangerous practice. It's an easy way out of making a difficult decision."

Tim still wasn't convinced. He asked further, "Don't you think workers ought to have some say in what happens to them? Since they are the ones who stand to lose their jobs, shouldn't they be allowed to play a role in these decisions?"

"Do you think any of the teachers appointed to this committee will be released? Of course not! And what do you expect, Tim? You think they are going to say it's fine for you to take away jobs from their union brothers and sisters? Of course not. I think you have a no-win situation here. And just for a moment, think about your personal role in all of this. You're the one who has to work with this committee. You're the one who has to reach the compromises. If they turn out to be bad decisions, and that's likely to be the case, who's going to get criticized for not protecting the school district? Dr. Pryor or you? I suggest you convince your superintendent to get directly involved in this committee. Let him be the one who reaches the compromises. If he doesn't see anything wrong with the committee provision, let him deal with it."

Tim was again troubled about the reduction-in-force matter. On the one hand, he respected Bill's expertise in labor relations. On the other hand, he admired Dr. Pryor, a leader he viewed as a model superintendent. Hence, the two persons whose opinions he most respected were taking opposite positions on an issue he would have to face.

At the administrative team meeting three days later, fiscal and demographic reports confirmed everyone's worst fears. Reductions would be necessary, and the number would be approximately 25 as earlier projected. Dr. Pryor instructed Tim to take immediate steps to form the ad hoc committee as stipulated in the collective-bargaining agreement. The superintendent also indicated that this matter would be made public at the next school board meeting.

Tim's self-confidence had been eroded by the different stances taken by Bill and Dr. Pryor. After weighing matters one more time, he decided not to follow his neighbor's advice. He would proceed as directed. That afternoon he called Jane Sparkman, president of the teachers' union, and notified her of the need to activate the committee. She reacted with surprise.

"I thought we were over these reductions. When is this going to stop? In the past we were cooperative. This time we may have to say no. Here we are just two months into a new school year and you are already talking about the need to let more teachers go next year."

Tim replied, "All I can tell you, Mrs. Sparkman, is that enrollment reports and financial data indicate that we have to make additional reductions. We will talk about the problem in the committee. Please let me know whom you will appoint so I can set the first meeting."

"Can you give me any idea about how many positions we will be talking about?" she asked.

Quietly Tim answered, "Maybe as many as 25."

"What! Are you serious? We are going to have some serious problems. I'll get back to you."

Tim called Bill at his office and told him what had just occurred. Bill responded confidently, "Isn't that what I predicted? Forget about what's happened in the past. Unions are very unpredictable groups. They respond solely on the basis of economic and political considerations that affect their well-being."

"What do you think I should do?" Tim asked.

Bill answered, "You have to convince your boss that this provision will not work. You are probably going to end up in court over this one. I'd play tough. Tell the union that you have no room for compromise, that you have to reduce 25 teachers, and that you welcome their input as to how it should be done. I would make it clear that they are only giving you advice, not making the decisions. Also, I'd be sure that they understand that the need to reduce 25 employees is not a negotiable item; you only want their input with regard to how it should be accomplished."

Tim hung up the phone and went immediately to see the superintendent. He informed his superior of his intention to be tough with the teachers. He relayed Mrs. Sparkman's negative reaction to his suggestion to form the committee and reasserted his belief that the contract language would not work. The disappointment on Dr. Pryor's face was obvious.

"Tim, maybe I expected too much from you. You have to understand that unions always say they can't agree to things. But somehow we always manage to work it out. This school district isn't U.S. Steel. Teachers are taxpayers. They have friends on the school board. They affect elections. We have learned to work together here in Shoreline. You need to learn that." With that sobering comment, the superintendent ended the brief discussion.

THE CHALLENGE

Place yourself in Tim's position. What would you do at this point?

KEY ISSUES/QUESTIONS

1. Why do you think Dr. Pryor and Bill have such different opinions about the effectiveness of the school district's policy regarding reduction in force?
2. To what extent are principles and practices of management in private industry applicable to public, professionally dominated organizations?
3. What is legitimate power? How does it compare to expert or referent power?
4. Tim was influenced by the advice he received from Bill. Why?
5. What type of power did Dr. Pryor have over Tim?
6. Is Bill's assessment correct that school administrators should not rely on past successes to direct their future actions in working with unions? Why or why not?
7. Assess Dr. Pryor's behavior in this case. Do you think he is a model superintendent? Why or why not?
8. Identify environmental (community) factors that you would weigh in deciding what to do.
9. Identify alternatives that are available to Tim and evaluate each of them.
10. Is Bill correct when he states that unions look out for their members and managers are supposed to look out for the organization?
11. Should efficiency be of equal importance to the Shoreline School District and Shoreline Metal Products? Why or why not?
12. What can you learn about an organization from analyzing the ways in which key decisions are made?
13. To what extent do you believe Tim should weigh past practices with regard to reduction-in-force decisions?
14. Do committees generally make better decisions than knowledgeable managers?

SUGGESTED READINGS

Allen, R., & Nixon, B. (1988). Developing a new approach to leadership. *Management Education and Development, 19*(3), 174–186.

Burke, R. (1983). Don't be a slave to seniority when developing RIF procedures. *American School Board Journal, 170*(7), 20–21.

Castetter, W. (1986). *The personnel function in educational administration* (4th ed., pp. 180–183). New York: Macmillan.

Chandler, T. (1984). Can theory Z be applied to the public schools? *Education, 104*(4), 343–345.

Chesler, N. (1991). Personnel cuts: Tough but effective. *School Administrator, 48*(8), 28.

Collins, P., & Nelson, D. (1983). Reducing the teacher workforce: A management perspective. *Journal of Law and Education, 12*(2), 249–272.

Conway, J. (1984). The myth, mystery and mastery of participative decision making in education. *Educational Administration Quarterly, 20*(3), 11–40.

Dunnerstick, R. (1987). If RIFs are in the cards for your schools, deal with them deftly. *American School Board Journal, 174*(1), 34.

Eberts, R. (1987). Union-negotiated employment rules and teacher quits. *Economics of Education Review, 6*(1), 15–25.

Hanson, E. (1991). *Educational administration and organizational behavior* (3rd ed., pp. 157–162). Boston: Allyn & Bacon.

Hartley, M. (1985). Leadership style and conflict resolution: No manager is an island. *Journal of Cooperative Education, 21*(2), 16–23.

Hendrickson, G. (1990). Where do we go after you get to yes? *Executive Educator, 12*(11), 16–17.

Herman, J. (1992). Dealing with crisis budgeting cutbacks and planning for more efficiency. *School Business Administrator, 58*(2), 35–36, 38–39.

Kerchner, C. (1993). Building the airplane as it rolls down the runway. *The School Administrator, 50*(10), 8–15.

Kowalski, T. (1982a). Don't be duped by the industrial mystique. *Executive Educator, 4*(11), 46.

Kowalski, T. (1982b). Organizational climate, conflict, and collective bargaining. *Contemporary Education, 54*(1), 27–30.

Kowalski, T., & Reitzug, U. (1993). *Contemporary school administration: An introduction.* New York: Longman (see chapters 7, 10, 16).

Lieberman, M. (1986). *Beyond public education.* New York: Praeger (see chapter 2).

Lieberman, A. (1988). Teachers and principals: Turf, tension, and new tasks. *Phi Delta Kappan, 69*(9), 948–953.

Lifton, F. (1992). The legal tangle of shared governance. *School Administrator, 49*(1), 16–19.

Nelson, R. (1991). Can corporate management work in schools? *Principal, 71*(2), 32–33.

Parkay, F. (1984). A conceptual model for quality-oriented educational leadership. *Planning and Changing, 15*(1), 3–9.

Rosen, M. (1993). Sharing power: A blueprint for collaboration. *Principal, 72*(3), 37–39.

Shedd, J., & Bacharach, S. (1991). *Tangled hierarchies: Teachers as professionals and the management of schools.* San Francisco: Jossey-Bass.

Smit, G. (1984). The effect of collective bargaining on governance in education. *Goverment Union Review, 5*(1), 28–34.

Snyder, K. & Anderson, R. (1987). What principals can learn from corporate management. *Principal, 66*(4), 22-26.

Threadgill, R. (1988). Analyzing the financial impact of teacher attrition and retirement. *Planning and Changing, 19*(3), 8-13.

Williams, M. (1985). The management of conflict. *New Directions for Higher Education, 13*(2), 33-36.

Wishnick, Y., & Wishnick, T. (1993). Collective bargaining and educational reform: Establishing a labor-management partnership. *Journal of Collective Negotiations in the Public Sector, 22*(1), 1-11.

Wood, C. (1982). Financial exigencies and the dismissal of public school teachers: A legal perspective. *Goverment Union Review, 3*(4), 49-66.

case 3

Setting Higher Standards

BACKGROUND INFORMATION

Since the early 1980s, school reform has permeated virtually every aspect of school administration. Dozens of reports critical of public elementary and secondary education received widespread media attention. As business and governmental leaders responded, two common perceptions were especially influential: (1) there was a strong link between education and America's ability to compete in a global economy, and (2) America's declining dominance in the global economy was associated with the sinking quality of public education.

Most of the reform initiatives during the 1980s were predicated on the notion that major improvements could be accomplished without significant modifications to organizational stuctures or cultures that were common in schools. Hence, recommendations frequently were restricted to intensification mandates that sought to make teachers and students simply do more of what they were already doing. More time in school, more homework, increased requirements for teacher licensure, and increased requirements for high school graduation exemplify efforts in this category.

Attempts to achieve excellence during the 1980s rekindled concerns for equity, especially among educators. Many superintendents and principals recognized that initiatives such as simply setting higher standards or providing rewards on the basis of standardized test scores were apt to exacerbate disparities that already existed among school districts. Even worse, efforts to improve education through intensification mandates made it less likely that more fundamental problems would be addressed. Issues such as poverty, deteriorating family conditions, and a lack of professional freedom for educators were almost entirely ignored.

This case is about school reform in the mid-1980s. A board member's demands for immediate action in the local school district result in the reassignment of the superintendent.

KEY AREAS FOR REFLECTION

1. Implications of reform initiatives developed in the 1980s
2. Differing perceptions of how schools should improve
3. The power of individual school board members
4. Political dimensions of the superintendency
5. Development and implementation of school policy

THE CASE

The Community

Simpson is a community with approximately 18,000 residents located in a southern state. Within the city limits there is a hospital, a community college, a manufacturing plant, and an array of small retail businesses. Located in a predominately farming area (dairy products and cotton), Simpson's population increased less than 1 percent in the past decade. Most citizens are content with things the way they are.

Taxes in this state are relatively low, and in Simpson they are below the state average. City officials, most of whom come from a dozen or so powerful families in the town, have almost discouraged the local chamber of commerce from trying to attract new business or industry. Most residents agree with their leaders that growth is likely to bring new problems, higher property taxes, and destroy the small-town qualities that make Simpson special. Besides, residents are within a one-hour drive of a much larger city if they want a greater variety of stores or restaurants.

The School District

The Simpson Public School District consists of seven elementary schools, a junior high school, and a high school. Enrolling a total of 3,476 students in grades kindergarten through 12, the district has had a stable enrollment for the last five years. In many ways, the public schools in Simpson are average. Student achievement scores, property taxes, and even the number of high school graduates going on to college are at or near the average for the state. The district is governed by a seven-member school board, and members are elected to four-year terms in a nonpartisan election held in May. The terms of individuals are staggered to prevent a majority of new board members from being seated in any one year.

The district superintendent, Jack Darble, has been employed by the local public schools for 27 years. For the last 12 years he has held the top administrative position. He is a soft-spoken individual who is remembered by many of his former students as an effective teacher and principal. His relationship with the teachers and administrative staff has remained very positive despite the presence of an aggressive teachers' union.

Education has never really been a topic of controversy in Simpson. Most citizens remain pleased with the schools, and this condition was verified by a recent survey of parents. Whereas parents gave all public schools across the United States a grade of *C* and schools within the state a grade of *C+*, they rated the local schools as *B+*. The comment of one parent exemplified the sentiments expressed by many on the survey: "I got an awfully good education here, and my kids are receiving the same benefits."

Many local residents are enthusiastic boosters of Simpson High School athletics, especially the school's highly successful football team. It is not uncommon for 3,000 or more to attend home games. The high school is a source of pride for many residents, and an annual homecoming parade attracts many former residents.

The School Board Election

Board members are elected to four-year terms in nonpartisan elections held every two years. There are seven members, and to avoid a majority being seated in any given year, the relationship of elections and terms is set as follows:

Seats 1, 2, and 3 are elected in the same election, and the members are seated to four-year terms commencing the following July 1.

Seats 4, 5, 6, and 7 are elected in the same election, held two years after the previous election, with members elected to seats 4, 5, and 6 seated to four-year terms commencing the following July 1 and board member 7 seated to a four-year term commencing one year from the following July 1.

Although each seat represents a specified geographic section of the school district, and although candidates must reside in the specified sections they seek to represent, all voters in the school district are allowed to vote for candidates in all seven districts.

The filing dates for candidacy occurred four months prior to the actual election. In this given year, seats 1, 2, and 3 were to be elected. One of the incumbents, Dave Petty in District 2, announced he would not seek another term. Another, Rose Connors, a biology instructor at the community college completing her first term as the representative of District 1, officially filed papers for candidacy on the first day that it was possible to do so. Joe Stinson, an insurance agent and the incumbent in District 3, filed approximately one week later. The remaining board members were as follows:

Dr. Peter Swaim, physician and current board president (District 6)

Mrs. Jane Mason, housewife and current board vice-president (District 7)

Mr. Jimmy Lawton, farmer (District 4)

Mr. Arnold Barker, farmer (District 5)

George Jenkins, owner of Jenkins Farm Supply, filed for the vacancy in District 2, and Mrs. Elizabeth Potter, housewife and sister-in-law of Mr. Jenkins, filed to run against Rose Connors in District 1. By the filing deadline, there were no other candidates. Hence, the only contested seat was in District 1 where Mrs. Potter was trying to defeat the incumbent, Mrs. Connors.

For the most part, there was little campaigning. There were no debates or public forums. Rose Connors distributed pamphlets in the community emphasizing her experience as an educator and board member. Even though Mr. Jenkins was unopposed in District 2, he spent money campaigning to make it clear that he was supporting Mrs. Potter. The two had posters printed and paid for several ads in the local newspaper. Their ads expressed the view that they would work as a team if elected. Joe Stinson remained quiet during the campaign period. He saw no need to spend money since he was unopposed, and he did not wish to endorse a candidate in District 1.

Among close friends, George Jenkins argued that his sister-in-law deserved to be elected because she was a lifelong resident of Simpson. He assured his friends that Mrs. Potter held views that were identical to his. He told loyal supporters, "If you want me on the board, you need to back Liz Potter. If I'm to get things done, I need her on the board."

Mrs. Connors moved to Simpson when she and her husband accepted teaching positions at the community college about seven years ago. She ran for the school board largely because no one else wanted the job. In her first election, she was unopposed. Over the four years on the school board, her relationships with the other board members were positive. Dr. Swaim, board president, saw her as one of the most effective members; however, he did not campaign on her behalf because he thought that doing so would be inappropriate.

George Jenkins was well known in Simpson, and he had "connections" in statewide politics. In the past ten years, however, he was unsuccessful in two bids to obtain a position in state government. The first involved a state senate seat. Although he had tremendous support from voters in Simpson, he received less than 25 percent of the votes outside of his home town and lost by a substantial margin. The second unsuccessful effort was a bid to get his party's nomination for state auditor. In that primary election, he received only 34 percent of the votes.

Perhaps past political disappointments were responsible for George's behavior in the school board election. He acted like a candidate engaged in a bitter contest rather than one who was unopposed. And when the election was over, he gave himself a victory party. He also claimed that he swept his sister-in-law into office, since Liz Potter defeated Rose Connors by 155 votes.

Postelection Activities

The school board election was held in early May and new members were not seated until the first board meeting in July. Nevertheless within three weeks after the election, George Jenkins began to make it clear that he had some things he wanted accomplished. He scheduled one-to-one visits with each of the five board members who would remain on the board after June 30.

It was common knowledge in the community that despite George's unsuccessful attempts in statewide politics, he was a close friend of the current governor. One reward of that friendship was his appointment two years previously to the governor's select task force on educational reform. It was this experience that caused him to seek a seat on the local school board. Service on the governor's task force was bittersweet for George. Although he relished the public exposure, he was tremendously frustrated when the task force's recommendations were soundly rejected by the state legislature. When this occurred, George wrote letters to the editors of all the major newspapers in the state claiming that the rejection was simply a product of blatant partisan politics (the majority in the legislature and the governor belong to different parties). He urged citizens to enact at the local level what his political opponents were unwilling to accept at the state level.

During the visits with the board members, George essentially repeated what he had said in his public letters after the legislature rejected the reform recommendations. But now, he added a new dimension—his disdain for the state teachers' union. He blamed this organization for distorting the work of the governor's commission, and he said that legislators who voted against the recommendations were pawns of organized labor.

As he visited with each of the board members, George distributed a packet containing the full text of the report of the state committee on which he had served, as well as digests of selected national reports on school reform. He urged them to study the material, and he made it clear that he intended to push for some or all of these initiatives once he was officially part of the school board. Only one board member, Dr. Swaim, expressed concern about George's premature efforts to influence the school board.

"You were just elected, and you'll have several years to introduce your ideas to other board members and the administration. Right now, I think you would be wise to take the time to study what has occurred in the school district and to identify areas where improvement is needed."

George Jenkins was not one who took advice well.

"Listen Doc, our schools are a mess. We don't have time to sit back and philosophize. It's time for action. I ran for the school board because I want to get things done. Hopefully, we'll work together to move forward."

After completing the visits to the five school board members, George went to see the school superintendent. Although the two knew each other, their previous contact had been pretty much limited to exchanging pleasantries at official functions. The one exception was when George Jenkins was serving on the governor's task force several years ago. He telephoned Mr. Darble to solicit his opinion on several educational matters that were being discussed by the committee. The superintendent was cooperative, and George thanked him for his help.

Superintendent Darble was not surprised when George Jenkins came to see him just three weeks after the election. The administrators in the school district expected the newly elected board member to become actively involved in the operations of the schools. The superintendent presumed that George wanted either to get to know him better or to find out more about the school district. After only two minutes of conversation, Mr. Darble became aware that his guest was there neither to build friendship nor to ask questions. In a straightforward manner, George again expressed his disdain for the state teachers' union and he laid out his plan for bringing educational reform to Simpson. The superintendent was stunned by the specificity of the five proposed actions:

1. All teachers were to receive two formal evaluations each school year. All those receiving less than satisfactory assessments would be identified at a public board meeting and forced to enter a remedial program.
2. All students scoring one grade level below current grade placement in either reading or mathematics competency would be retained in their present grade.
3. The school year would be extended five days this next school year and an additional five days the following school year.
4. Any student receiving a grade lower than a *C* in reading, mathematics, or science would be required to do remedial work in the summer.
5. All teachers would be required to assign daily homework—a minimum of one hour of work for elementary students and two hours of work for high school students.

Mr. Darble read the list twice after it was placed before him, and he responded carefully, "Mr. Jenkins, several of these ideas have some merit. But, we can't just charge out and change things like this overnight. We have policies, contracts, and the like. Besides, each of these ideas should be studied independently. There may be some dimensions of these recommendations that you have not considered."

"Well, Darble," responded Mr. Jenkins, "that's what's wrong with schools. If I sat around on my thumbs waiting for my employees and customers to tell me something was okay before I could do it, I would have been bankrupt years ago. I've made a success of my business by being ahead of everyone else. By God, we're going to make Simpson a model for the rest of the state. The governor will point to this community with pride and tell the public that here's one school district that works. We can show the state what could have been accomplished if the governor's recommendations had been followed two years ago."

"I just don't think your ideas can be implemented, especially not in the next few months," answered the superintendent. "I am willing to work with you and everyone else, but I want to do that in a proper manner."

"We will see, Mr. Darble. We will see." And with those words, George Jenkins turned and left the superintendent's office.

During the next month, George concentrated on three of the returning board members. After his visits, he decided that Dr. Swaim, Mr. Darble, and the board's vice president, Mrs. Mason, were not going to be cooperative. Thus, he intensified his efforts with Lawson, Barker, and Stinson.

The Incident

Under the law in this state, each school board holds a reorganization meeting in early July; new board members are given the oath of office and officers are elected for the fiscal year. The school attorney administered the oath to the two new members, and then he conducted the election of a new president. Mrs. Potter immediately nominated her brother-in-law, George Jenkins. Dr. Swaim subsequently nominated Mrs. Mason. To the surprise of those present, Jenkins was elected by a margin of 5 to 2. The fact that Mr. Stinson cast his vote for George Jenkins was the biggest surprise. Over the past few years, he had usually supported positions taken by the physician.

After being on board for only about five minutes, George was now the elected leader of the seven-member group. Dr. Swaim handed his successor the gavel and the agenda prepared by the superintendent for the remainder of the meeting. Mr. Jenkins's first order of business was to conduct an election for vice president. By the same 5 to 2 margin the other new board member, Mrs. Potter, was elected. Dr. Swaim and Mrs. Mason graciously congratulated the new officers and publicly announced that they would work to promote progress and harmony on the school board.

Putting the prepared agenda aside without even looking at it, George Jenkins announced that Mrs. Potter wanted to introduce a special item of business. She read from a prepared statement:

Ladies and gentlemen,

After considering many aspects of our community and school system, I think we need to move forward and improve our schools. In my mind this will be impossible unless we have leadership committed to change. That means a superintendent who is willing to take risks and not be intimidated by unions and other obstructionists. Mr. Darble has served this community for many years, and I appreciate his efforts. The time has come, however, for new leadership. Therefore, I move that Mr. Darble be reassigned to a teaching post at the high school for the remaining two years of his contract. This board shall honor the salary in that contract, and he will be assigned to special duties in the summer to assure that he is earning his salary.

There was an immediate second from board member Lawton. A hush fell over the meeting. Dr. Swaim asked to be recognized.

"This is outrageous. First of all, this item is not even on the agenda. Second, there are no justified reasons why Mr. Darble should be replaced. I object to these proceedings and ask our attorney to declare this matter out of order."

Before the attorney could speak, Mr. Jenkins slammed down his recently acquired gavel and said loudly, "I'm the one who decides what's in order at this meeting. Quite frankly, Doctor, you had two years as president and little was done to institute reform in this district. The time has come for bold action. We need to improve our schools, and unfortunate as it is, this is where we start."

Mrs. Mason requested to hear specific reasons why Mr. Darble should be reassigned. Neither Mrs. Potter nor those supporting her motion were willing to do so. The vote was 4 to 2 in favor of reassigning the superintendent— Mr. Stinson abstained.

Disbelief turned to anger and Dr. Swaim stood and pointed his finger at George Jenkins. "You are going to destroy this school system, and I will not be a party to it. I resign my seat on this board, and I hope that the teachers and taxpayers of this community will react strongly and swiftly to the injustice that has occurred here this evening." With that said, he left the meeting.

George Jenkins responded as Dr. Swaim walked from the room while being applauded by the teachers present at the meeting, "That's your choice, Doctor. Believe me, this action does not make me feel good. But my experiences dealing with education over the past two years have convinced me that change will only come if we take risks. School improvement is our goal, and Mr. Darble has already indicated to me that he really doesn't want to be part of any plan that moves ahead immediately."

Mr. Darble rose from his seat and said, "For nearly 30 years I have worked for this school system. I have always respected the authority of the school board. The action this evening is a complete surprise to me, and for that reason, I think it best that I not comment at this time." Then he too left the meeting.

THE CHALLENGE

Assess the options available to the superintendent. What would you do if you were in his place?

KEY ISSUES/QUESTIONS

1. To what extent were environmental factors (i.e., factors external to the school district as an organization) responsible for what occurred in this case?
2. Are public organizations more or less susceptible to environmental influences than are private organizations?

3. Why are many citizens so quick to criticize education and to accept simplistic solutions to problems confronting public schools?

4. Assess the superintendent's behavior following his first encounter with George Jenkins shortly after the board election. Would you have done anything differently?

5. At least two major legal issues are included in this case:
   a. a school board's ability to reassign a superintendent even though he has two years remaining on his contract, and
   b. a school board's ability to take such action even though the item is not on the agenda.

   Are laws regarding these two matters the same in most states? What are the laws in your home state?

6. What positive outcomes might result from this incident?

7. To what extent is the community at large responsible for what occurred in this case?

8. To what extent should the behavior of school board members be restricted? By whom should it be restricted?

9. To what extent do you believe that school board members get involved in the day-to-day operations of schools?

10. Identify potential motivators with regard to George Jenkins's behavior. Why did he run for the board? What exactly is he trying to accomplish?

11. Did the superintendent invite this action by his responses to George Jenkins when first confronted with the reform initiatives?

12. Is the superintendent's relationship with employees in the district an issue in this case? Why or why not?

SUGGESTED READINGS

Apple, M. (1991). Conservative agendas and progressive possibilities: Understanding the wider politics of curriculum and teaching. *Education and Urban Society, 23*(3), 279-291.

Bacal, E. (1986). Learn not to burn, or fulminate over school board trouble. *American School Board Journal, 173*(5), 29-30.

Berliner, D. (1993). Mythology and the American system of education. *Phi Delta Kappan, 74*(8), 632-640.

Carr, R. (1988). Second-wave reforms crest at local initiative. *School Administrator, 45*(7), 16-18.

Cuban, L. (1987). State-powered curriculum reform, measurement-driven instruction. *National Forum: National Phi Kappa Phi Journal, 67*(3), 22-24.

Darling-Hammond, L. (1992). Reframing the school reform agenda: New paradigms must restore discourse with local educators. *The School Administrator, 49*(10), 22-27.

Edwards, C. (1993). Restructuring to improve student performance. *NASSP Bulletin, 77*(553), 77-88.

Edwards, C. (1988). Setting school board goals: A model for accountability. *Educational Horizons, 66*(3), 117-118.

Grady, M., & Bryant, M. (1991). School board turmoil and superintendent turnover: What pushes them to the brink? *School Administrator, 48*(2), 19-26.

Hopkins, R. (1989). How to survive and succeed as the chief school executive. *The School Administrator, 9*(46), 15-17.

Hoy, W., & Ferguson, J. (1985). A theoretical framework and exploration of organizational effectiveness of schools. *Educational Administration Quarterly, 21*(2), 117–134.

Kowalski, T., & Reitzug, U. (1993). *Contemporary school administration: An introduction.* New York: Longman (see chapter 12).

Krajewski, R. (1983). Nine ways a superintendent can corral a maverick board member. *American School Board Journal, 170*(11), 29–30.

MacDougall, C. (1988). Boards need education, too! *Updating School Board Policies, 1*(5), 1–2.

McCarthy, M. (1993). Challenges to public school curriculum: New targets and strategies. *Phi Delta Kappan, 75*(1), 55–60.

Namit, C. (1987). How a crisis meeting can control school board trouble. *American School Board Journal, 174*(9), 36–37.

Peterson, P. (1985). Did the education commissions say anything? *Education and Urban Society, 17*(2), 126–144.

Rada, R. (1984). Community dissatisfaction and school governance. *Planning and Changing, 15*(4), 234–247.

Ravitch, D. (1993). Launching a revolution in standards and assessments. *Phi Delta Kappan, 74*(10), 767–772.

Schneider, E. (1992). Beyond politics and symbolism: America's schools in the years ahead. *Equity and Excellence, 25*(2-4), 156–191.

Shanker, A. (1985). The reform reports: Reaction from the front lines. *Education and Urban Society, 17*(2), 215–222.

Slaughter, S. (1988). Academic freedom and the state: Reflections on the uses of knowledge. *Journal of Higher Education, 59*(3), 241–262.

Tallerico, M. (1989). The dynamics of superintendent-school board relationships: A continuing challenge. *Urban Education, 24*(2), 215–232.

Turlington, R. (1985). How testing is changing education in Florida. *Educational Measurement: Issues and Practices, 4*(2), 9–11.

Wells, F. (1992). External pressures for reform and strategy formation at the district level: Superintendents' interpretations of state demands. *Educational Evaluation and Policy Analysis, 14*(3), 241–260.

Wiggins, G. (1993). Assessment: Authenticity, context, and validity. *Phi Delta Kappan, 75*(3), 200–214.

Wimpelberg, R., & Ginsberg, R. (1985). Are school districts responding to *A Nation at Risk? Education and Urban Society, 17*(2), 196–203.

Yeakey, C., & Johnston, G. (1985). High school reform: A critique and a broader construct of social reality. *Education and Urban Society, 17*(2), 157–170.

Lounge Talk

BACKGROUND INFORMATION

Employee behavior in schools and school systems is influenced to a large extent by the power individuals and groups exercise over each other. One of the strongest types of power, and one that has been receiving increasing levels of attention in the past 15 or so years, is referent power. Put simply, *referent power* is associated with liking or admiring another. For example, a leader may have power to influence others because he or she is perceived by subordinates and peers as a charismatic administrator—an ideal leader.

Interest in referent power has sparked research efforts that have contributed to theory building in the areas of transformational and charismatic leadership. As Yukl (1989) noted, these two terms

> . . . refer to the process of influencing major changes in the attitudes and assumptions of organization members and building commitment for the organization's mission and objectives. Transformational leadership is usually defined more broadly than charismatic leadership, but there is considerable overlap between the two conceptions. (p. 204)

The seminal work of Burns (1978) distinguished between transactional and transformational leadership. The two are seen as somewhat opposite positions of behavior. In reviewing the work of Burns, Kowalski and Reitzug (1993) wrote

> Transactional leadership involves an exchange between leader and follower for purposes of achieving individual objectives. For example, a principal may agree to let a teacher attend a national reading conference in

exchange for the teacher's work on a textbook-adoption committee. (p. 233)

Transactional leaders concentrate on the self-interests of subordinates in an attempt to motivate them to do desired things. Bennis and Nanus (1985) concluded that much of the work in organizations is accomplished by this type of interaction between leader and follower.

By contrast, transformational leadership has been described as

> . . . the pursuit of higher-level goals that are common to both leader and followers. There are two components to transformational leadership: (1) It elevates the motives of individuals toward a common goal. (2) It focuses on higher-order, intrinsic, and moral motives. (Kowalski & Reitzug, 1993, p. 233)

Transformational leadership is concerned with vision and culture. Change in schools, for example, is attempted by appealing to the professional commitment of teachers.

In this case, four teachers discuss the leadership behavior of a new principal. What becomes obvious is that the new principal is almost the complete opposite of her predecessor. Some of these differences are readily apparent (e.g., gender, experience), but others are more subtle. As you read the case, concentrate on trying to understand why these four teachers hold their respective views. Also try to relate the discussion to your personal experiences. Do either of these principals resemble administrators with whom you have been associated?

KEY AREAS FOR REFLECTION

1. Principal succession and the ability to create change
2. Teacher expectations of principal behavior
3. Various types of power and how they are used by leaders
4. The importance of culture and climate in relation to leadership behavior
5. Communication processes in schools
6. The importance of moral, professional, and ethical issues in transformational leadership

THE CASE

As Peter Weller walked into the teachers' lounge, there was a sudden silence. Only three teachers were in the room, and they were seated together at one of the small round tables placed randomly in the room. He looked at each of them hoping that someone would break the silence.

Finally he asked, "Okay, what's going on here? You guys look like you just got caught doing something terribly wrong."

Debra Lowler, Linda Mays, Jake Brumwell—the three teachers in the room—and Peter all had their preparation period during the second hour of the school day. Over the course of the year, they got to know each other quite well. It had become customary for them to convene for coffee—usually during the last 15 minutes of their preparation period.

"Peter," Linda answered, "We didn't know it was you. We were just discussing your favorite principal. Maybe she has a bug in this room and sent you in here to defend her! Just a joke, Peter, so don't get hostile."

Peter just smiled and walked over to the table with the coffeepot; he filled his cup and sat down with the others.

"Don't you people have better things to discuss? Now I realize that teachers just love to criticize principals. But come on now, let's ease up on Dr. Werner."

Colleen Werner became principal of Drewerton South High School less than a year ago. The school is only 14 years old and enrolls 1,050 students in a middle-class suburban community. She is only the second person to hold this administrative position at the school.

George Calbo, Dr. Werner's predecessor, retired a year ago. He is a tall man, approximately 6'5", whose presence is immediately noticed when he walks into a room. Prior to being named the first principal at South, he taught physical education and coached basketball at Drewerton Central (which was the only high school in the district at the time). Many of the teachers at South admired and respected him. He had a way of keeping everybody happy. He found ways to work out problems; he was a master at reaching compromises.

The selection of Colleen Werner to be the next principal at Drewerton South shocked many on the faculty. She and George Calbo were obviously very different. She was somewhat introverted, she came from the East Coast, she had just earned a Ph.D., and she was quite young—only 32 years old. Whereas George would spend much of his time walking the halls and talking to teachers in the lounge, Colleen was more apt to schedule her days in meticulous fashion. Whereas George was prone to make all the big decisions, Colleen delegated much of the managerial functions of the school to her two assistant principals. When George went to a football or basketball game, he made sure everyone knew he was there. He would walk through the stands shaking hands and slapping people on their backs. Colleen went to games, but you would really have to look to find her. She maintained a low profile, but she was always friendly to those who tried to engage her in conversation.

Peter Weller often found himself defending Dr. Werner during the coffee sessions with his three colleagues. He really didn't mind doing so, because he truly believed that she was an exceptional leader. He admired her courage to be the type of principal she wanted to be; he admired her professional approach to dealing with the faculty and the public; and he appreciated her candidness about the school and what needed to be done in the future.

"Well, what are you crucifying her for today?" Peter asked.

"Come on Peter," Jake answered. "You know we have to talk about some-body, and it might as well be Colleen."

"No, you talk about her almost every day. She's become an obsession for you three," Peter noted.

Debra Lowler, who is usually the person in the group with the least to say, spoke next. "I'll tell you what bothers me about her. It's those repeated com-ments about how we should be professionals, about why we should always do things for the kids, and about how we should be willing to volunteer for this and that. We never got any of that nonsense from George. He knew the score. He was a teacher for many years before becoming a principal. He had his feet on the ground."

"Yes," Linda chimed in, "George fought for teachers' rights. He made sure we got paid for doing extra things. He didn't want teachers to be abused."

"Don't you think that Colleen cares about people?" Peter asked. "Don't you think she wants to do what's best for students and faculty? Just because she doesn't go around praising everyone every minute of the day doesn't mean she's indifferent or cold."

Jake Brumwell teaches mathematics and coaches track and cross-country. In the group, he is probably Dr. Werner's biggest critic. Jake's age, 51, and his close relationship with the former principal are probably factors that contribute to his negative attitude toward her.

"Peter, this principal still has a lot to learn," Jake said. "She especially has a lot to learn about people and about getting things done. Just last week, for example, she called me into her office and asked if I would be willing to take a group of students camping in June. These are the kids that she has put in this special program—you know, the ones who are likely to quit school. She has already gotten two other teachers to agree to volunteer for this weekend camp-ing trip, and she wants to know if I'll go too. So, I ask her how much I would get paid. And she looks at me like I'm crazy. She says that it is something we are doing for the kids. She's going to pay for the van and the food, but that's all. So, I tell her I'm busy that weekend. I just don't like being put in these positions where I have to say no and end up looking like a bad guy."

Peter responded very quickly, "Did you know, Jake, that I'm one of those who volunteered?" Not waiting for an answer, he asked another question. "Did you know that Colleen, herself, was going to go? So, it wasn't like she was ask-ing you to do something that she wasn't doing herself."

Debra came to Jake's defense. "Sure, she's going. But she's on a 12-month contract. We're not."

"But she's not paid for working on weekends, is she?" Peter shot back.

Linda entered the conversation again. "Look, it's more than just asking us to give up our time. Colleen's whole approach toward running South High is very different—she doesn't do things the way George Calbo did them. I guess the best way to put it is that George was always looking out for us. He cared that teachers received fair compensation for what they did. He wasn't going to let anyone take advantage of us. It seems that Colleen only cares about the students—and the worse the students are, the more she seems to care about them. She's obsessed with saving lost causes. Now we all recognize that this is noble, but can she be a good principal if this is all she cares about?"

"Yeah, maybe if she tried to make us as happy as she tries to make the kids, she would be a lot better off," Jake added. "Personally, I think it would be better for her to pay attention to the best students. They are the ones who ought to be receiving special trips. What kinds of messages are sent to the kids when the very worst students, the troublemakers, are the ones who get all of the principal's attention?"

Peter was visibly frustrated by what he was hearing. He had been teaching for nearly 15 years, and it was at times like these that he reached back to remember why he had become a teacher in the first place.

"You three realize, don't you, that there are many teachers here at South who support Colleen and her leadership style?" Peter asked rhetorically. "It's not as if everybody thinks she is a disaster. Why don't you give her credit for some of the things she has accomplished in just a short period of time? What about her work with Deloris Hutchins?"

Deloris Hutchins taught home economics, and students and teachers at South viewed her to be one of the worst teachers at the school. Dr. Werner made Deloris her pet project during the first year of her principalship. She personally spent time helping her to improve her planning and instructional strategies. In return, Deloris has become one of Dr. Werner's primary supporters.

Peter answered his own question. "You know and I know that George Calbo simply protected Deloris. He didn't care whether she became a better teacher. He just wasn't going to let anyone touch one of 'his' teachers. That's all he cared about. Why didn't he raise concern about Deloris's students? Why didn't he help her become a better instructor instead of just making excuses for her poor per-formance? Ask Deloris whether Colleen is a good principal. Ask her which prin-cipal really cared about helping her. She told me a week ago that Dr. Werner is the best administrator she has ever known. She said that Colleen has helped her become a better teacher. To say that Colleen doesn't care about teachers is a lot of nonsense."

Jake replied to Peter, "See, that's what I was trying to say a minute ago. No matter whether it's teachers or students, she seems to care only about those who are doing poorly. What about some 'perks' for those of us who do a good job day after day. What do we get? I'll tell you. We get to give up a weekend to supervise a bunch of rowdies out in the woods! And if we say no, we're sud-denly uncaring teachers, insensitive human beings. I don't like the way this administrator operates; and I'll say again, she's not ready for a job like this."

Peter recognized that he was not going to gain any converts today. There had been many previous conversations like this one; although everyone leaves with the same convictions, they all seem to feel better having had the opportu-nity to vent their feelings. Strangely, the 15- to 20-minute daily debates seem to strengthen the bond among the four teachers.

"Well, colleagues," Peter said as he stood up, "time to get back to work. But before I do, I just wanted to let you know one last time that you are all wrong about Colleen. Give her a chance. She's a bright, energetic leader. Maybe she's not perfect, but who is?"

"Oh Peter," Linda said, "wipe that smile off your face. Don't you recognize when you have lost an argument. After all, three of us can't be wrong!"

"We all know that women are more flexible leaders," Debra interjected.

Jake now was smiling too, and he shot back, "Says who?"

"I say so," Debra answered sarcastically. "I've got scientific evidence. Seriously, maybe Colleen will see the light and become more like George Calbo. She is bright, and I think she really wants to do the right things. Let's give Peter credit for one good suggestion. Maybe we should give her more time before we declare her a lost cause."

The group always had a way of ending their discussions with a little humor. Maybe it was their way of assuring that no one's feelings were hurt.

Jake had the last word as the teachers left the lounge. "First thing you should learn, Debra, is that you never tell Peter he's right about anything. After all, we're his only friends and we have make sure that his overactive ego remains under control."

The four teachers laughed as they scattered down different hallways to their next classes.

THE CHALLENGE

Utilize your knowledge of leadership and organizational behavior to analyze the discussion that took place. Specifically, provide an explanation of why teachers in this school react to Dr. Werner so differently.

KEY ISSUES/QUESTIONS

1. Is it common for teachers in a school to have differing role expectations for a principal? What evidence do you have to support your response?

2. In the case, a charge is made that Dr. Werner spends an inordinate amount of her time trying to assist students and teachers experiencing problems. Assuming this is an accurate observation, are you troubled by that fact?

3. Compare and contrast *legitimate, expert,* and *referent* power. Based on the conversation held by the four teachers, can you make any judgments about the forms of power used by the past and present principals?

4. Succession in the principalship is a topic receiving added attention in the literature. Why is there growing interest in this topic?

5. What factors are associated with a new principal's ability to bring about significant change in a school?

6. Identify several theories that focus on transformational or charismatic leadership. Discuss the primary facets of these theories.

7. To what extent do the personal values and beliefs of teachers influence their judgments about school administrators?

8. One argument frequently made in collective bargaining is that teachers should not be expected to do "extra" work without additional compensation. In part, this position is predicated on the belief that teachers are not adequately compensated in the first place. What is your personal position on this matter?

9. What is your image of an ideal principal? What characteristics, skills, knowledge, and so forth, would this person possess?

10. Principals are involved in a wide range of duties. These include such responsibilities as managerial tasks (e.g., facility management, budgets), instructional leadership (e.g., developing new courses, working with teachers), student supervision (e.g., discipline), organizational tasks (e.g., scheduling), and public relations (e.g., being a representative of the school to the community). In general, which of these duties most influences teachers' perceptions of a principal?

11. Assume that you are seeking a position as assistant principal. Would you like to work for Dr. Werner? Why or why not?

12. Do you believe that Dr. Werner tries to lead by example? Why or why not?

13. What is meant by the symbolic nature of the principalship?

14. Is it more feasible for a new principal to set a vision and bring others to accept that vision or to reach a new vision democratically by building consensus over time?

SUGGESTED READINGS

Bass, B., & Avolio, B. (1989). Potential biases in leadership measures: How prototypes, leniency, and general satisfaction relate to ratings and rankings of transformational and transactional leadership constructs. *Educational and Psychological Measurement, 49*(3), 509-527.

Bennis, W., & Nannus, B. (1985). *Leaders: The strategies for taking charge.* New York: Harper & Row.

Blase, J. (1986). Leadership behavior of school principals in relation to teacher stress, satisfaction, and performance. *Journal of Humanistic Education and Development, 24*(4), 159-171.

Burns, J. (1978). *Leadership.* New York: Harper & Row.

Cunningham, W., & Gresso, D. (1993). *Cultural leadership: The culture of excellence in education* (pp. 41-50). Boston: Allyn & Bacon.

Erickson, H. (1985). Conflict and the female principal. *Phi Delta Kappan, 67,* 288-291.

Foster, W. (1988). The administrator as transformative intellectual. *Peabody Journal of Education, 66*(3), 5-18.

Hallinger, P. (1992). The evolving role of the American principals: From managerial to instructional to transformational leaders. *Journal of Educational Administration, 30*(3), 35-48.

Hart, A. (1991). Leader succession and socialization: A synthesis. *Review of Educational Research, 61,* 451-474.

Hart, A. (1993). *Principal succession: Establishing leadership in schools.* Albany, NY: State University of New York Press.

Kowalski, T., & Reitzug, U. (1993). *Contemporary school administration: An introduction.* New York: Longman (see chapter 10).

Krug, S. (1993). Leadership craft and the crafting of school leaders. *Phi Delta Kappan, 75*(3), 240-244.

Leithwood, K. (1992). The move toward transformational leadership. *Educational Leadership, 49*(5), 8-12.

Meadows, B. (1992). Nurturing cooperation and responsibility in a school environment. *Phi Delta Kappan, 73*(6), 480-481.

Ogawa, R. (1991). Enchantment, disenchantment, and accommodation: How a faculty made sense of the succession of its principal. *Educational Administration Quarterly, 27*(1), 30-60.

Owens, R. (1991). *Organizational behavior in education* (4th ed.). Boston: Allyn & Bacon (see chapter 6).

Reitzug, U., & Reeves, J. (1992). Miss Lincoln doesn't teach here: A descriptive narrative and conceptual analysis of a principal's symbolic leadership behavior. *Educational Administration Quarterly, 28*(2), 185-219.

Roesner, C. (1987). Principals' leadership behavior—Do you see yourself as your subordinates see you? *NASSP Bulletin, 71*(502), 68-71.

Rossmiller, R. (1992). The secondary school principal and teachers' quality of work life. *Educational Management and Administration, 20*(3), 132-146.

Sagar, R. (1992). Three principals who make a difference. *Educational Leadership, 49*(5), 13-18.

Sillins, H. (1992). Effective leadership for school reform. *Alberta Journal of Educational Research, 38*(4), 317-334.

Valentine, J., & Bowman, M. (1991). Effective principal, effective school: Does research support the assumption? *NASSP Bulletin, 75*(539), 1-7.

Wells, D. (1985). The perfect principal: A teacher's fantasy. *Principal, 65*(1), 27.

Wooster, M. (1991). First principals: The leadership vacuum in American schools. *Policy Review, 57,* 55-61.

Yukl, G. (1989). *Leadership in organizations* (2nd ed.). Englewood Cliffs, NJ: Prentice-Hall (see chapter 10).

An Assistant Principal Who Does Not Fit the Image

BACKGROUND INFORMATION

Individual employee behavior in a school is the product of many influences such as personal characteristics (e.g., personality, needs, values, and beliefs), role expectations, and organizational characteristics (i.e., the culture and climate of the school). Generally, individuals conform to role expectations, because such factors as rules, regulations, rewards, and punishments are almost always present to encourage conformity. But some individuals do not make this adjustment, and the result is role conflict—a disharmony between expectations and actual behavior.

There are numerous sources of role conflict (Owens, 1991). Discord could be created by differences between two individuals (a principal and a teacher do not agree on the role the teacher should assume), between an individual and a group (a principal and his or her faculty do not agree on the principal's role), between an individual and an organization (a principal does not adjust to rules and regulations that detail expected administrative behavior), or within a single individual (a new principal still clings to his or her former role as a teacher after entering administration).

Conflict can also be the product of uncertainty. Often, administrators receive mixed messages regarding their behavior. A good example involves risk taking. School district officials may verbally encourage principals to seek change by taking chances with new ideas, but they support a salary system that rewards those who avoid problems. In such instances, principals are often confused by an incongruity between what they are told to do and the consequences of their behavior.

To a large extent, this case involves role conflict and role ambiguity. But it also entails several other key issues. One of them is socialization or organizational enculturation. Miklos (1988) wrote that these terms involved

> . . . the ways in which the values, norms, rules, and operating proce-
> dures that govern the practice of administration are communicated and
> learned. (p. 65)

Generally socialization can be divided into two components: (1) that occurring prior to a specific administrative appointment, and (2) that occurring following the appointment. In the former, family life, college, graduate school, and teaching exemplify experiences that help shape administrative behavior. The latter occurs in the first few years after appointment to a specific leadership position. At this stage, both the organization and the individuals and groups within it communicate expectations.

School districts, like all other organizations, exhibit differences in role expectations and the intensity of socialization. This helps explain why some principals or superintendents are highly successful in some settings but not in others. School districts also differ in the degree to which they demand conformity. That is to say, punishment for nonconformity is not consistent across all organizations.

This case takes place in an affluent suburban community. An assistant high school principal who is seen as highly successful by his immediate supervisor is recommended for dismissal by central office staff. There are many different perspectives to this situation, and it is helpful to examine why individuals do not tend to react to this case in a uniform manner.

KEY AREAS FOR REFLECTION

1. Role theory (role conflict and role ambiguity)
2. Personal conflict related to assuming administrative positions
3. Socialization and its effect on administrative behavior
4. The effects of the community environment on role expectations
5. Many facets of determining success and failure in administration
6. Communication processes and their relationship to role conflict

THE CASE

The Community

Thomas Creek is an established suburb located approximately 12 miles from a major city in the western part of New York State. With its quiet, tree-lined streets and attractive homes, Thomas Creek is definitely upper middle class. Most adult residents are college graduates, many hold prominent management positions in corporations, and about 15 percent are self-employed professionals (e.g., lawyers, physicians, architects).

Although somewhat homogeneous with regard to family income, the community's population is diverse in other respects. Official census data provide the following population profile:

Caucasian—75 percent

Asian American—14 percent

African American—7 percent

Hispanic—2 percent

Other—2 percent

Unofficial data collected in a recent sociological study conducted by a local university indicated the following religious affiliations for the citizens of Thomas Creek:

Protestant—34 percent

Roman Catholic—26 percent

Other Christian—3 percent

Jewish—32 percent

Moslem—3 percent

Other or No Affiliation—2 percent

The overall population of the community is stable; very little land remains for new developments. When houses go on the market, they usually sell within two or three weeks.

The School System

The brochure prepared by the Thomas Creek Chamber of Commerce identifies the public school system as a major asset of the community. The K–12 system has developed an outstanding reputation. The high school, for example, recently won several citations from state and national groups for excellence in educational programming. Scholastic Aptitude Test scores for high school students are usually among the top 5 percent in the state. The Chamber of Commerce brochure includes the following statement: "Thomas Creek—a community where cultural diversity and public education have been made assets."

The public school system in Thomas Creek includes three elementary schools (K-5), a middle school (6-8), and a high school (9-12). The overall enrollment is 2,500 students. The number of students in the system declined steadily from 1976 when the total enrollment was 3,150. In the past two years, however, enrollments have remained relatively stable.

In addition to the public schools, two private elementary schools are located within the boundaries of the public school system: (1) St. Jerome Catholic School (K–6) and (2) Thomas Creek Academy (K–5). Virtually all of the students from St. Jerome enter the public schools after the sixth grade; only about 40 percent of those attending Thomas Creek Academy do so.

The High School

Although all the schools in Thomas Creek are considered well above average in per-pupil spending, it is the high school that is the "showpiece" of the community's commitment to education. The facility is attractive, and although now 27 years old, it has been constantly updated. Just recently fiber optics labs, two electronics classrooms, and two additional computer laboratories were added. The school looks like it was just built a few years ago.

The curriculum at the school is somewhat comprehensive. As one might expect, technical and vocational courses are not as prevalent here as they are in urban schools. The primary instructional thrust is college preparation, because approximately 80 percent of the graduates go on to four-year colleges and universities (another 10 percent enroll in two-year institutions). The school offers a comprehensive athletic program, having seven boys' and seven girls' athletic teams. With an enrollment of 870, the school also provides students access to special-interest clubs, fine arts activities, and community experiences (e.g., internships).

The staff at the high school is considered an asset. Most teachers have advanced degrees, and resignations are rare. In the past five years, there have been only three changes on the faculty. Unlike many other high schools in this part of the state, Thomas Creek has not been burdened with union-related problems. Only about 40 percent of the teachers at the high school belong to the teachers' association.

The Principal

Allen Miller accepted the principalship at Thomas Creek High School four years ago. Prior to this assignment, he was a high school principal in a Cleveland suburb. He is energetic and enthusiastic, frequently spending 12 hours a day on the job. Parents, students, teachers, and other administrators generally perceive Allen to be a forceful leader, a good listener, and a patient person. Basically, he is people-oriented, devoting much of his time to meeting with students, teachers, and parents. For example, his weekly coffee sessions with parents are highly publicized. By contrast, he spends very little time with what he calls the "administrivia" of running a high school—bus schedules, lunch programs, book rentals, and the like. He not only dislikes these assignments, he also feels that he is least effective when he is wearing the hat of "building manager." Hence, those assignments that Allen finds less desirable are relegated to his assistant principal, George Hopkins.

The Assistant Principal

George Hopkins has worked at Thomas Creek High School for the last 27 years. He was football coach and taught physical education prior to becoming an administrator five years ago. He is considered the "enforcer" by the students—the person in charge of discipline in the school. With his crewcut hair style and serious manner his outward appearance is in sharp contrast to Mr. Miller, who looks more like a corporate executive. Students often joke that Mr. Hopkins has two sets of clothing, wrinkled and more wrinkled. Despite differences in their appearance, the two administrators respect each other and maintain a congenial relationship. Allen has recommended George for the highest level of merit increase for the last four years. Allen recognizes his personal strengths and weaknesses and sees George as a perfect complement to his leadership style. Additionally, George feels comfortable with his duties and his working relationship with Allen.

Key Central Office Administrators

Dr. Valerie Daniels is the associate superintendent for instruction in the school district. She is a former elementary principal who has occupied her present position for two years. The superintendent is Dr. Ronald O'Brien, who also has been in his present post for just two years. Both administrators worked together in a district in Illinois prior to coming to Thomas Creek. In addition to these two positions, the central office includes a business manager and director of special services.

Allen's relationship with both of the top-ranking school district officials was extremely positive. Last year, Dr. O'Brien, with Dr. Daniels's support, nominated him for the award of outstanding high school principal in the state principals' association. In his letter of nomination, Dr. O'Brien wrote

> Allen Miller is an outstanding leader. He is a dedicated professional who provides a positive role model for the teachers and students. He represents the values and beliefs that make Thomas Creek High School one of the best secondary schools in the nation.

Allen had much more contact with Dr. Daniels than he did with Dr. O'Brien. The organizational arrangement of the district was such that principals reported directly to the associate superintendent for instruction. Dr. Daniels would visit the high school about once a month, unless there were special meetings or programs that caused her to be there more frequently. Additionally, she held meetings with all principals at her office once every two weeks. On occasion, Dr. O'Brien would attend these meetings, but over the course of a year, he probably would attend just five or six meetings. In the two years since Dr. O'Brien's arrival, Allen has had just three or four private meetings with the superintendent.

Evaluation Procedures

Performance evaluations for the school principals are conducted by the associate superintendent, who discusses the outcomes with individual principals in evaluation conferences. The superintendent typically is in attendance at these conferences, and one reason relates to salary decisions. Administrative salary increases are based exclusively on merit that is determined by the outcome of the annual evaluation, and even though the associate superintendent conducts the evaluation, it is the superintendent who makes salary increase determinations. For the most part, the administrative staff in the district likes the present procedure. They generally receive higher percentage increases than other employees.

As part of the evaluation process, principals are required to evaluate their assistants and to bring written documentation of that process to their own evaluation conferences. Each principal reviews subordinate evaluations with the associate superintendent and superintendent. The principal also makes a salary recommendation for assistant principals.

The Incident

Evaluation conferences for the principals are scheduled in late March of each year. When Allen Miller arrived five minutes early for his evaluation conference, his thoughts were on another matter. He presumed that this would be another routine session, so as he waited to be called into Dr. O'Brien's office, his mind was on the agenda for the seniors' honor banquet that would take place in three weeks. About 15 minutes after arriving, Dr. Daniels emerged from the superintendent's office.

"Good morning, Allen. Come in. We're trying to keep pretty much on schedule today, but as you can see, we're already a few minutes behind," she said.

Allen smiled, nodded, and entered the large office. He exchanged pleasantries with the superintendent and took his customary seat (every evaluation conference found the three participants occupying the same seats around a small conference table as if the chairs were reserved). It was 9:40 AM and Allen figured that as usual he would be back in his office at least by 11:00 AM.

After the greetings were completed, Dr. Daniels started the conference.

"Let's start with your evaluation of George Hopkins."

Mechanically, Allen ticked off the ratings he had given his assistant in the various categories of the standard evaluation form. Most ratings were in the "excellent" range; some were "above average"; and only one, personal appearance, was rated as "average."

"You know old coaches," Allen commented with a smile and a nod, "they seem to enjoy looking like old coaches."

The two central office administrators did not smile at Allen's comment, and being observant, he quickly retracted his grin. His comment about his assistant's appearance was followed by one of those awkward moments of silence. Allen quickly sensed that something was wrong. He felt uncomfortable, but he wanted one of the others to break the silence.

Dr. Daniels finally obliged when she looked squarely at him and said, "Allen, this is a special community. Thomas Creek High School is a special school. We should all feel fortunate this is the case. But to preserve these images, we must constantly be concerned about the images our administrators present to the general public. In this regard, George has become somewhat of an embarrassment. He never wears a suit, he looks like he shaves before he goes to bed rather than in the morning, and he is not involved in any community service activities. Visitors to the school could easily mistake him for a custodian."

Allen was shaken by this harsh assessment. He certainly could not argue that George had a problem with personal appearance, but he asked himself why this condition—which certainly was not new—had suddenly become such a big issue. He decided to verbalize his inquiry,

"If you felt this strongly about George, why did you approve a maximum merit raise for him last year?"

The superintendent decided to field the question. "We did it for you, Allen. We did it for you. We didn't want you to feel hurt because we wouldn't accept your recommendation. So we went along with it. Don't forget, we were both new administrators in this district. We had to depend on judgments made by our staff."

"So what does all this mean? Does it mean that you reject my recommendation that he again receive the top level of merit increase?" Allen asked.

"No. It is much more serious," Dr. Daniels answered. "It means that George has got to go. We have an opening at the middle school for a physical education teacher. He can be assigned there. We'll see that he gets some driver education work in the summer to help with his overall salary."

Allen was stunned by what he had just heard. He stared at his supervisor in disbelief. After about a minute, he collected his thoughts.

"You have to understand that you caught me completely off guard with this matter. I have to tell you, I don't think this is a proper decision," Allen asserted. "George is a good administrator. I could not get along without him and I mean that. If anything, he has never received the recognition he deserves. I doubt that I can be as effective with someone else being the assistant principal. He is loyal, he is dedicated, and he doesn't deserve this. And besides if this was so important, why didn't anyone say something to me before this conference?"

Dr. O'Brien again entered the conversation. "Allen, listen. You don't have to take the blame for this. We are willing to explain to the board that it is our decision. George won't be angry with you. He'll direct his outrage at me and perhaps Valerie—but not you. All we are asking from you is to be silent on the matter. It would not look good for you to be publicly fighting this decision."

"He's right, Allen," Dr. Daniels interjected. "You have a great thing going at Thomas Creek High School. But if you had an assistant whose image was in line with that of the school district, you could be doing even more. Believe me, Dr. O'Brien and I have given this a great deal of thought. There are many administrators who can handle discipline and other matters and still look like leaders."

Dr. O'Brien reached over and put is hand on Allen's shoulder. "We want your assurance that you will go along. We are just asking you not to comment on the matter publicly. We'll take care of the rest."

THE CHALLENGE

Place yourself in Allen's position. What would you do in this situation?

KEY ISSUES/QUESTIONS

1. To what extent do you believe the nature of the community plays a role in this case?
2. What aspects of organizational theory are helpful in determining why the personal appearance of an assistant principal is a critical element in this case?
3. What aspects of role theory are helpful in determining why the personal appearance of an assistant principal is a critical element in this case?
4. What does Allen have to gain by agreeing to do what the superintendent and associate superintendent are requesting?
5. What options does Allen have, if any, beyond either agreeing or not agreeing to do what his superiors have asked of him?
6. Discuss the socialization elements of this case. What significance do you give to the length of service in the district of the various administrators?
7. How do you think teachers at the high school might react if the assistant principal is reassigned? What elements of the case lead you to your response?
8. Evaluate the line relationship of principals in this school district. Do you think it is appropriate for them to be reporting directly to the associate superintendent? Why or why not?
9. Assess the behavior of the associate superintendent in this case. Is this a type of person to whom you would like to report?
10. Assess the behavior of the superintendent in this case. Is this a type of person to whom you would like to report?
11. To what extent did Allen err by assuming that this would be a routine conference?
12. Some experienced administrators might defend the action of the superintendent and assistant superintendent on the grounds that it is best to "act swiftly and forcefully" in controversial situations. Do you agree?
13. Discuss the differences between summative and formative evaluation. To what extent are the superintendent and associate superintendent supporting both processes in this case?
14. Who has contributed to role conflict in this case?

SUGGESTED READINGS

Calabrese, R., & Adams, C. (1987). A comparative analysis of alienation among secondary school administrators. *Planning and Changing, 18*(2), 90-97.

Calabrese, R., & Tucker-Ladd, P. (1991). The principal and assistant principal: A mentoring relationship. *NASSP Bulletin, 75*(533), 67-74.

Cantwell, Z. (1993). School-based leadership and the professional socialization of the assistant principal. *Urban Education, 28*(1), 49-68.

Drake, T., & Roe, W. (1994). *The principalship* (4th ed.). New York: Macmillan (see chapter 2).

Duke, D. (1992). Concepts of administrative effectiveness and the evaluation of school administrators. *Journal of Personnel Evaluation in Education, 6*(2), 103-121.

Fulton, O. (1987). Basic competencies of the assistant principal. *NASSP Bulletin, 71*(501), 52.

Hamner, T., & Turk, J. (1987). Organizational determinants of leader behavior and authority. *Journal of Applied Psychology, 72,* 647-682.

Hanson, E. (1991). *Educational administration and organizational behavior* (3rd ed., pp. 157-162). Boston: Allyn & Bacon.

Harrison, W., & Peterson, K. (1988). Evaluation of principals: The process can be improved. *NASSP Bulletin, 72*(508), 1-4.

Hess, F. (1985). The socialization of the assistant principal: From the perspective of the local district. *Education and Urban Society, 18*(1), 93-106.

Hoy, W., & Forsyth, P. (1986). *Effective supervision: Theory into practice* (pp. 120-122). New York: Random House.

Hoy, W., & Miskel, C. (1987). *Educational administration: Theory, research and practice* (3rd ed., pp. 76-79). New York: Random House.

Hoy, W., Newland, W., & Blaxovsky, R. (1977). Subordinate loyalty to superior, esprit, and aspects of bureaucratic structure. *Educational Administration Quarterly, 13*(1), 71-85.

Immegart, G. (1988). Leadership and leader behavior. In N. Boyan (Ed.), *Handbook of research on educational administration* (pp. 259-278). New York: Longman.

Kowalski, T., & Reitzug, U. (1993). *Contemporary school administration: An introduction.* New York: Longman (see chapters 7, 10).

Lang, R. (1986). The hidden dress code dilemma. *Clearing House, 59*(6), 277-279.

Manatt, R. (1987). Lessons from a comprehensive performance appraisal project. *Educational Leadership, 44*(7), 8-14.

Marshall, C. (1992). *The assistant principal: Leadership chores and challenges.* Newbury Park, CA: Corwin.

Marshall, C. (1985). Professional shock: The enculturation of the assistant principal. *Education and Urban Society, 18*(1), 28-58.

Marshall, C., & Greenfield, W. (1985). The socialization of the assistant principal: Implications for school leadership. *Education and Urban Society, 18*(1), 3-8.

McPherson, R., & Crowson, R. (1987). Sources of constraints and opportunities for discretion in the principalship. In J. Lane and H. Walberg (Eds.), *Effective school leadership* (pp. 129-156). Berkeley, CA: McCutchan.

Miklos, E. (1988). Administrator selection, career patterns, succession, and socialization. In N. Boyan (Ed.), *Handbook of research on educational administration* (pp. 53-76). New York: Longman.

Norton, M., & Kriekard, J. (1987). Real and ideal competencies for the assistant principal. *NASSP Bulletin, 71*(501), 23-30.

Owens, R. (1991). *Organizational behavior in education* (4th ed.). Boston: Allyn & Bacon (see chapter 3).

Peterson, K. (1984). Mechanisms of administrative control over managers in educational organizations. *Administrative Science Quarterly, 29,* 573-597.

Reed, D. (1985). The work of the secondary assistant principalship: A field study. *Education and Urban Society, 18*(1), 59-84.

Socialization of the assistant principal: Implications for school leadership (1985). *Urban Education, 18* (special theme issue).

Yukl, G. (1989). *Leadership in organizations* (2nd ed., pp. 151–157; 174–191). Englewood Cliffs, NJ: Prentice-Hall.

Using Committees to Make Key Decisions

BACKGROUND INFORMATION

At the very heart of leadership is the process of making decisions. While some may assume that this responsibility is solely an art, there is a great deal of scientific information illustrating how administrators make critical choices for their organizations and their own behavior. In reviewing research on this topic, Estler (1988) outlined four models of decision making: rational-bureaucratic, participatory, political, and organized anarchy. The first two relate to normative theory and the others to descriptive theory.

In trying to gain an understanding of how decisions are made in a school or school system, researchers have recognized that a number of variables play an important role. For example, the individual decision maker brings biases, beliefs, and previous experiences to the situation; the specific school or school district has some bearing on the matter; and the nature of the decision is certainly a cogent ingredient.

Managers in private industry have long sought rational and easily understood decision-making models that would reduce errors (and ultimately inefficiency). Peter Drucker (1974), for instance, reduced the process to five critical steps: defining the problem, analyzing the problem, developing alternative solutions, selecting a best solution, and taking action. But researchers, both in education and in other organizations, have increasingly realized that theories do not fully explain real behavior. Cultural elements of organizations, such as myths, symbols, and rituals, can help determine procedures and decisions. Hence, decisions may not focus solely on organizational or individual goals. The formation of a committee to make a key decision, for instance, may be influenced by a belief that all professionals should be represented in the process even if this alternative prolongs the decision or produces an inferior decision. While this may not make much sense managerially, it occurs frequently in everyday practice.

This case centers on a new superintendent's decision to create a committee to study a problem in the district. Some administrative staff are angered by the superintendent's action, and those who do not agree with the committee approach speculate on the superintendent's motives. Also at issue are perceptions of organizational life—especially as they relate to dividing functions among divisions of the school district. One key element is that the superintendent is new in the district, and the chief business official sees this as an opportunity to resolve what she considers to be a long-standing problem.

KEY AREAS FOR REFLECTION

1. Theories of decision making
2. Division of authority in school districts
3. Participatory approaches to problem solving
4. Subordinate expectations of a new superintendent
5. Perceptions of power among key administrators

THE CASE

The Community

Oxford County is located in a mid-Atlantic state. The county seat is Fullmer, a small city with about 45,000 residents. In recent years, there has been modest population growth—the overall county population increased by 5 percent from 1980 to 1990. In large measure, this increase was attributable to the in-migration of retirees. Senior citizens are attracted by the mild climate, scenic beauty, and the fact that the county is just far enough north to still have four distinctive seasons. Additionally, housing can be obtained at reasonable costs, property taxes are low (especially compared to the northeast and midwest), and there is little industry to create environmental problems.

Since the early 1980s, many counties in this state have been actively encouraging industrial development as a means of economic growth. Executives of both foreign and domestic companies have been courted by local officials. Therefore, the development of industrial parks, enterprise zones, and tax abatement programs are rather common in the region—but not in Oxford County. The Oxford County Chamber of Commerce has consciously pursued a different path. Tourism and the development of retirement villas have been the prime targets of this community.

Several relatively small manufacturing companies are located in Fullmer, but they were established more than 50 years ago. Periodically, executives of these companies express concerns that Oxford County ought to be more forward thinking about industrial development. There is a general fear that without further development, existing companies will face growing difficulties with infrastructures and taxes. For example, one of the companies in Fullmer, a candy factory, is currently examining relocating its plant in a neighboring county's modern industrial park. But to date, neither concerns nor threats has changed the desire to keep Oxford County a clean, environmentally safe community.

Six years ago, a new hospital was erected in Fullmer offering modern medical care to county residents. Its presence enhances the desirability of the county as a site for retirement villas. The hospital, costing more than $75 million, is considered one of the most modern in the state. The county planning board views the development of retirement complexes to be consistent with established values and beliefs that place a high priority on protecting the county's scenic environment.

The School District

The Oxford County School District is an all-county school system. It has a current enrollment of 21,500 students and operates the following attendance centers:

Two high schools, grades 9-12

Four middle schools, grades 6-8

Thirteen elementary schools, grades K-5

A vocational school (also includes an alternative program for secondary students not enrolled in a regular high school program)

Enrollment in the school system has declined just about 1 percent over the past decade, but in the last two years, kindergarten enrollments have declined by 7 percent.

The school district is governed by a seven-member board, each member being elected to represent a specified geographic area within the county. There are nine townships in the county. The seats on the board are distributed as follows:

Center Township (Fullmer)—2 seats

Abington Township—1 seat

Covington Township—1 seat

Delaware and Potter Townships—1 seat

Ealon and Mud Creek Townships—1 seat

Richards and Washington Townships—1 seat

The central office staff in the district has remained very stable over the past ten years. Data below exhibit the positions and tenure of the administrators at the director and assistant superintendent levels:

Name	Position	Years in Position	Years in District
Bob Andrevet	asst. supt./curr.	8	24
Pamela Davis	asst. supt./business	12	15
Jake Barnes	director/personnel	10	27
Neil Vickers	director/transportation	7	7
Iran Sults	director/maintenance	21	26
Anne Major	director/federal programs	9	16
Margo Jasik	director/special education	6	6

The superintendent, Dr. Rudy Quillen, is in his first year with the school district. He replaced Orville Cruthers, who served as the chief executive of the Oxford County School District for 18 years.

The Incident

Dr. Quillen arrived in Oxford County in mid-July after having completed three years as superintendent of a much smaller district (enrollment of 2,400 students) in a neighboring state. Several school board members from Oxford County met Dr. Quillen at a national convention over a year ago when he made a presentation on goal setting. They were so impressed with his presentation that they encouraged him to pursue the superintendent's job in their district, which they already knew would become vacant with the announced retirement of Mr. Cruthers. At age 38, Rudy Quillen was in good health, well experienced (over 12 years of administrative experience despite his young age), and eager to test his leadership ideas in a much larger school system.

One of the first controversies that faced the new superintendent centered on the use of petty cash funds by principals. These funds had been in place for as long as anyone could remember, but in recent years, there was an increasing number of legal questions about their purpose and use. Petty cash funds were employed by principals for emergency situations or the purchase of small items that had to be obtained in a timely fashion. Auditors periodically raised questions about their use but they never recommended their abolition—at least not formally.

The perpetuation of petty cash funds had become especially bothersome to the assistant superintendent for business, Pamela Davis. She thought the risks of having them far outweighed their potential benefits. On several occasions, she attempted to make this point to Mr. Cruthers, but to no avail. In the last two years of his tenure, he made it clear he would let someone else deal with this issue after he retired. With the employment of Dr. Quillen, Pamela saw a new window of opportunity to address one of her pet peeves. In fact, the topic of petty cash funds was raised in the first formal meeting the new superintendent had with his assistant superintendent for business. Perhaps more noteworthy for the superintendent, two school board members also voiced concerns about the petty cash funds—albeit informally and outside of school board meetings.

Petty cash funds exist in the district that previously employed Dr. Quillen, but they had never generated controversy there. He also personally used a petty cash fund when he was a principal, and it had not caused him any problems. Thus judging from personal experience, he was surprised that Pamela was so perplexed over this issue. In their conversations, he tried to find out if there had been specific problems in the past, and although she related some minor incidents, the superintendent concluded that her opposition to the funds was associated with the potentialities of problems rather than their actual existence. Even so, Dr. Quillen decided to seek advice from the state department of education and several other state agencies. Unfortunately, these inquiries failed to produce clear direction on the matter. The superintendent discovered that there were many opinions on the matter.

Dr. Quillen takes pride in being an open-minded administrator, and he did not want to offend a key official on his staff or ignore school board member inquiries. Hence, he placed the topic of petty cash funds on the agenda of the November meeting of the administrative team (principals and central office administrators constituted the administrative team). When Superintendent Quillen got to this item on the agenda, he outlined Pamela's concerns and shared the information he gathered via his telephone calls to state agencies. The superintendent pointed out that even several school board members asked why the funds were necessary.

Although Dr. Quillen expected some disagreement, he was shocked at the level of emotional intensity that was generated. All of the principals made it abundantly clear that they opposed abolition of the funds. Their position was fervently supported by the assistant superintendent for curriculum, Bob Andravet. Pamela Davis, as expected, took a very different posture. She restated that the funds served no useful purpose and that their very existence created a potential management problem. She conceded that they were legal, but she once again put forward the argument that they constituted an unnecessary risk. And for the first time, she offered an alternative.

"The principals say that they need the funds to make quick purchases. Well, I'm willing to set up a petty cash fund for the district. It will do the same thing your individual funds now do, but there will be more control," she said.

"That's just the problem," one of the principals answered. "More control. Every time we turn around, things are being centralized in this district. What makes you think you can do a better job of managing a petty cash fund?"

Seeing that nothing positive was apt to come from the discussion on this day, Dr. Quillen again took charge of the meeting.

"It's pretty obvious to me," he announced, "that we don't all agree on this matter. So maybe we should move on to the next agenda item, and we'll talk about petty cash funds another day."

Pamela Davis saw her window of opportunity becoming smaller. She did not want this issue returned to the back burner where it would again be forgotten. She felt that she needed to be assertive.

"There are important issues involved here. There are some serious management questions surrounding this practice, and we accomplish nothing by pretending it doesn't exist," she said with emotion. "Just because I stand alone on this issue doesn't make you right and me wrong. This isn't a matter that we should resolve by a show of hands. As administrators, we have a responsibility to do what is correct—not what is popular. At the very least, we need a detailed study of the issue. I'm willing to let the facts speak for themselves. Are you?"

Before any of the others could respond—and many were anxious to do so— the superintendent again seized the floor.

"First, I'm not in favor of just burying our heads in the sand. Pamela has a job to do and she's trying to do it. Her concerns are genuine. Second, I agree with her that issues such as this are not properly resolved by a straw vote. She makes an excellent point—we need to look at this issue more objectively and more extensively. Petty cash funds have existed in this school district for years and years. I don't suppose it will do much harm to wait another few months while we take a closer look. The question is, who is going to do the looking?"

Pamela answered immediately, "This is a fiscal matter. The responsibility for completing the study rests with my office. I'm the chief fiscal officer for the district."

Rich Kizer, a high school principal, strongly disagreed. "Pamela, your position on this matter is well known. How could you ever be objective about this issue? I recommend that Bob Andravet be responsible for doing it. After all, the principals report to him. Isn't he in the best position to balance the interests of the school district and the interests of individual principals?"

Skillfully, Dr. Quillen once again brought the debate to a halt before emotions became too heated. He said he would take the matter under advisement and announce his decision about the study of petty cash funds at the next meeting of the administrative team, which would be in two weeks. In the interim, he invited all parties to send him recommendations or suggestions.

At the next administrative team meeting, all those present anxiously awaited the superintendent's decision. Unlike his predecessor, Dr. Quillen was not prone to sharing his feelings on controversial matters with staff before he took a public stance on them. Thus, he was the only one in the room who knew what he would announce. This particular issue took on special meaning, because several of the principals and central office staff openly suggested that this action would reveal how the new superintendent approached problems. One principal speculated that Dr. Quillen would find a way to avoid making a decision; another said he would behave as a true bureaucrat and side with Pamela; still another said that he would be political and rule in favor of the principals.

To no one's disappointment, Dr. Quillen placed the item of petty cash funds at the top of the agenda.

"I have looked at this matter carefully," the superintendent began. "First, let me say that I am more convinced now than before that this issue should be thoroughly studied. If for no other reason, there are some contrasting perceptions and judgments about the need and effectiveness of petty cash funds. The comments I received over the past several weeks can be placed into two categories. One includes urgings that the study be headed by the assistant superintendent for curriculum. Those who recommend this alternative tend to see the political dimensions of the problem. Not surprisingly the other position is that the study should be completed by the assistant superintendent for business. Individuals embracing this position, and this includes at least two of our school board members, tend to see the managerial dimensions of this problem. After carefully considering all of the suggestions, I have decided that, given this problem and surrounding conditions, neither alternative is really best. Instead, I have decided to create an ad hoc committee consisting of two teachers, a parent who is an accountant, a high school senior, a parent who is an attorney, and Ann Major [director of federal programs]. Ann will serve as chair of the committee."

The group sat in silence. It was obvious they were caught off guard. One of the principals finally broke the silence by asking sarcastically, "This isn't a joke, is it?"

With a smile, Dr. Quillen answered. "No, it's no joke. Nor is it simply a way of avoiding taking sides. I truly believe that such a committee can do an objective job of looking at petty cash funds. Every person I named has an interest in this school district. Each is affected by critical decisions we make, and collectively, their views are valuable to us. Yet, each is sufficiently detached from the issue to assure objectivity."

Those in the room became convinced that the superintendent was in no mood for additional debate. No one offered further judgments on his decision, and he moved to the next item on the agenda.

After the meeting, Pamela Davis was the first to visit Dr. Quillen in his office. She expressed her disappointment in his decision and pleaded with him to reconsider the matter.

"If I knew that we would go off in this direction, I'm not sure I would have brought the issue up in the first place. There are two things that really bother me," she asserted. "First and most importantly, I see this as a slap in the face. Fiscal matters should be handled by my office. Otherwise, why have an assistant superintendent for business? Second, you should realize that the principals will work overtime to convince the teachers, students, and probably the parents that their position on this matter is correct. By creating this committee, you have reduced an important management issue to a political argument. I'm the one who faces the auditors when they raise questions about petty cash funds. Sooner or later we're going to have a real problem, and I wonder where all these principals and Bob will be when that happens?"

Dr. Quillen assured Pamela that this was not intended to be negative toward her or her position in the school district. He asked her to be patient and allow the process to run its course.

The superintendent also received a visit from Bob Andravet. He too was disappointed with the decision. He warned, "Dr. Quillen, the principals are really upset about all of this. They believe—no, we believe—that Pamela just wants to broaden her control over the operations of our schools. Principals already have to go to her with hats in hands begging for money. If they lose their petty cash funds, she will have even more to say about how the principals manage their schools. Your idea of a committee scares the principals because they think the committee members will be unduly influenced by simple management judgments. The committee members do not understand all the ramifications of school administration. They are apt to come down on the side of money management."

Dr. Quillen thanked Bob for his candidness, but as he had done with Pamela, he said he was committed to his decision.

THE CHALLENGE

Evaluate the decision made by Dr. Quillen. Would you have done something differently?

KEY ISSUES/QUESTIONS

1. Identify the range of options that are available to the superintendent at this point. What are the advantages and disadvantages of each?

2. Why do you think the assistant superintendents reacted so strongly in this matter? Do you believe that the organizational climate has anything to do with their reactions?

3. Some administrators might argue that Dr. Quillen should have attempted to reach a compromise between the two assistant superintendents so that they could have presented a united front to the principals. Do you agree that this would have been a better alternative than the one he pursued? Why or why not?

4. Are ad hoc committees effective? What are the strengths and weaknesses of this approach to dealing with problems?

5. Do you believe that the issue in question is serious enough for the superintendent to risk his working relationships with his top two assistants?

6. Identify some steps the superintendent can take to assure the board and professional staff that his idea of an ad hoc committee can work.

7. If you were a principal in this district, how would you interpret the superintendent's decision to use a committee? Does this decision provide insight into the new superintendent's leadership style?

8. Discuss the concept of project management. Does it have any relevance to this case?

9. In the early 1960s, research focusing on *career bound* versus *place bound* administrators emerged in the literature. Does this research have any value in analyzing behaviors in this case?

10. Should Dr. Quillen have been more sensitive to past practice? Why or why not?

11. Evaluate the issue of petty cash funds from two perspectives: (a) rational management and (b) political convenience. How are the two alike and different?

12. In what ways do elements of culture in a school district affect decision-making processes?

SUGGESTED READINGS

Black, J., & English, F. (1986). *What they don't tell you in schools of education about school administration.* Lancaster, PA: Technomic (see chapter 1).

Carlson, R. (1961). Succession and performance among school superintendents. *Administrative Science Quarterly, 6,* 210-227.

Crowson, R. (1987). The local school district superintendency: A puzzling role. *Educational Administration Quarterly, 23*(4), 49-69.

Cunningham, W., & Gresso, D. (1993). *Cultural leadership: The culture of excellence in education.* Boston: Allyn & Bacon (see chapter 9).

Drucker, P. (1974). *Management: Tasks, responsibilities, practices.* New York: Harper & Row.

Estler, S. (1988). Decision making. In N. Boyan (Ed.), *Handbook of research on educational administration* (pp. 305-320). New York: Longman.

Feld, M. (1988). The bureaucracy, the superintendent, and change. *Education and Urban Society, 47*(8), 417-444.

Goldman, C., & O'Shea, C. (1990). A culture for change. *Educational Leadership, 47*(8), 41-43.

Greenhalgh, J. (1978). *Practitioner's guide to school business management.* Boston: Allyn & Bacon (see chapter 2).

Hanson, E. (1991). *Educational administration and organizational behavior* (3rd ed.). Boston: Allyn & Bacon (see chapter 11).

Hughes, L., & Ubben, G. (1984). *The elementary principal's handbook* (2nd ed., pp. 304-309). Boston: Allyn & Bacon.

Ives, R. (1993). Shared decision making improves staff morale and efficiency. *NASSP Bulletin, 77*(550), 107-109.

Kessler, R. (1992). Shared decision making works! *Educational Leadership, 50*(1), 36-38.

Kowalski, T., & Reitzug, U. (1993). *Contemporary school administration: An introduction.* New York: Longman (see chapter 9).

Lakowski, G. (1987). Values and decision making in educational administration. *Educational Administration Quarterly, 23*(4), 70-82.

Lange, J. (1993). Site-based, shared decision making: A resource for restructuring. *NASSP Bulletin, 76*(549), 98-107.

McInerney, W. (1985). Participation in educational planning at the school district level. *Planning and Changing, 16,* 206-215.

Meadows, B. (1987). The influence of participants' values on group process and decision making. *North Central Association Quarterly, 61*(3), 440-443.

Meadows, B. (1992). Nurturing cooperation and responsibility in a school community. *Phi Delta Kappan, 73*(6), 480-481.

Meadows, B. (1990). The rewards and risks of shared leadership. *Phi Delta Kappan, 71*(7), 545-548.

Miklos, E. (1988). Administrator selection, career patterns, succession, and socialization. In N. Boyan (Ed.), *Handbook of research on educational administration* (pp. 53-76). New York: Longman.

Owens, R. (1991). *Organizational behavior in education* (4th ed.). Boston: Allyn & Bacon (see chapter 10).

Owens, R., & Lewis, E. (1976). Managing participation in organizational decisions. *Group and Organizational Studies, 1,* 55-56.

Pajak, E. (1989). *The central office supervisor of curriculum and instruction.* Boston: Allyn & Bacon (see chapter 8).

Russell, J., Cooper, B., & Greenblatt, R. (1992). How do you measure shared decision making? *Educational Leadership, 50*(1), 33–35.

Watson, P. (1986). Effective task forces: Getting a quality product in minimum time. *Planning and Changing, 17,* 131–145.

Yukl, G. (1989). *Leadership in organizations* (2nd ed.). Englewood Cliffs, NJ: Prentice-Hall (see chapter 3).

The Principal Changes Some Valued Rules

BACKGROUND INFORMATION

Much has been written about the school principal as a potential agent of change. This concept was especially popular in the late 1960s during a time when there were numerous attempts to radically change curriculum and instructional methods. Today, desires to create a new generation of American schools have rekindled the notion that the principalship can be the key to reshaping schools. In particular, efforts to decentralize authority and decision making (e.g., site-based management) have focused attention on the power and potentialities of formal leadership roles.

The idea that one administrator can radically improve a complex social institution is generally accepted by the public. An example of this is seen in the urban districts where a revolving door to the superintendent's office has resulted in an average tenure of approximately two and one-half years. It is less expensive and more politically expedient to create illusions of change by replacing the most visible leaders than it is to attack the real problems and deficiencies that plague our schools.

In reality, a principal's ability to quickly change a school's culture and climate is quite limited. Teachers, parents, and even students who have vested interests in the school are often reluctant to abandon long-standing values, beliefs, and practices. Change, especially top-down imposed change, is threatening.

In this case, a principal attempts to impose a new philosophy on an inner-city elementary school. His efforts to alter policy in two key areas, student retention and corporal punishment, meet with stiff opposition from the faculty. In analyzing the case, you should pay particular attention to interfacing means (how the principal attempted to impose change) and ends (the goals of the principal). Additionally, consider why a principal may be highly successful in one school, but using the same behaviors, may encounter conflict in another school.

KEY AREAS FOR REFLECTION

1. A principal's ability to impose change
2. Conflicting values and beliefs among educators
3. How groups and individuals interact and exchange power in schools
4. Communication processes between the principal and faculty
5. Organizational climate and culture

THE CASE

Oliver Wendell Holmes Elementary School is the third-oldest facility in this far-western major city. It is located in a neighborhood that has deteriorated substantially in the past three decades. The drab brick exterior and rectangular shape are constant reminders of the unimaginative nature of school facility design in the 1940s. The cracked sidewalks are soiled with endless works of graffiti, written in English and Spanish and displaying every color of the rainbow. The playground is covered with weeds and litter, and the broken swings and teeter-totters attest to the fact that school officials no longer attempt to keep the area functional.

John Lattimore has been principal of Holmes Elementary School for the past three years. He is a veteran administrator, having served at three other elementary schools in the district prior to this assignment. In total, he has been an educator for 31 years, 22 of them as a principal. When the principalship at Holmes became vacant, John was the only sitting principal in the district who sought the post. Most of his colleagues were completely puzzled by this decision. He was assigned to a school in one of the city's best neighborhoods, and more importantly, the parents, students, and teachers there strongly supported him. Why then would he want to give this up to become principal in one of the city's worst schools?

John's motivation was formally questioned by central office administrators who had the responsibility of selecting a new principal for Holmes. In his interview with the superintendent and assistant superintendent for elementary education, John provided a brief and direct answer. "I'm ready for a new challenge. I think Holmes will benefit from my leadership, and I will benefit from the change in scenery." Given that experienced administrators were not standing in line for the job at Holmes Elementary, Dr. William Gray, the superintendent, was only too happy to oblige Mr. Lattimore.

The three years at Holmes Elementary School seemed to pass very quickly for John. The first year was essentially an adjustment period. He tried to meet most of the parents, learn every child's name, and develop a positive working relationship with the faculty. The second year was marked by substantial changes in rules and regulations. In particular, John tried: (1) to revamp the school's discipline program, one that had relied heavily on corporal punishment and suspensions, and (2) to alter the practice of retaining a significant number of students, especially in first grade. The third year is best described as a quagmire of conflict. A significant number of teachers and parents voiced strong objections to what they perceived as the principal's "liberal approaches" to managing student conduct and establishing academic standards.

Dissatisfaction with Mr. Lattimore's leadership style and decisions became pervasive. A group of parents signed a petition demanding that he be transferred to another school. Slightly over one-half of the faculty agreed with this suggestion, and they signed a letter of no confidence that was forwarded to the assistant superintendent for elementary education, Dr. Janelle Danton. They also sent a copy of the letter to the superintendent.

Clearly, those who opposed the principal cited his beliefs regarding discipline and grade retention as a major concern. But they also voiced discontent with his style of administration. John's strategy for bringing about change included (1) announcing his intentions to the staff in formal meetings and (2) inviting teachers to voice their support or opposition—but only if they did so individually and face-to-face in meetings with him. In their letter of no confidence, the teachers expressed dissatisfaction with both the principal's ideas and his methods:

Dear Dr. Danton:

Undoubtedly you receive many complaints from teachers who disagree with their principals. Please do not consider this letter to be one of those routine grievances. Over the past two and one-half years, the teachers at Oliver Wendell Holmes Elementary School have observed the leadership capabilities of Mr. John Lattimore. While he is a friendly, industrious, and intelligent person, his approach to dealing with children at this school simply is ineffective.

Most of the children who attend Holmes come from one-parent families living below the poverty level. Many receive little or no direction with regard to their personal behavior outside of school. Even the parents and guardians of the students recognize that the school must be a major force in providing discipline for the children. Since arriving at our school, Mr. Lattimore has gradually changed all of the established regulations related to discipline. He has made it impossible to administer corporal punishment or to utilize suspensions. He encourages social promotions.

While we do not dispute his judgment that these children lack love and understanding, we reject his belief that the school can be the parent, the psychologist, the social worker, and the friend that each troubled child needs. Allowing disruptive children to remain in school deprives other children of their opportunities to learn.

We learn about changes after the principal has already made a decision. We are never asked to join him in studying needed changes or to democratically participate in making decisions. We are not permitted to voice concerns as a group—only as individuals.

It is with heavy hearts that we must notify you that we have no confidence in Mr. John Lattimore to be principal of Oliver Wendell Holmes Elementary School. Perhaps his talents can be utilized more productively in another assignment. He is a good person who means well. He cannot, however, effectively lead this school. We ask that he be removed as principal as soon as possible.

Respectfully,
(signed by 18 of the 26 teachers)
cc: Dr. Gray, superintendent
    Ms. Hutchins, president of the local teachers' union

Although John knew there was some dissatisfaction with his leadership style, he had underestimated the intensity and extent of the discontent. His eyes were opened, however, when Dr. Danton sent him a copy of the letter. The district has 87 elementary schools, most in inner-city neighborhoods. Complaints about principals are not uncommon; but a letter of no confidence signed by most of the teachers at a school was indeed rare. Attached to the copy of the letter was a note from Dr. Danton:

John,

See me at 8:00 AM tomorrow morning at my office. It is urgent we discuss this immediately. The union has already called Dr. Gray demanding action on this matter.

J.D.

John Lattimore opened the discussion with his supervisor by stating that he was surprised and hurt by the letter of no confidence. He also told Dr. Danton that he was angry. He felt that the teachers had been most discourteous in not coming to him first.

"You mean you had no idea there was this level of concern among your staff members?" Dr. Danton asked.

"Well," John responded, "several teachers voiced displeasure with my changing some rules and regulations related to discipline. You know how that goes, Janelle, you were a principal. Teachers don't always agree with you, and we have to respect the fact that everyone is entitled to an opinion. Unfortunately, someone has to be in charge; someone has to make the difficult decisions. No, I knew there was some displeasure; I just didn't think it was so widespread."

John Lattimore and Janelle Danton were old friends. They served as fellow elementary principals for nearly a decade, and John wrote a letter of support when she applied for her current position. Their mutual respect and friendship made the meeting even more difficult.

"John, didn't you discuss the rules and regulations with them before you made changes? Did you give them an opportunity for input?" Dr. Danton inquired.

"The changes were discussed. We never voted on them, but they were discussed. I thought most of the teachers were willing to give a different approach a chance. Listen, I've been around these children for a long time—and so have you. Their lives are filled with grief and disappointments. Why should school become another enemy, just another miserable experience? Maybe, just maybe, by showing some love and compassion for these children we could turn a few lives around. Maybe we could convince a few children that someone cares. Isn't that important? What do we accomplish when we suspend a child from school? We're punishing the parent, not the child. How will we ever teach these children to be responsible for their own behavior if we constantly impose negative reinforcements on them?"

"What about this issue of social promotions?" asked the assistant superintendent.

"Failing children who are already at risk simply does not work. They prefer to say that I favor social promotions. I prefer to say that I condemn failing children when it just makes it more likely they will be unsuccessful."

Dr. Danton looked directly at him and asked, "John, would you consider taking another assignment at this time? I can arrange for you to work with me here in the central office. I need a director of pupil personnel services. It would mean an increase in salary, and it would be a good way to resolve this problem. Now I don't want you to think that I'm just trying to get you out of the school. I really would like to have you here working with me in the central office. Lord knows, you've earned it. You have put in your time in the trenches. What do you think?"

"Janelle, you know the answer. I've had other opportunities to work here in the central office. That's not my cup of tea. I want to be with the kids. No, I'm sorry. I'm not going to run away from this. I think I am right and if you give me the time, I think I can turn the parents and teachers around. Why is everyone so sure that my changes won't be successful? I thought the principal was supposed to be the leader. All I'm asking for is the opportunity to do my job."

"But John, I don't know if we have time. Dr. Gray may demand that we resolve this right away. Let me think about it for a day or so. I'll call as soon as I make a decision. And John, you should know that I can't make any promises here. Dr. Gray doesn't want another big fight with the union." With that being said, John got up from his chair and nodded that he understood. He shook Dr. Danton's hand while he smiled and then he left.

After the principal left her office, Dr. Danton remembered that Mr. Lattimore also belonged to a union. The principals' union in the school district was every bit as strong as the teachers' union. She wished that her friend had been more compromising and accepted her offer.

THE CHALLENGE

Analyze Mr. Lattimore's behavior in this case. What advice would you give him regarding his future?

KEY ISSUES/QUESTIONS

1. Identify the range of options available to the assistant superintendent in this matter. Identify the advantages and disadvantages of these options.
2. If you were the principal and wanted to change rules and regulations regarding discipline, would you have required consensus from the teachers to do so? Why or why not?
3. Do you believe it was proper for Dr. Danton to offer the principal a job in central administration to resolve the issue? Why or why not?
4. Is the principal correct in his judgment that corporal punishment and suspensions provide negative reinforcement that deters the development of self-discipline?
5. Discuss the rights of the troubled child in relation to classmates. Are the teachers correct in their contention that permitting a disruptive child to remain in the classroom deprives other students of their opportunity to learn?
6. What weight should be given to the fact that many parents are also unhappy with the principal's positions on discipline?
7. What information is not provided in this case that you consider important to reaching a decision?
8. Identify the advantages and disadvantages of Dr. Danton following the recommendation of the disgruntled teachers to remove Mr. Lattimore as principal.
9. What can be assumed about the teachers who did not sign the letter of no confidence?
10. Can you suggest any positive action that might bring the parents, teachers, and principal together to address this problem?
11. Do the goals of the principal justify his means in this case?
12. What elements of organizational theory are cogent to this case?
13. Imagine that you are John Lattimore. What plan would you develop that might convince Dr. Danton to allow you to remain at Holmes?

SUGGESTED READINGS

Auer, M., & Nisenholz, B. (1987). Humanistic processes and bureaucratic structures—Are they compatible? *NASSP Bulletin, 71*(495), 96-101.

Blase, J. (1991). The micropolitical orientation of teachers toward closed school principals. *Education and Urban Society, 23*(4), 356-378.

Blase, J. (1985). The phenomenology of teacher stress: Implications for organizational theory and research. *Administrator's Notebook, 31*(7), 1-4.

Blase, J. (1984). Teacher coping and school principal behaviors. *Contemporary Education, 5*(1), 21-25.

Bridgeland, W., & Duane, E. (1987). Elementary school principals and their political settings. *Urban Review, 19*(4), 191-200.

Carey, M. (1986). School discipline: Better to be loved or feared? *Momentum, 17*(2), 20-21.

Crocker, R., & Brooker, G. (1986). Classroom control and student outcomes in grades 2 and 5. *American Educational Research Journal, 23*(1), 1-11.

Cunningham, W., & Gresso, D. (1993). *Cultural leadership: The culture of excellence in education.* Boston: Allyn & Bacon (see chapters 4, 5).

Curwin, R., & Mendler, A. (1988). Packaged discipline programs: Let the buyer beware. *Educational Leadership, 46*(6), 68-71.

Docking, R. (1985). Changing teacher pupil control ideology and teacher anxiety. *Journal of Education for Teaching, 11*(1), 63-76.

Drake, T., & Roe, W. (1994). *The principalship* (4th ed.). New York: Macmillan (see chapter 16).

Erickson, H. (1988). The boy who couldn't be disciplined. *Principal, 67*(5), 36-37.

Fine, M., & Holt, P. (1983). Corporal punishment in the family: A systems perspective. *Psychology in the Schools, 20*(1) 85-92.

Fris, J. (1992). Principals' encounters with conflict: Tactics they and others use. *Alberta Journal of Educational Research, 38*(1), 65-78.

Gaziel, H. (1990). School bureaucratic structure, locus of control, and alienation among primary teachers. *Research in Education,* (44), 55-66.

Gottredson, D. (1987). An evaluation of an organizational development approach to reducing school disorders. *Evaluation Review, 11*(6), 739-763.

Gotts, E., & Purnell, R. (1987). Practicing school-family relations in urban settings. *Education and Urban Society, 19*(2), 212-218.

Guthrie, J., & Reed, R. (1986). *Educational administration and policy* (pp. 325-344). Englewood Cliffs, NJ: Prentice-Hall.

Hartzell, G., & Petrie, T. (1992). The principal and discipline: Working with school structures, teachers, and students. *The Clearing House, 65*(6), 376-380.

Hoy, W., Tarter, C., & Witkoskie, L. (1992). Faculty trust in colleagues: Linking the principal with school effectiveness. *Journal of Research and Development in Education, 26*(1), 38-45.

Johnston, G. & Venable, B. (1986). A study of teacher loyalty to the principal: Rule administration and hierarchical influence of the principal. *Educational Administration Quarterly, 22*(4), 4-27.

Kimbrough, R., & Burkett, C. (1990). *The principalship: Concepts and practices* (pp. 129-151). Englewood Cliffs, NJ: Prentice Hall.

Kowalski, T., & Reitzug, U. (1993). *Contemporary school administration: An introduction.* New York: Longman (see chapters 9, 10).

Lane, B. A. (1992). Cultural leaders in effective schools: The builders and brokers of excellence. *NASSP Bulletin, 76*(541), 85-96.

Laughter, K. (1988). Nothing was ever Timothy's fault. *Learning, 16*(9), 38-40.

Lowe, R., & Gervais, R. (1984). Tackling a problem school. *Principal, 63*(5), 8-12.

Lunenburg, F. (1987). Another face of school climate. *Illinois Student Journal, 67*(1), 3-10.

Maynard, B. (1983). Is your discipline policy part of your discipline problem? *Executive Educator, 5*(3), 26-27.

McDaniel, T. (1986). School discipline in perspective. *Clearing House, 59*(8), 369-370.

Meadows, B. (1987). The influence of participants' values on group process and decision making. *North Central Association Quarterly, 61*(3), 440-443.

Menacker, J. (1988). Legislating school discipline: The application of a systemwide discipline code for schools in a large urban district. *Urban Education, 23*(1), 12-23.

Menacker, J., Weldon, W., & Hurwitz, E. (1989). School order and safety as community issues. *Phi Delta Kappan, 71*(1), 39-40, 55-56.

Moore, W., & Cooper, H. (1984). Correlations between teacher and student background and teacher perceptions of discipline problems and disciplinary techniques. *Psychology in the Schools, 21*(3), 386-392.

Neuman, S. (1992). Editorial: The negative consequences of the self-esteem movement. *Alberta Journal of Educational Research, 38*(4), 251-253.

Prestine, N. (1993). Shared decision making in restructuring essential schools: The role of the principal. *Planning and Changing, 22*(3-4), 160-177.

Reitman, A. (1988). Corporal punishment in schools—The ultimate violence. *Children's Legal Rights Journal, 9*(33), 6-13.

Reitzug, U. (1989). Principal-teacher interactions in instructionally effective and ordinary elementary schools. *Urban Education, 24*(1), 38-58.

Rosen, M. (1993). Sharing power: A blueprint for collaboration. *Principal, 72*(3), 37-39.

Sashkin, M. (1988). The visionary principal: School leadership for the next century. *Education and Urban Society, 20*(3), 239-249.

Sergiovanni, T. (1991). *The principalship: A reflective practice perspective.* Boston: Allyn & Bacon (see chapters 5, 8).

Sikes, P. (1992). Imposed change and the experienced teacher. In M. Fullan and A. Hargreaves (Eds.), *Teacher development and educational change* (pp. 36-55). Bristol, PA: Falmer Press.

Slavin, R., & Madden, N. (1989). What works for students at risk: A research synthesis. *Educational Leadership, 46*(5), 4-13.

Smylie, M. (1992). Teacher participation in school decision making: Assessing willingness to participate. *Educational Evaluation and Policy Analysis, 14*(1), 53-67.

Snyder, K., & Anderson, R. (1986). *Managing productive schools: Toward an ecology* (pp. 111-123). Orlando, FL: Academic Press College Division.

Thomas, W. (1988). To solve "the discipline problem," mix clear rules with consistent consequences. *American School Board Journal, 175*(6), 30-31.

Thompson, S. (1991). School culture in transformation. *Equity and Choice, 8*(1), 19-24.

Valverde, L. (1988). Principals creating better schools in minority communities. *Education and Urban Society, 2*(4), 319-326.

Vasiloff, B. (1983). The teacher's vital role in developing student discipline. *Momentum, 13*(4), 23-26.

Wager, B. (1993). No more suspension: Creating a shared ethical culture. *Educational Leadership, 50*(4), 34-37.

Wynne, E. (1988). Character building: Transmitting values in schools. *Curriculum Review, 26*(1), 18-22.

Wynne, E. (1986). Character development: Renewing an old commitment. *Principal, 65*(3), 28-31.

case 8

An Effort to Study Site-Based Management

BACKGROUND INFORMATION

Criticisms of public education during the 1980s and early 1990s resulted in a number of conclusions about elementary and secondary schools. Among the more cogent were the following:

1. In many school systems, authority remained centralized and this condition served to block meaningful change.
2. Schools could not improve significantly by simply doing more of what they were already doing.
3. Teachers and schools needed fewer, not more, controls to become effective.
4. Meaningful improvement was more likely to occur at the school rather than school district or state levels.

Collectively, these judgments increased interest in concepts of decentralization, and none became more popular than site-based management.

Despite its popularity, not all educators readily embrace site-based management as a positive concept. In part, this is evidenced by the fact that many school districts have made no attempt to move in this direction. Some critics believe that resistance to decentralization within school districts is simply a product of power-hungry superintendents refusing to relinquish bureaucratic control. But more enlightened observers realize that centralization, especially in the past 40 or 50 years, has been prompted by increased concerns for litigation. For instance, laws governing equal protection and equal rights lead superintendents to insist on uniform and proper employment practices. When administrative decision making is dispersed to schools, some argue that the potential for legal problems increases significantly.

Although this case entails site-based management, it also has the primary focus of organizational change. A superintendent wants to move to decentralized governance, and a number of key staff members resist. Thus both the process of seeking change and the targeted change emerge as issues affecting behavior.

To some extent, change is encountered in all school districts; however, the ways in which these institutions react to, encourage, and manage the process vary substantially (Kowalski & Reitzug, 1993). In one school district, massive change can be pursued with little dispute, whereas in another district, even minor alterations spawn substantial resistance. One explanation is that all organizations possess unique cultures and climates that make them relatively open or closed to change. The following questions are also central to the understanding of attempted change: What is to be changed? Why is the change being proposed? How will the change occur? How will change affect individuals and groups in the school district? To what degree is the change supported and likely to be sustained?

As you read this case, try to identify elements of organizational life that either encourage or discourage change. Try to understand why some of the administrators are resistant to even studying possible change. As you complete your analysis, attempt to separate procedural issues (i.e., issues related to the proposed change process) from substantive issues (i.e., site-based management itself).

KEY AREAS FOR REFLECTION

1. Processes for studying possible change in school districts
2. Why principals and other administrators may oppose decentralization
3. Why administrators and teachers may oppose organizational change
4. Why districts have unique cultures and climates and how this condition affects responses to proposed change
5. The advantages and disadvantages of decentralization

THE CASE

Lora Mipps has been secretary to the superintendent of the Lewis Public Schools for 31 years. In that period, she has outlasted eight superintendents, all of whom brought unique personalities and leadership styles to the school district. She thought about that fact as she listened to the shouting coming from behind the closed door of the superintendent's office. As the voices became louder, she started to wonder if she was about to see her ninth boss depart.

Dr. George Pisak arrived in Lewis, a quiet community of 18,000 located in the "sunbelt," just 15 months ago. He accepted the superintendency with the local public schools here because he wanted new challenges and opportunities for personal and professional growth. For the previous 12 years, he occupied the position of assistant superintendent for instruction in a large school system located in a neighboring southern state. George believed that anyone who became a superintendent today was taking risks; however, since their two children were grown and out of college, George and his wife, Estelle, thought that they were now in a position to take some risks.

The Pisaks moved to Lewis well aware of the history of the school system. The longest tenure of a superintendent in recent times was five years, and in the past six years, three different individuals have occupied this post. In part, the instability was linked to the fact that school board members found it virtually impossible to be reelected. School board elections attracted many candidates, an average of about four or five for every vacant seat. In the past three elections, no incumbent has won.

When George was contacted by Ken Hollman, a former professor, about the job in Lewis, he initially indicated that he was not interested. The reputation of the district was well known in this region of the country. Dr. Hollman's employment as a consultant was due to the realization that the district had difficulty attracting good candidates. But Ken Hollman did not accept an answer of no easily. A week after his initial telephone call to George, he called a second time. This conversation was more productive, and the two agreed to meet for lunch to discuss the job in Lewis.

During their meeting, Dr. Hollman outlined six reasons why he thought George should pursue this opportunity:

1. The school district desperately needed someone who could provide fresh leadership ideas. Of the four most recent superintendents, three were promoted from within the district. Each of these three eventually met with insurmountable problems as the composition of the school board changed.
2. The school board now realizes that the superintendent must be allowed to be in charge of the day-to-day operations of the system. They want someone who can lead as well as manage and someone who understands instructional programs.
3. The board recognizes the poor reputation of the district and that to hire a quality leader, they would have to offer an attractive salary.
4. The community of Lewis is divided from a socioeconomic standpoint. To a large degree, this condition is responsible for the shifts in school board composition and initiatives. The board is now controlled by upper-middle-class and middle-class residents, and they are committed to long-range reforms.
5. After all the turmoil in the district, conditions are favorable for a superintendent to meet with high levels of success.
6. The board is willing to let the superintendent replace any and all of the current administrative staff if such decisions are deemed necessary.

George acknowledged that he and his wife were interested in relocating, preferably to a city smaller than the one in which they were living. He also explained that for the first time in his career, he was interested in becoming a superintendent. Yet, George continued to express concerns that Lewis provided the opportunities he was seeking.

Dr. Hollman can be a very convincing individual; and besides, he knew George very well. He taught him and served as his dissertation advisor when George was pursuing his Ed.D. degree. Dr. Hollman recognized that George was intelligent, capable, and industrious—but very cautious. He knew that if he was to get him to pursue this job, he had to emphasize the opportunities. He felt that if George would agree to pursue the position, his reason would most likely be professional commitment. His strategy worked and before their luncheon concluded, George agreed to submit his application.

Dr. Hollman told the board that Dr. Pisak was their leading candidate and assured them he was the perfect person for the job. Dr. Pisak had two interviews for the position, and he was particularly impressed that the board confirmed that they would give the superintendent nearly complete control of the district. Three days after his second interview, the board president called and offered him the position. Dr. Pisak's only concern was how each board member would vote on his appointment. The board president told him that four members would definitely vote to approve his employment; he said he was unsure about the fifth member. He agreed to accept the position.

The board voted four to one to hire George. The one negative vote was cast by Billy Foster, a board member who was a close friend of the previous superintendent. George received a three-year contract at a salary approximately $20,000 greater than his predecessor's. In an interview with the local newspaper, Mr. Foster called the salary for the new superintendent "outrageous." The unhappy board member told the reporter, "We have families in Lewis who can't afford to feed their children. Yet, we take public money and pay a superintendent $90,000. The voters will have a chance to say how they feel during the next school board election."

The four board members who supported Dr. Pisak were most helpful in his first few months in Lewis. They attempted to offset the negative statements of Billy Foster, and they introduced George to many of the leaders in the community. During the first few months in Lewis, George was invited to speak to service clubs, church groups, and just about every other type of gathering. In the northern part of Lewis, the area of town with the more affluent neighborhoods, his reception was warm and friendly. In the southern half of Lewis, "the other side of the tracks," his reception was mixed.

The first six months in Lewis convinced George that he was dealing with two very different communities. The school board was now controlled by the "northern" faction and the patrons in the southern half of the school district resented it. George felt that this resentment had little to do with educational programs or initiatives; he judged it to be a form of class jealousy. The superintendent concluded that if he could create a greater sense of ownership among the residents in the southern part of the city, they would be less inclined to feel alienated by his and the school board's actions.

In reviewing ideas that prove useful to his goal, George became especially interested in a concept called *site-based management*. He visited Salt Lake City, Utah, and Hammond, Indiana—cities where iterations of the concept were already in place. Through his friend, Dr. Hollman, he obtained the names of several professors who were advocates of site-based management. After collecting information from experts and visiting programs already in place, George decided that site-based management was the ideal concept for trying to reduce the alienation of the residents in the southern part of his school district.

During a staff meeting in early April, George revealed (1) his concerns about political divisions in the community, (2) his goal of finding a way of giving parents and taxpayers a greater sense of ownership in their schools, and (3) that he had selected site-based management as the vehicle for reaching this goal. During the long discussion that followed, George discerned that at least half of the administrative staff had either never heard of site-based management or knew little about the concept. Even more discomforting were indications that most of those who knew something about site-based management were not supportive. But George was not discouraged. In the weeks following the meeting, he distributed copies of journal articles and materials from school districts he had visited detailing the potentialities of site-based management; he sent several principals to visit schools that were implementing this program; and he assured his staff that he fully intended to move forward in trying to give individual schools more control in their day-to-day operations.

At an administrative staff meeting in early May, the three principals who visited other schools reported on their experiences. Their comments included both perceived advantages and disadvantages, and there was little evidence of enthusiasm. George then asked for reactions to the materials he had distributed. A few favorable remarks were made, but for the most part, the administrators expressed skepticism.

Somewhat disappointed, George told his staff, "You have been very open with me about my idea, and I appreciate that. But I still feel strongly that this is an avenue we should pursue. Therefore, I am going to recommend to the school board that we complete a detailed feasibility study regarding the implementation of site-based management. I'll suggest a committee that includes parents, teachers, and administrators, and I will recommend that the board retain a consultant to work with the committee."

Reactions to his comments were immediate. Three of the eight elementary principals said that they supported the idea of doing a feasibility study, four others took the opposite position, and one indicated that he still did not know enough about the concept to have an opinion. All three secondary principals opposed the study, and the two assistant superintendents were divided on the issue.

George reacted, "I must admit, I did not expect this much opposition to just looking at the idea objectively. Again, I thank you for your candor, and I will give this matter further thought."

After talking again to several of the experts referred to him by Dr. Hollman and several superintendents who were engaged in site-based management programs, George decided to move forward with the recommendation to conduct the study. He prepared the following recommendation to be placed in the school board packets:

Lewis School Board Meeting:

Topic: Feasibility Study for the Implementation of Site-Based Management.

Superintendent Recommendation: (a) The board authorize that Dr. Shirley Lowe and Dr. Paul Swartz, professors at the state university, be retained as consultants to assist the district in completing this feasibility study. Each consultant shall receive a fee of $8,000. (b) The board authorize the formation of a task force to oversee the feasibility study with the following composition: two administrative staff members (appointed by the superintendent), five teachers (appointed by the superintendent), one school board member (appointed by the board president), and five patrons (each board member making an appointment).

Background Information: The Lewis School District has experienced pronounced changes in school board membership. Frequently these changes have been accompanied by radical shifts in philosophy. My judgment is that the socioeconomic divisions of the community are largely responsible for this pattern. The changes in school board membership also result in administrative changes, particularly in the superintendency. If stability is not achieved, it will be extremely difficult to engage in long-range planning and to initiate programs that will improve our schools. It is my opinion that we must find ways of letting parents and other taxpayers in all parts of our school system have a greater voice in decisions.

Site-based management is a concept that permits this to occur. By establishing school councils composed of all elements of the school/ community (i.e., teachers, administrators, parents, students), we will hopefully gain the support of most patrons in moving forward with reforms. In fairness to my administrative staff, I should tell you that a majority is not enthusiastic about the study.

The feasibility study will generate data that will permit us to examine more closely the advantages and disadvantages of site-based management in our district. The study is not designed to produce a final decision on this matter. We may well decide, after looking at the data, that site-based management will not work here. I urge you to support the study so that we can make informed choices in the future. The study will be completed in six to eight months and will include attitude surveys of both staff and community.

The recommendation was distributed to board members, and the item was placed on the agenda for the regular board meeting that was to take place four days later. When the high school principal, Ernie Duggon, saw the agenda, he called all of the other principals and asked them to attend a meeting at his house that evening. Nine of the 11 principals attended. Duggon outlined his dismay that the new superintendent was moving ahead with this idea even though most administrators in the district were opposed to it. A petition was developed and signed by those attending the meeting urging the superintendent to retract his recommendation. It read as follows:

As building level administrators in Lewis, we respectfully request that you reconsider your recommendation regarding a feasibility study for implementing site-based management in our district. We offer three fundamental reasons for our request:

1. Site-based management is a controversial movement that has not worked well in some communities. It diminishes the control of principals over their schools.
2. Placing teachers and parents in positions where they can make major decisions will only generate more conflict in a community that has had more than its share over the past six years.
3. The money and human resources that would be devoted to this study could be better utilized studying ways we can improve our existing curriculum.

We believe that we have been loyal to you. We have not opposed your ideas in the community, nor have we undermined any of your initiatives. The administrative staff in this district is overwhelmingly opposed to your idea of having a study. Won't you respect our viewpoint?

After reading the petition, George called his two assistant superintendents to his office and told them he wanted to find out who instigated this matter. He then called the board president and told him about the petition.

"Look," George said over the telephone, "I didn't come here to be pushed in the corner by a bunch of principals who aren't even open-minded enough to look at an idea. I hope you meant what you said when you told me I could get rid of any or all of these staff members."

At 3:30 PM, the two assistant superintendents appeared in George's office. The one who had previously voiced opposition to the study made it clear that he was not part of this petition, and he assured his boss that he did not agree with the tactics. Later that day the two assistant superintendents told George that they had learned via the grapevine that the high school principal was the organizer.

Ernie Duggon was summoned to the superintendent's office the next morning for a meeting. When he received the call from the superintendent's secretary, he figured that it was about the petition and asked if he could bring several other principals with him.

"No, Mr. Duggon," the secretary answered, "Dr. Pisak was specific that he wanted to see you alone."

Ernie Duggon came to the meeting determined not to back down from the superintendent. As both individuals had expected, the meeting was not pleasant. George accused Ernie of being a troublemaker; Ernie accused George of being insensitive to his staff's feelings. As the meeting progressed, the shouting became louder.

Sitting outside the closed door to the superintendent's office, Mrs. Mipps, the secretary, had recollections of other such heated arguments. That is why she wondered if yet another superintendent was about to have a short stay in Lewis.

THE CHALLENGE

Place yourself in Dr. George Pisak's position. What would you do at this point?

KEY ISSUES/QUESTIONS

1. Assess the judgment the superintendent is making about the nature of the community and the relationship between a socioeconomic polarization and problems in the school district.

2. Was it proper for Dr. Hollman to talk Dr. Pisak into applying for the superintendency in Lewis? Was it ethical for him to appeal to George's sense of professional commitment?

3. At times superintendents ask staff for input when there is little chance that they will follow suggestions that contradict their intentions. Should they do this? Do you think that George did this?

4. Do you think that site-based management has the potential of giving parents and taxpayers a greater sense of ownership?

5. To what extent do environmental conditions (community) and organizational climate affect the implementation of decentralization concepts such as site-based management?

6. Evaluate the behavior of the high school principal in this matter. What is your mental image of this individual?

7. Do you believe that the rapid turnover of superintendents in the district affected the behavior of the principals who signed the petition? Could their behavior have been affected by their knowing that this was Dr. Pisak's first superintendency?

8. Do you think that the superintendent did an adequate job of trying to educate his staff about site-based management?

9. If you were a principal in this school district, would you have signed the petition presented to the superintendent? Why or why not?

10. Are there any conditions in the community or school district that suggest that the superintendent was correct in moving quickly to recommend a feasibility study?

11. Given the information in this case, how do you believe the board will react if (a) the superintendent moves forward with his recommendation in spite of the petition, or (b) he decides to withdraw the recommendation because of the petition?

12. If you were the superintendent, would you fire the high school principal? If so, what would be your reasons for doing so? If not, would you pursue any other actions against him?

13. If you were superintendent in this district and wanted to pursue site-based management, what other tactics might you have used?

SUGGESTED READINGS

Black, J., & English, F. (1986). *What they don't tell you in schools of education about school administration* (pp. 15-17). Lancaster, PA: Technomics.

Brieschke, P. (1985). Principals in schools: Insubordination in discretionary decision making. *Educational Forum, 49*(2), 157-169.

Caldwell, S. (1988). School-based improvement—Are we ready? *Educational Leadership, 46*(2), 50-53.

Caldwell, S., & Wood, F. (1992). Breaking ground in restructuring. *Educational Leadership 50*(1), 41, 44.

Cawalti, G. (1989). The elements of site-based management. *Educational Leadership, 46*(8), 46.

David, J. (1989). Synthesis of research on school-based management. *Educational Leadership, 46*(8), 45-53.

Guthrie, J. (1986). School based management: The next needed education reform. *Phi Delta Kappan, 68*(4), 305-309.

Guthrie, J., & Reed, R. (1986). *Educational administration and policy* (pp. 16-18). Englewood Cliffs, NJ: Prentice-Hall.

Hanson, E. (1991). *Educational administration and organizational behavior* (3rd ed., pp. 64-66, 82-87). Boston: Allyn & Bacon.

Harrison, C., Killion, J., & Mitchell, J. (1989). Site-based management: The realities of implementation. *Educational Leadership, 46*(8), 55-60.

Herman, J., & Herman, J. (1992). Educational administration: School-based management. *The Clearing House, 65*(5), 261-263.

Hoy, W., & Forsyth, P. (1986). *Effective supervision: Theory into practice* (pp. 168-177). New York: Random House.

Kowalski, T., & Reitzug, U. (1993). *Contemporary school administration: An introduction.* New York: Longman (see chapters 9, 13).

Kritek, W., & Schneider, G. (1993-94). Site-based management and decentralization. *National Forum of Educational Administration and Supervision Journal, 11*(1), 3-20.

Lawler, E. (1986). *High involvement management.* San Francisco: Jossey-Bass (see chapter 1).

Lewis, A. (1989). *Restructuring American schools.* Arlington, VA: American Association of School Administrators (see chapter 9).

McWalters, P. (1988). New realities call for new rules. *School Administrator, 4*(8), 13-15.

Ratzki, A. (1988). Creating a school community: One model of how it can be done. *American Educator: The Professional Journal of the American Federation of Teachers, 12*(1), 10-17, 38-43.

Scarr, L. (1988). Lake Washington master plan: A system for growth. *Educational Leadership, 46*(2), 13-16.

Sergiovanni, T. (1987). *The principalship: A reflective practice perspective* (pp. 323-329). Boston: Allyn & Bacon.

Stover, D. (1989). But some principals feel threatened. *The Executive Educator, 11*(1), 17.

Wicks, T., & Pankake, A. (1989-90). Board of education and superintendent: The team that "empowers" effectiveness. *National Forum of Educational Administration and Supervision Journal, 7*(1), 117-123.

Wohlstetter, P., & Odden, A. (1992). Rethinking school-based management policy and research. *Educational Administration Quarterly, 28*(4), 529-549.

Yatvin, J. (1992). Memoir of a team player. *Educational Leadership, 49*(5), 50-52.

Yukl, G. (1989). *Leadership in organizations* (2nd ed., pp. 112-119). Englewood Cliffs, NJ: Prentice-Hall.

Zerchykov, R. (1985). Why school councils? *Equity and Choice, 2*(1), 37-38.

Involving Teachers in Employment Decisions

BACKGROUND INFORMATION

One of the positive outgrowths of educational reform efforts has been a renewed interest in empowering teachers to be true professionals. In bureaucratic-like schools, power and authority are highly centralized and remain in the hands of principals and assistant principals. Such closed environments tend to alienate teachers, because they are unable to function as true professionals (i.e., to have some degree of autonomy in performing their duties).

The extent to which principals are autocratic is an important aspect of leadership. Authoritarian and democratic represent the extremes of a behavior continuum. You should not think of administrators as being either one extreme or the other, but rather as tending to be more authoritarian or more democratic. Autocratic leaders allow little or no subordinate participation in decision making, because such involvement is seen as counterproductive, threatening, potentially disruptive, or inefficient. Democratic leaders, by contrast, seek involvement and consensus. While reviews of research have indicated that satisfaction and morale are likely to be higher in democratically led groups, data regarding productivity have produced mixed results (Kowalski & Reitzug, 1993). Even though there is limited empirical support linking participatory decision making and outcomes (Estler, 1988), a myriad of ethical, moral, and professional concerns make authoritarian leadership a valid concern in school administration.

In this case, a newly employed principal seeks to involve teachers in the employment of peers. This is a practice that has not been used in the school system previously, and her decision sparks concerns and anger from other administrators. One of the issues that emerges relates to communication within a school system. Should a principal, for example, seek permission to do something that is not prohibited, either legally or in policy, but is contrary to standard practice? To what extent is a principal's supervisor responsible for assuring that standard practices are followed in employment? Such questions emerge as the principal's decision to allow teachers to participate in peer employment is criticized.

The case also illuminates the systemic nature of decisions. When the principal decides to involve teachers in employment interviews, she probably never considered that there might be implications for collective bargaining. School districts, like all organizations, are systems made up of individuals and groups; any action within the system has the potential of affecting other parts.

This case also sparks questions about the symbolic nature of administrative communications and behavior. Individuals and groups within a school district interpret the actions taken by top-level officials. In this case, both the actions of the principal (involving teachers in employment interviews) and the superintendent (sending a letter of reprimand) are likely to transmit symbolic messages.

KEY AREAS FOR REFLECTION

1. Teacher professionalism (empowerment)
2. Participatory decision making
3. Organizations as integrated systems
4. Democratic versus authoritarian leadership
5. Organizational communication processes
6. The symbolic importance of communication and administrative actions

THE CASE

The Community

Davidtown is located in the heart of farming country in a midwestern state. Unlike many similar towns, it has experienced steady growth through the 1970s and 1980s. In part, population increases are attributable to the following conditions: (1) Davidtown is a county seat, (2) it has a hospital that serves a four-county area, (3) the local chamber of commerce has been successful in bringing five new companies to the community in the last 10 years, (4) it is located on a major interstate highway, and (5) it is the site of a public community college and a private four-year college.

The population of Davidtown is currently 24,300—a 40 percent increase in 20 years. New subdivisions are being erected continuously, and a new shopping mall opened just three years ago. A recent fact book about the state described Davidtown as "a prosperous, growing, middle-class community." A newspaper article highlighting community leaders noted that only one of five members of the city council had resided in Davidtown for more than ten years. This statistic is perhaps most descriptive of the demographic changes that have occurred.

The School District and School Board

The boundaries for the Davidtown Community School District go beyond the town and include four rural townships. Many students in the system live on farms. The diversity of the school system is reflected in the composition of the school board. Joe Marshall, an attorney with the largest law firm in the county, is the board president; Lisle Atwood owns a farm implement business in Davidtown; Mary Ingalls is a teller in one of the local banks; Jim Maigthorn and Bryon Trumski are self-employed farmers; Lowell Ridovich is the plant manager at a local manufacturing company; and Deloris Simpson is a housewife and part-time English instructor at the community college. The two farmers on the board have been reelected twice. The other board members are all serving first terms.

The district includes a high school, two middle schools, and eight elementary schools. Four of the elementary schools are located in Davidtown, and the other four are dispersed in the outlying townships. Six of the school buildings have been erected or remodeled in the past 15 years. Each of these projects caused controversy between the residents of Davidtown and other school district taxpayers. Those residing in rural areas have generally opposed facility projects, largely on the grounds that large landowners shoulder a disproportionate share of the financial burden.

Central Office Administrators

Will Guyberger has been superintendent of this district for seven years. Previously, he was the principal of Davidtown High School—a post he held for eight years. Superintendent Guyberger is considered a competent leader and he has many supporters in the community.

The assistant superintendent for business, Howard Grangal, has 22 years of experience in the district. His wife owns and operates a small business in Davidtown. The assistant superintendent for instruction, Dr. Patricia McDowd, has been employed by the school system for only two years. Her appointment caused a major battle among school board members. She was the first administrator in recent times to be employed in a top-level position from outside the school system. When Joe Marshall and Deloris Simpson became board members, they argued that the school district needed some new ideas. They felt that relying solely on internal promotions was counterproductive to that goal. Their views played a key role in Dr. McDowd's employment.

Employing a New High School Principal

For the first time since Will Guyberger left the principalship of Davidtown High School seven years ago, the school faced the task of finding a new principal. Aaron Ketchie, who replaced Will, had decided to retire.

The school district received 47 applications for the position of high school principal. Among the applicants were the school's two current assistant principals and the middle school principal. The task of coordinating the search was delegated to the assistant superintendent for instruction, Dr. McDowd. This was not an unexpected assignment since Superintendent Guyberger frequently delegates important tasks to his two assistants. Additionally, principals report directly to the assistant superintendent for instruction, so there was nothing unusual about Dr. McDowd coordinating the search.

Prior to coming to Davidtown two years ago, Pat McDowd was working in a neighboring state. During her brief period of employment with the schools here, most of the principals had accepted her as one of the "team," but most still considered her to be an "outsider." The vacancy at the high school was her first opportunity to replace a principal. She welcomed this challenge and personally felt that a change of leadership would be good for the high school and school system. She decided to advertise the vacancy nationally in professional journals and newspapers—something that had never been done before by the Davidtown school system. Neither the superintendent nor the school board objected.

In conducting the screening of the written materials submitted by the applicants, Dr. McDowd conferred with both the superintendent and the assistant superintendent for business. She felt that both had a vested interest in this appointment, because they too had to work closely with whomever was selected.

Although neither Mr. Guyberger nor Mr. Grangal overtly supported individual candidates, it became readily apparent to Dr. McDowd that they favored employing someone from within the school system. In a recent meeting with them, Will Guyberger said, "I'm really pleased that we have all these candidates for the high school principalship. But you know, Pat, I can't see how any of them could be any better than the administrators who are already in this district."

Howard Grangal certainly agreed. "Not only are our own candidates outstanding, they are loyal employees as well. I hope we don't forget that."

Six candidates were selected as finalists, including the middle school principal and one of the high school assistant principals. Each accepted the invitation to interview. Interviews were conducted by the two assistant superintendents and the superintendent. Pat requested that her two colleagues complete evaluation forms of each candidate and they obliged. After the interviews, two remaining candidates withdrew from the search. One was the middle school principal, who concluded he had little chance of being selected. From the remaining four, Dr. McDowd eventually recommended Dr. Sharon White. Dr. White was only 33 years old, but she had been working as an assistant principal at a state university laboratory school. Politically, this was not an easy decision. Pat knew that she would be accused of being biased for picking someone very much like herself. Additionally, she assumed that many of the present administrators would react negatively to the selection of a person from outside the system.

Even though Superintendent Guyberger did not agree with the choice, he felt compelled to support it. In an executive meeting with the school board, he said that he favored hiring the assistant from the high school, but that he had to weigh his personal choice against the principle of delegating authority to his assistants. After he said this, board member Ridovich leaned over and whispered in the ear of the board president, "And he realizes that if he didn't support Pat's decision, he'd have a problem with us!"

Even though Will Guyberger and Howard Grangal were disappointed that Pat did not pick the assistant from the high school, they agreed that her choice, Dr. White, was impressive and intelligent.

The Incident

Sharon White became the first female secondary school principal (two women hold posts as elementary school principals) and the youngest person (age 33) to ever be appointed to a principalship in the Davidtown school district. She recently completed her doctorate in educational leadership, and her two years at the laboratory school constitute her total experience in school administration. Prior to becoming an assistant principal, Dr. White taught high school English for seven years.

The first semester at Davidtown High School was a successful and pleasant experience for Dr. White. The faculty, students, and parents were impressed with her pleasant personality and sincere enthusiasm. Even the two assistant principals who had competed for the principalship became convinced that she was a capable leader.

Sharon's style of leadership is distinctively different from that of her predecessor. She views herself as an instructional leader and devotes much of her time to interacting with teachers, students, and parents (e.g., visiting classrooms, attending virtually all of the extracurricular events). Management tasks are largely delegated to the two assistant principals; however, Dr. White maintains an active role in dealing with discipline problems. She constantly seeks input from teachers, and most react positively to this leadership style.

In March, two faculty members at the high school indicated that they would not return for the following school year. Dr. White submitted their resignations with a request to retain their positions. She also requested two additional positions, citing enrollment increases as the reason. Within two weeks, she received permission to fill all four positions.

Traditionally, principals in Davidtown have been given authority to select their own teaching staffs. Final decisions are subject to approval by the assistant superintendent for instruction and the superintendent, who also interview finalists for professional positions. The principal submits a recommendation to the assistant superintendent for instruction, she consults with the assistant superintendent for business regarding funding, and the recommendation is then forwarded to the superintendent.

In late April, Dr. White was in her office at the high school interviewing a candidate for a teaching position. At about 9:00 AM her secretary received a telephone call from Superintendent Guyberger requesting a change in his designated time to interview the same candidate.

"Could you change my appointment with the math candidate today from 3:00 PM to 10:30 AM?" the superintendent inquired.

The secretary responded, "I don't think that's possible because the math department will be interviewing the candidate from 10:00 to 11:00 AM."

There was a pause, and after collecting his thoughts the superintendent asked, "What is the math department doing interviewing candidates for teaching positions? I don't understand."

The secretary realized that this was not a question the superintendent really expected her to answer, but to be safe, she told him he would have to ask Dr. White.

The superintendent then called Assistant Superintendent Howard Grangal and asked him if he knew anything about teachers being involved in employment interviews at the high school.

Howard said he knew nothing about it. He added a personal note, "I hope this is not going on. Among other things, it sets a bad precedent."

Mr. Guyberger quickly summoned his other assistant, Dr. Pat McDowd, to his office.

"Did you know that Sharon White is involving teachers in the interviews for teaching vacancies at the high school?"

"No, she never discussed it with me," Dr. McDowd responded. "Are you sure? You really think the teachers are playing a formal role in the process?"

The superintendent shared his telephone conversation with her and then directed her to investigate the issue and report back to him. It did not take long for Dr. McDowd to determine that Sharon White had indeed decided to let teachers become involved in the interviewing process.

When asked why she was doing this, Sharon gave two reasons: (1) the time had come to recognize that teachers are true professionals and should be treated as such, and (2) the process was used at the laboratory school where it worked very well. Sharon also told her supervisor that she believed in being a democratic leader. She went on to add, "Teachers need to have some input regarding who will work with them. Physicians typically decide who gets hospital privileges. Lawyers decide whether they let someone in their firm. Why shouldn't teachers have the same opportunity for input? When I was a teacher, I appreciated being treated as a professional. I intend to treat teachers the way that I wanted to be treated."

Dr. McDowd pointed out that the involvement of teachers in employment interviews was neither an established nor an accepted practice in the school district.

"None of the principals is doing this except you. Mr. Guyberger is concerned about possible repercussions. For example, will teacher involvement become an issue in collective bargaining? Will teachers demand that all principals let teachers play a role in hiring new teachers? And how will the school board react when they find out about this? These questions bother us," explained the assistant superintendent.

Dr. White responded to the concern. "I talked to the faculty about their roles in this process. They assure me that their involvement will not be made a political issue. Secondly, the recommendation for employment will still be mine. I take full responsibility for any recommendation that comes to your office."

"Did you ask your two assistant principals what they thought about involving teachers in hiring procedures?" the assistant superintendent inquired.

"Yes, we talked about it. They raised concerns privately with me but indicated that they thought the decision was mine. They told me that no other school in the system did what I was proposing. But I work best when I have the confidence of my faculty. I trust them and they trust me. If you permit each principal to have latitude in employing faculty, why don't you trust my methods in reaching employment decisions?"

Dr. McDowd reported the conversation to the superintendent. Mr. Guyberger dwelled on the fact that the principal's decision could cause problems in negotiations with the teachers' union. The issue of faculty participation in employment interviews has been discussed occasionally over the last three years at the bargaining table, and in each instance, the board negotiator took the firm position that employment was a management responsibility.

"Sharon is being a bit naive if she thinks that the union is going to ignore this issue simply because some of her teachers told her it would not be used in collective bargaining," surmised the superintendent. "My guess is that they'll use it and point out that it was successful. They'll indicate that if teacher involvement doesn't work in another school, it's the principal's fault—certainly not the fault of the teachers. Our other principals are going to hit the ceiling when they find out about this."

The two officials continued to discuss the issue for some time. They were joined by Assistant Superintendent Grangal, who was especially interested in the matter since he serves on the board's negotiations team. He suggested that they telephone the board's chief negotiator, an attorney named Roscoe Ferdinand, and get his opinion on the matter. Mr. Ferdinand, they discovered, was out of town and unavailable for several days.

Mr. Guyberger continued to voice his concerns regarding the potential negative effects on collective bargaining, and his position was reinforced by Howard Grangal. Eventually the three central office administrators agreed that something had to be done. The two men favored sending a letter of reprimand to Dr. White. Such a letter would provide evidence that the involvement at the high school was not a practice condoned by the central administration. Dr. McDowd objected. She thought their reaction was impulsive and excessive; and she believed that Dr. White was doing a very good job. Despite her objections, the superintendent drafted a letter the next day.

Dr. Sharon White:

Since you decided to involve your faculty in employment interviews without consulting your supervisor, and since this action involves a practice that is a matter of disagreement between the Davidtown Teachers Association and the board of education, we find it necessary to issue this reprimand. This reprimand focuses solely on your judgments and actions in this matter. Issuing this letter is most difficult given that this problem is inconsistent with your outstanding performance as principal over the last year. In the future, you should consult with the assistant superintendent for instruction and/or the superintendent on all decisions that have direct implications for either school board policy or negotiated agreements with the DTA.

W. Guyberger, superintendent

After seeing the draft, Dr. McDowd again asked the superintendent if he would consider another way of dealing with the problem. She offered to meet with Dr. White and the high school faculty to explain that the practice would not be allowed in the future. But the superintendent had his mind made up.

"No," he told her, "I think we have to go on record. I suggest you meet with Sharon and try to explain to her why this letter was necessary. She'll understand that it is not a reflection on the total job she is doing. After all, she is doing a very good job in all other areas. "

THE CHALLENGE

Assume you are the high school principal. What would be your reactions to receiving this letter?

KEY ISSUES/QUESTIONS

1. Do you see any linkage between the changing demographic conditions in the community and the problem that emerges in this case?

2. What alternatives could have been pursued by the superintendent or the assistant superintendent for instruction in dealing with this issue?

3. What values and beliefs lead administrators to believe that teachers should not be involved in employment decisions?

4. Given the current school board, do you think there is a possibility that the superintendent's actions will ignite a reaction from individual board members?

5. To what extent should the assistant superintendent of instruction be held accountable for what occurred in this case?

6. Describe what is meant by teacher empowerment. In general, do you agree with the principal's judgment that teacher empowerment is a positive goal? Why or why not?

7. Evaluate the principal's position that since she is responsible for employment recommendations, she ought to be given the latitude to determine who will be involved in the interviewing process.

8. Assess the position taken by the two assistant principals in this case. Do you think they helped the principal?

9. Suppose the principal had received a verbal rather than a written reprimand. Do you believe it would have had the same effect?

10. What symbolic messages are given to employees in the school district in this case?

11. Would you like to work in this school district? Why or why not?

12. Clearly there were some differences of opinion among the three top level administrators with regard to employing a high school principal. Is this fact cogent to the problem that emerges and the letter of reprimand?

SUGGESTED READINGS

Belasco, J., & Alutto, J. (1972). Decisional participation and teacher satisfaction. *Educational Administration Quarterly, 8*(1), 44-58.

Boyan, N. (1988). Describing and explaining administrative behavior. In N. Boyan (Ed.), *Handbook of research on educational administration* (pp. 77-97). New York: Longman.

Bredeson, P. (1983). The secondary school principal's role in personnel screening and selection. *High School Journal, 67*, 6-10.

Castetter, W. (1992). *The personnel function in educational administration* (5th ed.). New York: Macmillan (see chapter 9).

Conway, J. (1984). The myth, mystery, and mastery of participative decision making in education. *Educational Administration Quarterly, 20*(3), 11-40.

Cunningham, W., & Gresso, D. (1993). *Cultural leadership: The culture of excellence in education.* Boston: Allyn & Bacon (see chapter 5).

Estler, S. (1988). Decision making. In N. Boyan (Ed.), *Handbook of research on educational administration* (pp. 305-319). New York: Longman.

Gilberg, J. (1988). Managerial attitudes toward participative management programs: Myths and realities. *Public Personnel Management, 17*(2), 109-123.

Kowalski, T., & Reitzug, U. (1993). *Contemporary school administration: An introduction.* New York: Longman (see chapters 10, 13).

Lewis, A. (1989). *Restructuring America's schools.* Arlington, VA: American Association of School Administrators (see chapter 4).

Lindle, J., & Shrock, J. (1993). School-based decision-making councils and the hiring process. *NASSP Bulletin, 77*(551), 71-76.

Lugg, C., & Boyd, W. (1993). Leadership for collaboration: Reducing risk and fostering resilience. *Educational Leadership, 75*(3), 253-258.

Macguire, J. (1983). Faculty participation in interviewing teacher candidates. *Clearing House, 56*(7), 330-331.

Martin, C. (1993). Hiring the right person: Techniques for principals. *NASSP Bulletin, 77*(550), 79-83.

McPherson, R., & Crowson, R. (1987). Sources of constraints and opportunities for discretion in the principalship. In J. Lane & H. Waldberg (Eds.), *Effective school leadership: Policy and process* (pp. 129-156). Berkeley, CA: McCutchan.

Owens, R., & Lewis, E. (1976). Managing participation in organizational decisions. *Group and Organizational Studies, 1*(1), 56-66.

Pigford, A. (1989). How to hire teachers that fit. *The School Administrator, 10*(46), 38, 43.

Snyder, K., & Anderson, R. (1986). *Managing productive schools: Toward an ecology.* Orlando, FL: Academic Press College Division (see chapter 1).

Wendel, F., & Breed, R. (1988). Improving the selection of principals. An analysis of approaches. *NASSP Bulletin, 72*(508), 35-38.

Zirkel, P., & Gluckman, I. (1986). Letters of reprimand: The important questions. *NASSP Bulletin, 70*(491), 99-102.

A Matter of Honor

BACKGROUND INFORMATION

If principals were cold, unfeeling managers capable of always making objective and rational decisions, their preparation for practice would largely entail training rather than education. Despite decades of attempts to make school leadership a precise science, researchers repeatedly find that practitioners often behave emotionally, irrationally, and unpredictably.

Sergiovanni (1991) aptly observed that there are three dimensions to leadership behavior. He labeled them the *heart*, the *head*, and the *hand*. Principals are influenced by their personal beliefs, values, dreams, and commitments (the heart). They are also directed by professional knowledge (the head) and actions or leadership styles (the hand). Perhaps the greatest difficulties for practitioners arise when these dimensions are in disharmony. For instance, professional, political, and legal factors may direct principals to certain decisions, but from a moral perspective, they *feel* that different courses of action may be best.

In this case, a minority student is caught plagiarizing a book report in her English class. The teacher, invoking school district policy, recommends that the student be given a failing grade for the semester. This student happens to be a gifted althlete who has received an appointment to one of the service academies. A failing grade in English would almost certainly mean that her appointment would be rescinded.

As the case unfolds, the principal finds that he must choose between supporting the teacher's recommendation to fail the student and supporting a compromise solution suggested by the student's attorney. Although he favors the latter (as does the school district's attorney), he is concerned that he will have extreme difficulties with the teachers' union if he opts for this alternative.

Howlett (1991) wrote that "ethics begin where laws and doctrines of right and wrong leave off" (p. 19). Hodgkinson (1991) noted that "values, morals, and ethics are the very stuff of leadership and administrative life" (p. 11). In the real world of school administration, ethics can take several forms. These include nonroutine issues of morality and nonroutine issues of professional practice (Kowalski & Reitzug, 1993). For instance, a principal may face intense pressure to dismiss a teacher because she is not liked by students and parents. Yet, the principal believes that the teacher is effective and can improve her skills in human relations if given proper guidance. Should he make a political decision or a moral decision?

Matters of student discipline often entail political, professional, and ethical entanglements. How does one know whether the punishment is just and ethical? How does one know whether the punishment will really help the student? The school? Society? What considerations need to be given to setting precedent? What obligations does a principal have to follow a teacher's recommendation on punishment? Consider these questions as you read this case.

KEY AREAS FOR REFLECTION

1. The ethical and moral dimensions of practice
2. Student discipline
3. The political nature of controversial decisions
4. Balancing personal feeling with professional obligations

THE CASE

The Community

Newton, Michigan, has fallen on hard times in recent years. The local economy was devastated when two automobile-related factories, a transmission plant and a battery plant, closed. Union strife, lower domestic automobile sales, high labor costs, and automation contributed to their demise. The parent companies diverted much of the work from Newton to new operations they opened in Mexico—a pattern that had become all too common and exasperating for Michigan residents.

As might be expected, this industrial retrenchment spawned an exodus of citizens, and the city's population dropped from 45,500 to slightly over 38,000 in the past nine years. Many who remained were bitter. Some displaced workers were fortunate enough to qualify for early retirement, but many others were forced to either leave Newton or take jobs that paid only a fraction of the salaries they had made previously. Present-day Newton stands in sharp contrast to its glory days.

Following World War II, Newton grew rapidly. A steady stream of new residents were attracted by the high salaries in newly created industries. Many of the immigrants came from southern states such as Tennessee and Alabama—places where industrial growth had been minimal. Others came from large industrial cities such as Chicago, Detroit, and Pittsburgh. Many of these new residents were of eastern European extraction. During the 1960s and 1970s, a number of Hispanic families settled in Newton. They had come to Michigan originally to work in the farm fields as migrant workers, but the high salaries were sufficient to induce them to stay. Hence, Newton became a mini-Detroit or Pittsburgh—a melting pot of racial and ethnic backgrounds.

The Union Influence

The vast majority of the labor force in Newton worked in factories that had some ties to the automobile industry. Virtually all these laborers were loyal members of the local autoworkers' union. By the mid-1960s, the union was the most powerful political, social, and economic force in the community. During those more prosperous years, union leaders were more influential than even the mayor or city council members. They were highly respected and supported, and everyone knew that they had the power to get things done.

Beyond the traditional role of protecting worker rights and negotiating contracts, the local union played a very positive social role in Newton. For example, union leaders long ago realized that their organization could not prosper if there was racial strife. Great strides were taken to make the union hall a place where everybody was welcome and equal. The union became a catalyst for forging friendships that crossed racial and ethnic lines. Union officials were always very outspoken about promoting integrated neighborhoods and schools.

In the early 1980s, jobs in Newton started to disappear, and as they did, the union started losing some of its glamour and power. By the time the factories actually closed, union membership had dropped by over 50 percent. The loss of dues caused serious financial problems that forced union officials to pay less attention to civic matters. Gone were the once-a-month socials that provided free kegs of beer, gone was the annual Fourth of July picnic, and gone was the annual Christmas party that provided gifts to the children and grandchildren of union members. The union leaders now had to concentrate on their own organization's survival.

A New Mayor

In the midst of all of its economic and social problems, residents of Newton looked to the past when they elected a new mayor. Stanley Diviak, a 63-year-old retired tool-and-dye maker, was something of a folk hero in the town. From 1965 to 1978, he served as president of the local autoworkers' union, and many residents fondly remembered those years as the very best.

Stanley was a tough hard-working individual. Even though he wielded more power than anyone in Newton for 13 years, he had made only a handful of enemies. He personified the values that many residents held important. He always kept his word, he always helped his friends, he was a devoted father and grandfather, he went to church regularly, and he was never afraid to say what he believed.

During the election, in which Stanley faced only token opposition from a 24-year-old lawyer who was the Republican candidate, no one ever considered that the outcome was in doubt. Rather than discussing the merits of the candidates, the discussions at Gloria's Diner or Kelsey's Bar revolved around myths that made Stanley an even greater folk hero. Many believed that things would have been different had Stanley not given up the union presidency. Talk about a global economy or changing market trends for automobiles was usually not tolerated, especially after everyone had had a few beers.

Following his election, Stanley appointed many of his former union associates to key positions in the city administration, and he made sure that his appointees reflected the cultural diversity of Newton. Second, he appointed a special committee to examine prospects of attracting new industry to the town. And third, he announced that the traditional Fourth of July picnic would be back—this time sponsored by city government.

Newton High School

If you were to ask someone about the Newton public schools, chances are great that the response would somehow involve the high school's athletic teams. The high school still occupies a two-story building erected in 1958 just four blocks from the center of town. As you walk through the front entrance, the first thing you see is a huge trophy case that is overflowing with tarnished cups and plaques. Pictures of athletes from years past line the hallways.

The school's principal, Nick Furtoski, has lived in Newton virtually all of his life. Except for the time he spent going to college and two years in the Army, he has lived in the same house that was built by his parents prior to World War II. He played football for Newton High in the 1950s and helped the school earn its first state gridiron championship. Over time, he has become the authority on Newton High School history.

The principal's love for his school is obvious, but his greatest pleasure comes from bragging about the athletic heroes of the past. No visitor can escape without hearing about the seven graduates of Newton High School who made it in the National Football League, or the three who played professional baseball. He will take you down the hall and show you Ann Smith's picture—she won a silver medal in the 1972 Olympics. And before you say good-bye, he will puff up his chest and tell you about the 13 graduates who last year received some form of athletic scholarship. But beyond all the bravado and enthusiasm, one can detect that even Nick Furtoski realizes that the best days of Newton High are probably in the past.

The Newton School District

Overall the school district has declined from about 8,500 to just over 6,000 students. Superintendent Andrew Sposis has survived seven difficult years. During his tenure, he has recommended the closing of three schools, and although each closing was approved by the school board, none was greeted with enthusiasm by the community. The superintendent has had to reduce staff every year he has been in office, but the most difficult experiences of his tenure stemmed from employee union problems. Twice since becoming superintendent, the teachers have gone on strike, and two years ago, the custodians' union followed suit.

Virtually all administrators in the district obtained their positions through internal promotions. This includes Superintendent Sposis, who has never worked in another school system. Over the past 29 years, he has been a teacher, elementary school principal, assistant superintendent for business, and superintendent.

The school board is composed of five members selected through nonpartisan elections. Members serve three-year terms. In the past 10 years, the entire board has changed. Only one member who was in office when Superintendent Sposis was employed remains on the board. The current board consists of the following members:

Casimir Barchek, a postal worker

Yolanda Cody, a nurse

Matthew Miskiewicz, a tool-and-die maker

Angela Sanchez, a housewife

Dr. Darnell Turner, a dentist

Mr. Miskiewicz is president of the board and Dr. Turner is the vice-president. Both Mrs. Cody and Dr. Turner are African Americans; Mrs. Sanchez is a Hispanic. Matt Miskiewicz is Mayor Diviak's brother-in-law.

THE INCIDENT

Nancy Allison is a senior at Newton High School. She is a *B* student, an outstanding athlete, one of the most popular students in the school, and she is an African American. By the end of her junior year, she had been named all-state in basketball and track and was inundated with scholarship offers from over 40 universities. In the fall of her senior year, she was elected homecoming queen, but this honor was far less important than the one she received some five months later. In early March, a special delivery letter came to her home from the United States Naval Academy. Nancy had received an appointment to this prestigious institution.

The news of Nancy's accomplishment spread throughout Newton. Her picture appeared on the front page of the local newspaper above the story giving all the details. She was quoted as saying, "There is no doubt in my mind that I'm going to accept the appointment. I look forward to attending the Academy." In a community desperate for good news, Nancy's appointment to the Naval Academy was cause for rejoicing.

However, about two weeks after receiving her letter of appointment, her life took a dramatic turn. On the morning of March 15, Janice Durnitz, an English teacher at Newton High School, asked for an emergency appointment with the principal. Mr. Furtoski, who was in the cafeteria having lunch with several teachers, was summoned by his secretary. She told him that Mrs. Durnitz insisted on seeing him immediately. On returning to his office, the principal greeted his visitor with his usual smile.

"Good afternoon, Janice. What could be so important as to take me away from my late lunch?" he asked.

"I've got very bad news," she responded.

The smile left the administrator's face as he motioned for Janice to enter his office. Once she was inside, he quickly shut the door.

Janice had not even settled in a chair before she said, "Nancy Allison is in my honors English class and up until last week was doing quite well."

"Well, what's the problem?" inquired the principal.

"One requirement of honors English is to complete a critique of a contemporary novel. The assignment was given at the beginning of the semester. Two days ago was the deadline for submitting the project. Nancy was the last one in class to submit her work. In fact, she turned it in a day late. I read her paper last night, and I think there is a serious problem."

"Well, what exactly is this problem?" Mr. Furtoski inquired.

"There is no doubt that Nancy is guilty of plagiarism. The material in her critique clearly verifies this," responded the teacher. "I checked it carefully."

"You are absolutely sure about this?" asked the principal. "It could just be a coincidence."

"It's no coincidence," asserted Mrs. Durnitz. "The material comes straight from a review that appeared in a literary magazine three months ago. It's just her bad luck that I subscribe to it. I checked her work against the review three times hoping that I would find some evidence that I was mistaken. I'm afraid it's plagiarism, and as you well know, the school district policy clearly states that a student caught plagiarizing automatically fails the course."

"What does she say about it?" the principal asked.

"She doesn't deny that she took the material from the magazine. She says she did not know that was wrong. Now, I just can't believe that. Nancy is too bright not to realize you can't copy something word for word and submit it as your own work. She said that since she agreed with the review, she saw no harm in using it."

Mr. Furtoski was obviously shaken by the teacher's revelation. A pained look came over his face and he seemed to stare off into space. The teacher could see he was at a loss for words. Finally, after about a minute, he broke his silence.

"Well, what do you plan to do about this?" he asked.

"I have no choice, Nick. Nancy has to fail the course. That's the policy," she answered.

"Janice, we have worked together for over 15 years. We have never had a student at Newton High School flunk a course because of plagiarism. Hell, half the people in this town don't even know what the word means. Isn't there some way we can seek an alternative? Can't we give her the benefit of the doubt? Maybe she didn't know she was breaking the rules. You know that if you give her an *F*, and especially an *F* for plagiarism, they will probably withdraw her appointment to the Academy. In fact, she will have to go to summer school to make up the credit, and she can't do that and report to the Academy on time. Couldn't we just give her some form of discipline and let her make up the work?" the administrator pleaded.

"Look, Nick. I didn't make the rules, but if I had had the chance, I would have made the rule just the way it is. Plagiarism is cheating. It is a serious offense. What message do we give this student if we just slap her wrist? No, I plan to follow the policy. If that means she doesn't get into the Naval Academy, that's her fault. She should have thought about that before she copied someone else's work." With those parting comments, the teacher turned and walked out of the principal's office.

Mr. Furtoski shut the door to his office and slumped in the chair behind his desk. He sat quietly staring out his window, and after about 15 minutes he called the superintendent. As he waited for Mr. Sposis to come on the line, he kept asking himself what he should do. His first thoughts were to support Mrs. Durnitz, but emotionally he didn't agree with giving Nancy an *F*. His feelings were affected by the fact that he knew Nancy quite well. He knew her parents. They were good people, and her not going to the Academy would be devastating to them. He asked himself if Nancy's life should be ruined because of one mistake. Was giving her an *F* in the best interests of the high school and the town? When the superintendent came on the line, Nick gave him the full story.

Mr. Sposis responded, "This is just what I need, Nick! Do you know what will happen if this student doesn't go to the Naval Academy? The damn roof on your building and mine will be blown sky high. The mayor has been talking about her appointment every chance he gets. He had the whole Allison family to city hall for a picture-taking session a week ago. There has got to be a way out of this. What do you think, Nick?"

"There is no doubt that Mrs. Durnitz is not going to back down. She's not the type. She can be real stubborn. I don't know if she doesn't like Nancy or if it's something else. But she made it clear to me that she plans to give her an *F*. And I don't think you or I could talk her out of it."

"Can't you come up with some alternative?"

"I suggested an alternative. But Mrs. Durnitz will have no part of it. You know that changing her grade will cause all kinds of hell with the union. You know that, don't you?"

The conversation between the two administrators went on for another 10 minutes. Nick shared his emotions and noted that he was inclined to find a way out, but he just couldn't see how that could be done. The conversation concluded with Mr. Sposis saying that he would share the matter with the school board when they met in a few days.

The matter with Nancy was being kept secret at the school. The principal told Mrs. Durnitz and Nancy not to talk to anyone about the incident. Both agreed to remain silent until a final decision had been reached.

When Mr. Sposis informed the school board, the attorney for the district, June VanSilten, was present. She was annoyed that the superintendent had not bothered to call her about this matter prior to the meeting. After listening to the details, she said that the school district might have difficulty with this matter if the student received a failing grade. She was not more specific. The African-American board members expressed immediate concern. The attorney cautioned them not to get involved in the matter because of due process considerations. If the student was given a failing grade, and if she appealed that decision, the board might get involved officially at a later time.

After the board meeting, Superintendent Sposis called the principal and told him that a decision would have to be made. First, Mrs. Durnitz was to make her decision, then Mr. Furtoski would have to decide whether to support her action. The superintendent explained that everyone needed to be careful about violating procedures since the student and her parents may pursue legal action.

After meeting with Mrs. Durnitz and again pleading with her to reconsider, the teacher placed her decision in writing. She said that because Nancy Allison had plagiarized a book report, she would receive an *F* in the honors English class. A copy of the teacher's decision was given to Tony Prado, president of the teachers' union and a teacher at one of the elementary schools.

The following day, Mr. Furtoski received a telephone call from Mr. Prado. The principal was told that the union expected him to uphold Mrs. Durnitz. Mr. Prado made it clear that he saw this as a critical issue, because it involved a teacher's responsibility to follow policy and to be responsible for student grades.

Nick talked to several faculty friends whom he trusted, and each told him to back Mrs. Durnitz. Although he felt that a compromise would be better and congruent with his instincts, he decided not to reverse the teacher's decision.

News of the incident quickly spread through the community. The reactions were mixed—largely along racial lines. Mr. and Mrs. Allison were furious with the teacher and the principal. Their decision to give a failing grade was appealed to the superintendent.

A hearing was held as prescribed by school district policy. The student, her parents and their attorney, the principal, and the teacher attended. The superintendent served as the hearing officer. At the conclusion, the superintendent denied the appeal. He did so on the grounds that the policy was clear and that the student had not denied copying the report.

Mr. and Mrs. Allison arranged to do an extensive interview with the local newspaper. They charged Mrs. Durnitz, Mr. Furtoski, and Mr. Sposis with racism.

The father said, "If this had been a white football player, do you think this would be happening? Isn't it strange that when they decide to make an example of someone, it just happens to be an African-American female who is probably the best known student in the school?"

The school board was briefed more fully on the matter in executive session two days following the hearing. It appeared that the board was divided three to two, with the majority supporting the position of the superintendent. The two dissenting board members joined the parents in suggesting to the media that racial issues may possibly be involved in the case. In just a few weeks, the incident with Nancy Allison had divided the community, the school board, and even students and teachers at the school.

Nancy's parents decided not to appeal the matter to the school board, sensing that such an effort would be futile and time consuming. Rather, they instructed their attorney to file a lawsuit naming the three educators and the school board as defendants.

The school district's attorney, Ms. VanSilten, had felt uncomfortable about this matter from the very beginning. Now that the suit had been filed, she warned the board that they may not be able to win. The board, however, was bitterly divided, and the three who supported the decision refused to change their position. They argued that they needed to defend the actions of the teacher and administrators because they had officially followed board policy.

Three weeks after initiating legal action, Nancy's parents, through their attorney, offered a compromise. The Allisons feared that the litigation would drag on for some time and that their daughter would not be able to enroll at the Academy as scheduled. They offered to withdraw the lawsuit if Nancy would be allowed to retake the English class with another teacher. Phillip Jones, a member of the English department and an African American, offered to direct an independent study for Nancy at night and on weekends so that she could graduate on time. Additionally, Nancy would not be allowed to participate in any social events at the school for the remainder of the semester. Nancy's lawyer argued that this was a more appropriate punishment than receiving an *F*.

The school district's attorney urged the principal and superintendent to accept the compromise.

"This litigation could cost the school district a great deal of money and time. And there is a good chance that we won't win. Here is an opportunity for everyone to walk away with their heads held high," she told them.

The board president called an executive session and instructed the superintendent to have the principal present. The board president read the letter from the Allisons' attorney offering the compromise solution. He noted that Mayor Diviak knew about the offer and was urging everyone to take it. All of the board members said they could live with the compromise; but they would not force the administration to change the grade. Only Mr. Furtoski could do that.

"Nick, what do you think?" the board president asked. "We don't want to leave you hanging, but this compromise may be best for everyone."

THE CHALLENGE

Place yourself in the principal's position. What would you do?

KEY ISSUES/QUESTIONS

1. Identify the possible alternatives that the principal may pursue in this matter. Evaluate the merits of each of them.

2. Assess the behavior of Mrs. Durnitz in this case. Did she behave professionally? Ethically?

3. To what extent do you think the economic environment of the school district (the community) affects this situation?

4. Identify the moral and ethical dilemma facing the principal.

5. Most of the administrators in Newton acquired their positions via internal promotions. Do you think this has any bearing on this case?

6. What, if anything, would you have done differently if you were principal after first learning about the charges of plagiarism?

7. As principal, what weight would you give to the following?
   a. Division on the school board
   b. The opinion of the school district attorney
   c. The superintendent's position with the school board and community
   d. The teachers' union
   e. Racial and economic issues in the community

8. Can you think of any solutions other than the one proposed by the parents?

9. What is your assessment of the superintendent in this case? Should he have behaved differently?

10. Do you think it is important to this case that the principal is a "hometown boy"? Why or why not?

11. Do you think that most principals are influenced by their moral convictions and ethical dimensions of practice?

12. Should policies be absolutes or guidelines? Explain your position.

13. What do think will be the repercussions if the principal decides to reject the compromise?

14. Do you agree that students with good records should have their futures damaged because of one mistake? Would this have been a different matter if Nancy had been caught using cocaine?

15. Should the principal and superintendent have consulted with the school attorney before even discussing this matter with the school board?

SUGGESTED READINGS

Bartlett, L. (1987). Academic evaluation and student discipline don't mix: A critical review. *Journal of Law and Education, 16*(2), 155-165.

Browlee, G. (1987). Coping with plagiarism requires several strategies. *Journalism Educator, 41*(4), 25-29.

Cunningham, W. C., & Gresso, D. W. (1993). *Cultural leadership: The culture of excellence in education.* Boston: Allyn & Bacon (see chapter 2).

Dant, D. (1986). Plagiarism in high school: A survey. *English Journal, 75*(2), 81-84.

Drum, A. (1986). Responding to plagiarism. *College Composition and Communication, 37*(2), 241-243.

Fass, R. A. (1986). By honor bound: Encouraging academic honesty. *Educational Record, 67*(4), 32-36.

Fris, J. (1992). Principals' encounters with conflict: Tactics they and others use. *Alberta Journal of Educational Research, 38*(1), 65-78.

Geosits, M., & Kirk, W. (1983). Sowing the seeds of plagiarism. *Principal, 62*(5), 35-38.

Hobbs, G. J. (1992). The legality of reducing student grades as a disciplinary measure. *The Clearing House, 65,* 284-285.

Hodgkinson, C. (1991). *Educational leadership: The moral art.* Albany, NY: State University of New York Press.

Howlett, P. (1991). How you can stay on the straight and narrow. *Executive Educator, 13*(2), 19-21, 35.

Kowalski, T. J., & Reitzug, U. C. (1993). *Contemporary school administration: An introduction.* New York: Longman (see chapters 9, 15).

Martin, B. (1984). Plagiarism and responsibility. *Journal of Tertiary Educational Administration, 6*(2), 183-190.

Owens, R. G. (1992). *Organizational behavior in education* (4th ed.). Boston: Allyn & Bacon (see chapter 9).

Peterson, P. (1984). Plagiarism: It can happen to you. *Quill and Scroll, 58*(4), 15.

Sauer, R. (1983). Coping with copiers. *English Journal, 72*(4), 50-52.

Sergiovanni, T. J. (1991). *The principalship: A reflective practice perspective* (2nd ed.). Boston: Allyn & Bacon (see chapter 15).

Shea, J. (1987). When borrowing becomes burglary. *Currents, 13*(1), 38-42.

Skom, E. (1986). Plagiarism: Quite a rather bad little crime. *AAHE Bulletin* (October 3), 7.

Sterling, G. (1991). Plagiarism and the worm of accountability. *Reading Improvement, 28*(3), 138-140.

The Closed Door Policy

BACKGROUND INFORMATION

Researchers have long studied the effects of leadership behavior on organizations. In many school systems, it is the superintendent who sets the tone for expected behavior and outlines the goals that are to be accomplished. Early studies of leadership concentrated on personal traits or desired behaviors, but more recently, research has focused on examining behavior in conjunction with situational factors (i.e., the settings in which the behavior occurs).

The behavior of a superintendent or principal is the product of many influences, one of which entails perceptions of organizational life. If an individual leader believes that bureaucratic-like structures are most effective, this conviction will influence most or all decisions that are made. In school administration, a profession where practitioners are likely to change employers several times, this is a weighty consideration. For example, each time a principal moves to a new school or new school district, he or she faces somewhat different values, beliefs, practices, and leadership expectations. Success often depends on one's ability to understand these differences and to make adjustments that will allow for productive behavior.

The development of contingency theories in educational administration reflects the awareness that behavior needs to be examined in conjunction with situational variables. These theories describe the degree to which leaders are preoccupied with tasks versus people or with autocratic versus democratic leadership. A task-oriented leader, for example, may be unwilling to make policy exceptions regardless of the human circumstances involved; an autocratic leader may be unwilling to involve others in decisions because he believes this will lead to conflict. Determining the appropriateness of behavior requires a contextual analysis.

In this case, a newly employed superintendent isolates himself from his staff. Employees, even central office administrators, find it difficult to make appointments with him. Yet, this behavior occurs in a relatively small school district where one might expect that staff would have high levels of interaction. The superintendent's behavior becomes a critical issue when an employee seeks approval for a grant proposal. Frustrated by numerous barriers, the employee must make a decision that brings personal and organizational interests face-to-face.

KEY AREAS FOR REFLECTION

1. Leadership behavior
2. Analysis of behavior in an organizational context
3. Communication processes
4. Conflict between personal and organizational interests
5. Delegating authority

THE CASE

The Community

Placid Falls is a suburban community that emerged in the early 1950s. Located approximately 35 miles from New York City, it is considered a community of choice by many upper-class families. Houses in the community, when they become available on the market, sell for approximately $450,000 to $850,000. The 1990 census set the population at 7,631 residents, and the average family income is over $200,000 per year.

There is no additional land available for development in the community. The governmental structure of Placid Falls includes a five-member town council, a mayor, and a town manager. The council members are elected to four-year terms as is the mayor. The mayor's position is considered to be a part-time assignment, and currently the office is held by a retired physician. The town manager holds a master's degree in public administration, and he actually runs the day-to-day functions of local government.

The School District

The Placid Falls Public School District consists of four schools: two elementary schools (grades K-5), a middle school (grades 6-8), and a high school (grades 9-12). The total enrollment in the school district is approximately 1,800. Enrollments have declined slightly in the past decade, about 1 percent per year.

The local schools have historically been a source of pride for residents. In fact, many families located here because of the public school system. Approximately 90 percent of the graduates of the high school enroll in four-year institutions of higher learning; about one-third of the graduating class will enroll in highly selective, prestigious colleges and universities. Thus academic competition in the schools, especially at the high school, is usually intense. Precollegiate programs are stressed and few students ever opt to take vocational courses (most of which have to be taken at an area vocational school located 20 miles away).

The faculty and administration in the district also have a positive image. Both local residents and officials in the state department of education perceive the professional staff to be among the very best in the state. Nearly 15 percent of the teachers and 75 percent of the administrators have completed doctoral degrees. Salaries are among the highest in the state, and this has been judged to be an important factor that helps to attract outstanding educators to work in Placid Falls. Only a handful of the school district's employees, however, live in the community. Per-pupil expenditures in the school system are among the highest in the state.

The Superintendent

Three years ago when the superintendency in Placid Falls was vacant, 123 candidates applied. More important than the quantity of the candidates was the quality of the applicant pool. Dr. George Frieman, a well-known professor at a large university and a placement consultant with a national reputation, was retained by the school board to assist with the search. He developed an applicant pool that did not disappoint the Placid Falls school board. The ten candidates interviewed by the school board included some of the best-known superintendents in the United States. This was somewhat remarkable considering the relatively small enrollment in the district.

The school board invited three finalists to have second interviews. After examining each, the board offered the position to Dr. Andrew Sagossi, a superintendent of a large county school system in North Carolina. One of the novel experiences for the board was to negotiate with Dr. Sagossi's attorney in reaching an employment contract. One board member said it reminded him of negotiating with a professional athlete's agent. After making a number of concessions, the board agreed to a four-year contract with generous fringe benefits and an annual salary of $123,000.

Leaving a school district of over 25,000 students to move to a school district with fewer than 2,000 students may seem difficult to understand for many upwardly mobile administrators. Historically, school administrators have tended to equate career growth with ascension to progressively larger school districts. A closer examination of the facts provides insights into possible reasons for Dr. Sagossi's decision. The salary was over $20,000 higher than what he was being paid in North Carolina. Having grown up in New York City, he also was interested in "coming back home." A number of his relatives, including his mother, still resided in the metropolitan area. But perhaps his greatest motivation for taking the position in Placid Falls had to do with his plans for retirement. He needed five more years to reach maximum benefits in the state retirement system.

In publicly stating his reasons for becoming superintendent of Placid Falls, Dr. Sagossi never mentioned salary, family, or retirement. Rather he emphasized his desire to work in a community where education was appreciated and supported. In his final interview with the school board he told them, "I have been superintendent in several large school systems. I can no longer equate success with the size of the organization I manage. The quality of the work experience is now much more important to me. In a community such as Placid Falls, the superintendent has a much greater opportunity to work with community and state leaders to coordinate the efforts of the local schools. I am tired of fighting battles that relate to whether public schools should even exist. This is a community where you obviously appreciate good administrators and good teachers."

The Administrative Staff

At the time of Dr. Sagossi's appointment, the administrative staff in the district included the following individuals:

> Assistant superintendent for business—Dr. Al Yanko
> High school principal—Dr. Neil Larson
> Middle school principal—Mr. Joe O'Bannion
> Elementary principals—Dr. Wilma Tucko and Ms. Andrea Kline

One position, assistant superintendent for instruction, had just been filled. The person employed, Dr. Joan Myers, would be starting on July 1, the same date that Dr. Sagossi would start his employment. She replaced an individual who resigned in the middle of the school year to accept a superintendency in another school district.

All of the administrative staff, with the exception of the newly employed assistant superintendent, had been with the school district for more than 15 years. All were former teachers in the system.

The New Assistant Superintendent

Joan Myers was born and raised in a suburban New Jersey community. She is the oldest of three children in a rather close-knit family. Her parents are now retired. Her father practiced dentistry for 37 years and her mother was a marketing executive for a large department store. Her upper-middle-class homelife offered many cultural and educational opportunities. As an undergraduate, she attended a prestigious liberal arts college in New England. It was during her sophomore year there that she decided to major in social science education—a decision that was accepted but not cheered by her parents. They had hoped that she would pursue dentistry and enter the family-owned practice.

While teaching for six years in a high school, Joan finished her master's degree in school administration in Philadelphia. After completing her studies and receiving a principal's license, she accepted a position as an assistant principal in a large high school in western New York State. After just two years there, she resigned to accept a doctoral fellowship at a large state university.

Doctoral study was an exciting experience for Joan. She enjoyed the climate of the campus, and she found the opportunity to take courses without holding a full-time job to be a pleasant contrast from her experience as a master's degree student. One year after starting doctoral studies, she married Robert, a practicing attorney who taught part-time at the university. She ultimately spent two and a half years completing her graduate studies.

The position of assistant superintendent in Placid Falls was ideal for her. First, her husband had taken a position as a corporate attorney for a holding company that had offices in Manhattan. Second, Dr. Myers's primary goal was to be an assistant superintendent for instruction. When she first saw the listing for the vacancy in Placid Falls, however, she was reluctant to apply. With only two years of administrative experience, and that at the level of assistant principal, she did not think she would be competitive for the job. Fortunately, she convinced herself that she had nothing to lose. Her first surprise was a telephone call inviting her for an interview. The second surprise was that during the interviews the school officials made it clear they were looking for potential, not necessarily extensive experience. The third surprise was being offered the position. Dr. Myers was actually recommended for employment by Dr. Sagossi's predecessor. He told her that he would be retiring in a few months, but this fact did not bother her. Joan felt confident that the district would hire another outstanding superintendent.

Compared to the two other school districts where Joan had worked, Placid Falls seemed to be Utopia. There just didn't seem to be many of those nasty problems that plagued most other public school systems. Employees were happy; salaries were among the highest in the metropolitan area; and given the size of the school district, there were adequate numbers of administrators, teachers, and support staff.

Dr. Joan Myers has many strengths. Among the more obvious are her outgoing personality and her ability to motivate those around her. She generates an excitement about education. Although her title in the school system is "assistant superintendent," she basically is a staff administrator. That is, she does not have line authority for the principals. She works cooperatively with administrators and teachers on curriculum projects and serves as a resource person to assist with the development of instructional materials.

The New Superintendent

During the first two to three weeks in Placid Falls, Dr. Sagossi held several administrative staff meetings and met with administrators individually. During these sessions, he outlined expectations and developed several general goals that he had for the school system. In several ways, he appeared to the administrative staff to be like his predecessor—confident, articulate, and capable.

After those first weeks, however, the administrative staff saw little of Dr. Sagossi. Even the secretaries in the central office started to comment that he was away from his office frequently. And when he was at the office, he was not very visible. He either had appointments or worked with his personal secretary. This was an aspect of Dr. Sagossi's behavior that set him apart from his predecessor. The former superintendent rarely was away from the central office; he made a point of sticking his head in offices and saying good morning each day when he arrived; he enjoyed taking a coffee break with the secretaries and other administrators.

A number of the employees began to question what Dr. Sagossi was doing with his time. Dr. Yanko, the assistant superintendent for business, tried to explain that the new superintendent was very "community oriented." He told employees that unlike his predecessor, Dr. Sagossi preferred to spend his time working with civic and governmental leaders. He also noted that the superintendent believed in delegating authority; thus, he expected his two assistants to deal with everyday management problems.

After just two months in Placid Falls, Dr. Sagossi announced that he had plans to seek the presidency of the state superintendents' association the following year. He had many contacts in the state, and he believed he had a good chance to win. Additionally, the new superintendent accepted appointments to several boards of directors. These included a local bank, the United Way, and the alumni association of his alma mater.

The Problem

In December, Dr. Myers attended a national conference on gifted and talented education. There she met Maggie Zerich, a program officer with a midwestern foundation who was attending in relation to a project her employer was funding in six school districts. The project involved mentoring relationships for highly talented middle grade students. The two met purely by chance as they were seated next to each other at a luncheon.

During their initial encounter, Dr. Myers learned that Ms. Zerich was looking for several more school districts to become part of the middle-school mentoring project.

"Exactly what does this program involve?" Dr. Myers asked the foundation official.

"The primary purpose is to examine the benefits of taking students in the seventh grade and linking them with mentors for two years," Ms. Zerich answered. "The mentors are usually government officials, business leaders, physicians, engineers, and lawyers who live in the community. The students spend approximately three hours per week working with their mentors on approved projects. Our major interest is to find out if these encounters have a positive effect on the students. For example, will mentoring affect curricular choices later in high school? Will it affect career choices?"

Ms. Zerich detected that Dr. Myers was highly interested, and after learning more about Placid Falls, she invited her to submit a proposal to become part of the project. Dr. Myers left the conference full of excitement. She could hardly wait to tell Dr. Sagossi about the opportunity. She felt getting the grant would be a feather in her cap—proof that she could make positive contributions to the school district. Her one concern involved time parameters. Maggie Zerich needed the proposal within five weeks so that it could be reviewed in time for the upcoming funding cycle.

When Dr. Myers returned to Placid Falls, she immediately outlined what needed to be done to complete the proposal. First, she had to talk to Joe O'Bannion, the middle school principal, to assure his support and cooperation. Second, she had to determine a method for selecting students to participate in the program. Third, she had to build a pool of prospective mentors. Fourth, she had to identify a consultant who would conduct the research portion of the project (the foundation required that the investigator be a person not employed by the school district). Her final major task was to get Dr. Sagossi to agree to provide $30,000 in matching funds for the project. The first four tasks were accomplished with little difficulty; the final one proved to be more cumbersome.

The first day back from the conference, December 7th, Dr. Myers walked across the hall to Dr. Sagossi's office in hopes of telling him about the mentoring project. Miss Halston, his secretary, told her that the superintendent was out of town at a conference and would not return until December 12th. Fearing that not seeing the superintendent until then would deter her planning, she then went to see Dr. Yanko, the administrator who controlled the budget. She explained the proposal and asked if he could approve the $30,000 needed for the school district's share of the funding.

"Only the boss and the school board can approve that kind of expenditure," Dr. Yanko told her. "Proposals for outside funding must be approved by the school board before they are submitted to funding agencies. And as you know, nothing goes to the school board for consideration unless Dr. Sagossi has reviewed the material and decides to make a positive recommendation. When do you have to submit this?"

"I think the last date is January 12th," Dr. Myers replied.

"Well, you still have the January board meeting. Let's see; the first Wednesday in January is the 3rd. You'll be okay."

After the conversation with her colleague, Dr. Myers went back to Miss Halston to establish an appointment with the superintendent after he returned to the district. The secretary scheduled an appointment for 10:00 AM on December 13th. She explained that December 12th would not be possible because the superintendent had a standard practice of not scheduling appointments on the day he returns to the district after an absence of more than two days.

Dr. Myers continued working on the proposal. In a way she thought the delay in seeing the superintendent could be beneficial because her work on the project would be nearly completed by the time she met with him. This would permit her to discuss the funding proposal in detail.

Dr. Myers saw Dr. Sagossi briefly on Wednesday the 12th, the day he returned to Placid Falls. The two exchanged greetings in the hallway of the administrative office, but she did not have an opportunity to bring up the proposal. The following morning, there was an administrative staff meeting at 8:00 AM. Such meetings were not regularly scheduled and were held only whenDr. Sagossi determined they were necessary. The meeting on the 13th was devoted to a series of state-level reports the superintendent wanted to share with his administrative team. The meeting ended at approximately 9:30 AM. At promptly 9:55 AM, Joan arrived at Dr. Sagossi's office for her 10:00 AM appointment.

Miss Halston said, "I was just getting ready to call you, Dr. Myers. I'm afraid I'm going to have to change your appointment. Dr. Sagossi just received a telephone call that his mother is quite ill. He said he will be back in the office on Monday and he recommended that you should meet with him sometime that morning. His calendar is pretty clear, and I'm sure he'll be able to chat with you then."

On Monday morning about 9:00 AM, Dr. Myers again tried to see the superintendent. This time Miss Halston told her that the board president was with the superintendent and that she didn't know how long they would be together. Dr. Myers reminded the secretary that Dr. Sagossi was supposed to be able to see her and asked that she see him just as soon as the two men were finished with their conference.

At about 10:30 AM, Miss Halston called Dr. Myers and apologized on behalf of the superintendent. She told Dr. Myers that a problem had surfaced and that it would be necessary to schedule an appointment for the next day. Dr. Myers looked at her calendar and realized that she had to go to a meeting regarding textbook adoptions in the state capital on Tuesday.

"How about Wednesday?" asked Dr. Myers. "Is he available on Wednesday?"

"No," the secretary answered. "He is scheduled to be at the university for an alumni board meeting all that day. He will be back on Thursday."

At this point, Dr. Myers was both frustrated and angry. She told Miss Halston, "Look, this is important. This is not General Motors. I find it difficult to understand why I can't arrange to see the superintendent for just 30 minutes. There are thousands of dollars at stake, not to mention an excellent educational opportunity. I'm sure that if Dr. Sagossi knew why I wanted to see him, he would find the time."

"Dr. Myers," replied the secretary, "I don't make the rules. I just do my job. Let me talk to Dr. Sagossi to see if he can see you before the end of the week."

Fifteen minutes later the secretary called back and informed Dr. Myers that she should talk to Dr. Yanko about the matter.

"Tell Dr. Sagossi that I have already done that and he told me I had to talk to the superintendent," Joan impatiently responded. "Tell him I will send him something in writing and perhaps he can respond after he reads it."

After putting down the telephone, Dr. Myers realized that school would be dismissing for the holiday break in just four days. Further, she realized that the agenda for the January 3rd board meeting was probably being prepared. She went to the superintendent's office to see when board materials would be distributed for the January 3rd meeting. The secretary informed her that the packets, which included the agenda, would be distributed as always one week before the meeting. Because Dr. Sagossi was going on vacation to Florida for 10 days commencing the 23rd of December, he intended to complete the board packets by the afternoon of Friday the 22nd. Once again, Dr. Myers pleaded her case, indicating that it was extremely important to see the superintendent about the grant proposal. Again she was told that she would have to make an appointment.

"Look, the only possible date left is Thursday, December 21st. What if something else comes up and he cancels the appointment again?" Dr. Myers asked.

The secretary looked at her and said slowly, "Dr. Sagossi is a busy person. You cannot expect that he will see you whenever you like. If you have deadlines on a grant proposal, you should have talked to him about it weeks ago."

Dejected, Dr. Myers walked back to her office.

THE CHALLENGE

Place yourself in Dr. Myers's position. What would you do at this point?

KEY ISSUES/QUESTIONS

1. What options does Dr. Myers have in this situation? What are the advantages and disadvantages of each?
2. Assess the climate in this school system based on what you learned from reading this case.
3. Assess the leadership style of the superintendent based on what you learned from reading this case.
4. Describe the differences between a "line" and a "staff" position in a school district. Does the fact that Dr. Myers functions in a staff capacity have any effect on this case?
5. Given the availability of the superintendent, do you believe that he should delegate more authority to his assistant superintendents?
6. Is the type of leadership behavior exhibited in this case more likely to occur in community environments such as Placid Falls? Why or why not?
7. Would you like to work in Placid Falls? Why or why not?
8. Are Dr. Myers's background and assignments typical or atypical for women who occupy central office positions?
9. Do you think Dr. Myers is being treated differently by the superintendent because she is a woman?
10. To what extent do you believe that Dr. Myers's background and experience are issues in this matter?
11. In this case, there is mention of employee questions about the superintendent's schedule. Do you think it is common for employees to closely scrutinize the behavior of a new administrator, especially during the first few months of employment?
12. Is there sufficient information to determine whether the superintendent is oriented more toward people or tasks?

13. Do you believe that most school systems have provisions that permit projects to be developed quickly or that most are mired in rules and regulations?

14. In what ways could the superintendent communicate his priorities to this staff so that they better understand his behavior?

SUGGESTED READINGS

Abrams, J. (1987). How superintendents can work better with others. *Education Digest, 52*(10), 26-28.

Bass, B., & Valenzi, E. (1974). Contingent aspects of effective management styles. In J. Hunt & L. Larson (Eds.), *Contingency approaches to leadership* (pp. 130-152). Carbondale, IL: Southern Illinois University Press.

Chalker, D., & Hurley, S. (1993). Beastly people. *Executive Educator, 15*(1), 24-26.

Comer, D. (1991). Organizational newcomers' acquisition of information from peers. *Management Communication Quarterly, 5*(1), 64-89.

DeRoche, E. (1985). *How administrators solve problems.* Englewood Cliffs, NJ: Prentice-Hall (see chapter 3).

Duignan, P. (1980). Administration behavior of school superintendents: A descriptive study. *Journal of Educational Administration, 18*(1), 5-26.

Duttweiler, P. (1988). The dysfunctions of bureaucratic structure. *Educational Policy and Practice,* Issue 3.

Eblen, A. (1987). Communication, leadership, and organizational commitment. *Central States Speech Journal, 38*(3-4), 181-195.

Garland, P., & O'Reily, R. (1976). The effect of leader-member interaction in organizational effectiveness. *Educational Administration Quarterly, 12*(3), 9-30.

Geddes, D. (1993). Empowerment through communication: Key people-to-people and organizational success. *People and Education, 1*(1), 76-104.

Gouldner, A. (1970). About the functions of bureaucratic rules. In W. Scott (Ed.), *Social processes and social structures* (pp. 320-328). New York: Holt, Rinehart, & Winston.

Hanson, E. (1991). *Educational administration and organizational behavior* (3rd ed.). Boston: Allyn & Bacon (see chapter 9).

Hoy, W., & Miskel, C. (1987). *Educational administration: Theory, research, and practice* (3rd ed.). New York: Random House (see chapter 11).

Hoy, W., Newland, W., & Blaxovsky, R. (1977). Subordinate loyalty to superior, esprit, and aspects of bureaucratic structure. *Educational Administration Quarterly, 13*(1), 71-85.

Immegart, G. (1988). Leadership and leader behavior. In N. Boyan (Ed.), *Handbook of research on educational administration* (pp. 259-278). New York: Longman.

Kowalski, T., & Reitzug, U. (1993). *Contemporary school adminstration: An introduction.* New York: Longman (see chapters 7, 10).

Loose, W., & McManus, J. (1987). Corporate management techniques in the superintendent's office. *Thrust, 16*(7), 11-13.

O'Reilly, C., & Pondy, L. (1979). Organizational communication. In S. Kerr (Ed.), *Organizational behavior* (pp. 119-150). Columbus, OH: Grid.

Pajak, E. (1989). *The central office supervisor of curriculum and instruction.* Boston: Allyn & Bacon (see chapter 10).

Vroom, V., & Jago, A. (1988). *The new leadership: Managing participation in organizations.* Englewood Cliffs, NJ: Prentice-Hall (see chapter 7).

case 12

Captain Punishment

BACKGROUND INFORMATION

One of the challenges of public school administration is facing many different expectations that are held by students, parents, central office administrators, and employees. Both the position and environment in which the position functions play a part in establishing role perceptions. Largely for this reason, community standards, school goals, and demographic variables often intertwine to create role expectations for a principal in an affluent suburban school that are substantially different from those developed for an inner-city school principal. Additionally, one's personal values, beliefs, experiences, and biases influence self-perceptions of role.

Role conflict emerges when a school administrator is confronted with divergent expectations. This is a condition in which the administrator finds that compliance with one anticipated behavior may make it difficult (or impossible) to be in compliance with others. An example of role conflict is often seen during teachers' strikes. Many faculty expect their principal to be supportive of their cause—or at the very least, to be understanding and neutral. By contrast, the superintendent and school board expect the principal to support management positions and to exhibit overt behaviors that leave no doubt that principals are part of the management team.

When confronted with role conflict, administrators may exhibit a range of behaviors, one of which is to consciously accept one expectation over the other. Other possibilities include withdrawing from the situation (e.g., resigning), seeking to reconcile differences in the expectations, avoiding a decision in the hopes that the matter will pass, or deciding to explain behavior on the basis of school district policies or administrative rules (e.g., explaining that they have no freedom to make a decision).

This case involves a middle school principal who is confronted with differing role expectations. The issue is the use of corporal punishment. While many parents desire the principal to be a tough disciplinarian, others expect him to make professionally based decisions (i.e., decisions driven by professional knowledge). In this regard, decision making is one of the focal points of the case. Should administrators make decisions based on intuition and personal experience, or should they integrate professional knowledge with past experiences?

Another dimension of the case involves perceptions of success. People tend to be more tolerant of certain behaviors if they see the general outcomes to be positive—essentially that the ends justify the means. An example of this pattern is frequently observed in athletics. A coach who is highly successful in winning games may be able to exhibit behaviors that otherwise would result in rebukes, reprimands, or even dismissal. People are more tolerant because they like being associated with a winning team. In this case, some are reluctant to question the principal's behavior because the school he leads is considered to be successful.

KEY AREAS FOR REFLECTION

1. Role expectations
2. Role conflict
3. Relationship between behavior and organizational outcomes
4. Expectations for decision-making processes
5. The effects of community environment on role expectations of principals

THE CASE

Rogers Middle School is located in a major city in a southwestern state. The school came into existence seven years ago as a result of population growth. The school facility is attractive and well maintained, and it has become a source of pride for many families in the neighborhoods surrounding it. Those neighborhoods consist primarily of low-cost housing—prefabricated structures erected on small lots. Although these buildings are less than 20 years old, they already are showing signs of deterioration.

Students at Rogers mirror the heterogeneous population of this growing metropolitan area. Many of the students are bilingual. A recent study found that 14 different languages are spoken by boys and girls who attend the school. A statistical report prepared for the central administration of the school system identified the following breakdown of enrollment:

Hispanic—41 percent
African American—15 percent
Caucasian—24 percent

Native American—9 percent

Indochinese—9 percent

Other—2 percent

A profile of the school's professional staff is quite different. About two-thirds of the teachers, counselors, and administrators are Caucasian.

Rogers Middle School contains grades 6–8. The total enrollment of the school is 1,150, and there is no additional space to accommodate more pupils. When the school first opened, it enrolled just over 700 pupils, and since that time, enrollment has increased every year.

Comparatively, Rogers is considered a very good school. Average scores on standardized tests are the highest of any of the middle schools in the district. Athletic teams and other extracurricular programs have an established record of success. The school perennially has fewer suspensions and expulsions than other middle schools in the district. Much of the credit for these accomplishments is directed toward the principal, Pete Sanchez.

Ever since he was an elementary school student in southern New Mexico, Pete Sanchez wanted to be a teacher. One of nine children, he found it impossible to attend college after graduating from high school. Like his siblings, he went to work in a local factory right after high school graduation when he was 18 years old. But unlike many of his peers, Pete did not forget his dream. Over a span of seven years, he drove 45 miles twice a week to take night classes at a state university. By doing so, he managed to complete the equivalent of three years of full-time study. When he reached this point with his studies, he quit his job, obtained a student loan, and enrolled as a full-time student. Free from the burdens of working in a factory all day and going to school at night, he made all A's, including an A in student teaching during that final year of undergraduate studies.

Several of Pete's professors encouraged him to enroll in graduate school. But he had a burning desire to teach, and his wife had become pregnant during the final months of college studies. Thus, he accepted a high school teaching position in a neighboring state. There he taught mathematics and assumed two coaching responsibilities—assistant football coach and head track coach. During the 12 years he spent at this high school, he managed to complete a master's degree and obtained certification as a secondary school principal. The following year, he accepted a position as assistant principal in a high school in another district.

As an assistant principal, Pete was responsible for student discipline. According to his immediate supervisor, he did his job very well. He was stern, but consistent in delving out penalties. His use of a paddle on serious offenders earned him the nickname "Captain Punishment."

Just three years after accepting his first administrative position, Pete was employed as the principal of Rogers Middle School. His reputation as a "no nonsense" disciplinarian followed him. In large measure his philosophy for dealing with problem students stemmed from his observation that many students lacked proper guidance and direction outside of school. He felt that school provided the only hope for many of these students, and he did not want them to lose this opportunity. Above all, he felt that many of these students had to learn to respect authority if they were to succeed in life. He felt a good whack on the bottom with his walnut paddle, dubbed the "Board of Education," would leave a lasting impression that they had to be responsible for their behavior.

Rogers Middle School has one of the most active parent groups of all the schools in the district, including the elementary schools. Pete Sanchez spends a great deal of time with the parent committees he established since becoming the school's first and only principal. He has been very skillful in involving parents—in making them feel that they are part of the school. He once told his immediate supervisor, Dr. Penelope Mackee, "When you have so many children coming from one-parent families, it is important to get that one parent involved in the school."

One of these committees reviews matters related to student discipline; it consists of seven parents and three teachers. On several occasions, this committee reviewed the issue of corporal punishment. And each time the topic emerged, Pete expressed his convictions that, properly administered, paddling had a positive effect on students of this age. He also shared his belief that a strong discipline program was partially responsible for the school's overall success. Each time the matter of corporal punishment came up for review, the committee gave the principal near unanimous support to continue using his paddle when he deemed it was necessary.

Both a city newspaper and a local television station did special stories focusing on Rogers Middle School and its principal, Pete Sanchez. He was portrayed accurately as a "no nonsense" administrator who believed in firm discipline. The stories even referred to his nickname, Captain Punishment. One mother interviewed for the television segment said, "Mr. Sanchez understands my children. He teaches them that they have to obey rules. They don't have a father at home, so I'm glad that the principal provides direction at school. My kids have a lot of respect for Mr. Sanchez."

Despite publicity about the use of corporal punishment at the school, the superintendent and other central office administrators remained silent on the issue. And even though nearly half of the school's faculty opposed such disciplinary actions, most remained silent in public. One of the exceptions was a veteran social studies teacher, Aaron Carson. He too has been at Rogers since the school opened. He relocated to the Southwest after teaching in Virginia for three years—a move prompted by chronic asthma.

Mr. Carson first challenged the principal's behavior about four years ago in a faculty meeting. At that time, he received little support from his colleagues and the matter was pretty much ignored. Two years later, he again brought the issue to a faculty meeting, and this time he came armed with articles from professional journals that fortified his position. Several teachers supported him, but a decision was made that the principal and Mr. Carson ought to discuss their differences outside the faculty meetings. Most of the teachers simply did not want to talk about corporal punishment. Although two subsequent meetings between the two men allowed for a fuller exchange of ideas, neither changed his views. And although he felt strongly about the matter, Aaron Carson did not make his protestations public—that is, not until the incident with Jimmy Longbow.

Every student at Rogers Middle School knew Jimmy Longbow. He was a gifted athlete but prone to get into trouble. Jimmy lived with his mother and two sisters. His father passed away several years ago. Jimmy was a student in Aaron Carson's social studies class. It was one of the few classes in which he was making a better than average grade. Aaron saw something in Jimmy that he liked. Maybe he saw a little of himself—a rebellious child, growing up in poverty, without a father, and with a big chip on his shoulder. Aaron remembers all too well his own childhood in Brooklyn, New York. Life was tough, and you had to grow up in a hurry.

One of Jimmy's other teachers was Ned Draycroft. Jimmy hated Mr. Draycroft's English class. Poetry, short stories, and diagramming sentences were all things Jimmy didn't like. One day Jimmy was receiving a tongue-lashing from Mr. Draycroft for not doing his homework. It was a day when Mr. Draycroft was in an especially bad mood. When Mr. Draycroft finally ended his three-minute diatribe, Jimmy looked him squarely in the eye and said, "This stuff is all crap. Why don't you teach us something that's important?"

The students could see the veins pop out in Mr. Draycroft's neck. He stood in front of the rebellious student and shook his finger. "You, young man, are going to the office. I have had it with you. Maybe a dozen good whacks from the 'Board of Education' will teach you not to be so impudent."

Mr. Draycroft took Jimmy to the office and told the principal what had happened. Jimmy and Mr. Sanchez were not strangers. According to the school grapevine, Jimmy was more familiar with the "Board of Education" than any other student in the school.

"Jimmy," Mr. Sanchez began, "when are you going to learn? You mess up, you're going to get it. You can't just shoot your mouth off any time you feel like it. It's about time you grew up. But as we see by this incident, you're not there yet. So, you have to be treated like a second-grader."

The principal then issued his customary order in these situations, directing the student to empty his back pockets, to bend over, and to hold his ankles. But this time, Jimmy refused to comply.

"You're not going to hit me with that paddle again," he told the principal. "You can take your school and shove it."

With that, Jimmy ran from the office and the school building. Before anyone could catch him, he was gone. The principal called Jimmy's mother, who was a waitress in a local diner. She left work immediately to see if she could find her son, but the effort proved fruitless. Jimmy did not come home that night, nor the next, nor the next.

Various accounts of the incident spread quickly through the school. Aaron Carson found out about it in the teachers' lounge. He immediately called Jimmy's mother and asked if he could stop by the house to talk to her. The two had spoken with each other on several occasions about Jimmy's progress at school, so they were not total strangers. Mrs. Longbow trusted Mr. Carson and she shared with him the details of the incident as they were relayed to her by the principal. Aaron assured her that he would do what he could to find Jimmy and indicated he planned to talk to the principal as well.

When Aaron Carson and Pete Sanchez met the next day in the principal's office, the exchange of words was anything but pleasant. Aaron accused the principal of being a bully and a terrible administrator. The principal countered by describing the teacher as a "bleeding heart." It was obvious that the two had very different perceptions about how to handle problem children. Thus it was no surprise that the two ended the meeting the same way they started it, shouting unpleasant remarks to each other.

Aaron decided to take the matter to Mr. Sanchez's supervisor, Dr. Mackee. He quickly discovered that she was not about to take any action against the principal. She dismissed the matter as rather routine, suggesting that the dispute between the principal and teacher ought to be settled at the school level. Aaron's perception of his meeting with Dr. Mackee was that she was too insecure to take action against a principal who had become somewhat of a legend and hero in the city. The encounter with her only made Aaron angrier and more determined to see that something was done about this situation. He decided to state his case in the media. He wrote the following letter to the editor of the major newspaper in the city:

The public needs to know the story of Jimmy Longbow, a young Native American student at Rogers Middle School who is now a runaway. Jimmy is no angel, but neither is he some type of second-class citizen who should be whipped every time he does something improper. Corporal punishment is a practice that has been discontinued in most American public schools, but it is alive and well at Rogers Middle School. Jimmy Longbow is now somewhere on the streets because his teachers and his principal thought that brutality was more effective than counseling and constructive behavior modification. Parents of Rogers Middle School students and citizens of this community, wake up! Wake up before it is too late. Let your school board members know what you think about corporal punishment. Let's put a stop to this. Hopefully, Jimmy Longbow will come home, reenter school, and prove that he can be successful. Let's do something before there are more tragic stories.

Sincerely,
Aaron Carson,
Social studies teacher, Rogers Middle School

The letter spawned over 300 calls from angry citizens to the school board who supported Mr. Carson's position. The newspaper focused on the story and did a three-part report on what had occurred with Jimmy Longbow. The stories were great copy, and the "Jimmy Longbow incident" became a popular topic throughout the city. Conversely, a large number of parents, especially Rogers Middle School parents, came to the defense of Mr. Sanchez. They wrote their own letters to the newspaper detailing the great work that the principal had done for the school and pledging their support for his leadership. Some supporters of the principal attacked Aaron Carson, labeling him a troublemaker who was simply jealous of Mr. Sanchez's successes.

School board members became increasingly disturbed by the telephone calls and negative publicity. They demanded that the issue be discussed at the next school board meeting. When the newspaper reported that the board had decided to examine the issue publicly, the parent committees at Rogers Middle School started passing the following petition:

We the undersigned fully support the leadership of Mr. Pete Sanchez. He has made Rogers Middle School the most successful school in our district. We believe it is unfair to judge him on the basis of one incident. It is unfair for him to be blamed for what happened to Jimmy Longbow. We urge you, our representatives on the school board, to proclaim your support for a great principal. Further, we believe that in the best interests of Rogers, Mr. Carson should be transferred to another school.

In one week, nearly 70 percent of the Rogers parents signed the petition. Copies were mailed to each board member and to the superintendent, Dr. Fred Lopson, three days before the board meeting.

The meeting drew more than 400 supporters of Mr. Sanchez. Dr. Lopson began his review of the situation by reminding the board members that existing policy did not prohibit corporal punishment. He further pointed out the distinguished record of the school and the massive parental support enjoyed by its principal. The superintendent also expressed his personal sadness that Jimmy Longbow had run away from home.

George Manulita, a board member and a Native American, asked to be recognized after the superintendent concluded his remarks.

"I think we are all aware of Mr. Sanchez's successes," he said. "That is, in my opinion, not the real issue here. I want to know what we are going to do about allowing corporal punishment in our schools. It's unfortunate that this incident with the student at Rogers Middle School occurred. Hopefully, he will be found and he will return to school. But our concern as board members should now focus on the future. I want to know, Dr. Lopson, what you recommend with regard to policies governing corporal punishment. Do you think we should continue to permit such activity? Should we pass new policy to prohibit it?"

Mr. Manulita's questions were answered with shouts of "no" from most in the audience.

Darren Marshall, another board member, was next to speak.

"I don't disagree that we ought to think about policies when necessary. But let's keep in mind that we're talking about one of our best schools. Do we want to present yet another barrier to our administrators, especially when this administrator, Mr. Sanchez, is getting the job done? I'm more concerned about a teacher who writes derogatory letters to the newspaper about his principal. What are we going to do about this, Mr. Superintendent?"

This time the crowd applauded and started to chant, "Mr. Sanchez, Mr. Sanchez."

THE CHALLENGE

Analyze the behavior of all of the administrators in this case. Who really is responsible for this problem?

KEY ISSUES/QUESTIONS

1. Behavior in schools is affected by three critical factors: individuals, groups, and structure. Discuss how each of these plays a part in the behavior that is detailed in this case. How are each of these likely to influence the superintendent's decision?

2. What are your impressions of Mr. Sanchez? Would you like to be a teacher in this school?

3. In what ways might the principal's personal life affect his philosophy toward discipline?

4. What are your impressions of the teacher who wrote the letter to the newspaper? Is he a hero or troublemaker?

5. What are your impressions of the assistant superintendent, Dr. Mackee? Did she adequately address her responsibilities in this incident?

6. What does the literature say about the effectiveness of corporal punishment?

7. How does corporal punishment fit with the goals of middle grade education?

8. Do you believe that every school district should have a policy on the use of corporal punishment? Why or why not?

9. Based on what you read in this case, can you identify different role expectations of the principal? What are they?

10. In this case, the principal uses committees to involve parents in the educational process. Do you consider this to be a good idea for a middle school? Why or why not?

11. In your opinion, do most principals attempt to integrate research and theory into their practice?

12. Is the real issue corporal punishment? If the school board bans its use, do you think the culture of the school will change?

SUGGESTED READINGS

Andrews, R,. & Soder, R. (1987). Principal leadership and student achievement. *Educational Leadership, 44*(6), 9–11.

Ashbaugh, C., & Kasten, K. (1984). A typology of operant values in school administration. *Planning and Changing, 15*(4), 195–208.

Barbour, N. (1991). Ban the hickory stick. *Childhood Education, 68*(2), 69-70.

Boyan, N. (1988). Describing and explaining administrator behavior. In N. Boyan (Ed.), *Handbook of research on educational administration* (pp. 77-97). New York: Longman.

Campbell-Evans, G. (1990). Nature and influence of values in principal decision making. *Alberta Journal of Educational Research, 37*(2), 167-178.

Carey, M. (1986). School discipline: Better to be loved or feared? *Momentum, 17*(2), 20-21.

Curwin, R., & Mendler, A. (1988). *Discipline with dignity.* Arlington, VA: Association for Supervision and Curriculum Development.

Eberts, R., & Stone, J. (1988). Student achievement in public schools: Do principals make a difference? *Economics of Education Review, 7*(3), 291-299.

Erickson, H. (1988). The boy who couldn't be disciplined. *Principal, 67*(5), 36-37.

Glassman, N. (1986). Student achievement and the school principal. *Education Evaluation and Policy Analysis, 7*(2), 283-296.

Glickman, C. (1991). Pretending not to know what we know. *Educational Leadership, 48*(8), 4-10.

Grasmick, H. (1992). Support for corporal punishment in the schools: A comparison of the effects of socioeconomic status and religion. *Social Science Quarterly, 73*(1), 177-187.

Gusky, D. (1992). Spare the child. *Teacher Magazine, 3*(5), 16-19.

Hyman, R., & Rathbone, C. (1993a). *Corporal punishment in schools: Reading the law.* NOLPE Monograph Series, No. 48.

Hyman, R., & Rathbone, C. (1993b). *The principals's decision: A teaching monograph on corporal punishment.* NOLPE Monograph Series, No. 48a.

Kowalski, T., & Reitzug, U. (1993). *Contemporary school administration: An introduction.* New York: Longman (see chapters 11, 14).

Kritsonis, W., & Adams, S. (1985-86). School discipline: Could I be part of the problem? *National Forum of Educational Administration and Supervision, 2*(2), 68-72.

Lowe, R., & Gervais, R. (1984). Tackling a problem school. *Principal, 63*(5), 8-12.

Maurer, A. (1981). *Paddles away: A psychological study of physical punishment in schools.* Palo Alto, CA: R & E Research Associates.

McDaniel, T. (1986). School discipline in perspective. *Clearing House, 59*(8), 369-370.

McFadden, A. (1992). A study of race and gender bias in the punishment of children. *Education and Treatment of Children, 15*(2), 140-146.

Nolte, M. (1985). Before you take a paddling in court, read this corporal punishment advice. *American School Board Journal, 173*(7), 27, 35.

Paquet, R. (1982). *Judicial rulings, state statutes, and state administrative regulations dealing with the use of corporal punishment in public schools.* Palo Alto, CA: R & E Research Associates.

Pearce, A. (1992). Investigating allegations of inappropriate physical punishment of students by school employees. *School Law Bulletin, 23*(2), 15-21.

Pitcher, G., & Poland, S. (1992). *Crisis intervention in the schools.* New York: Guilford Press.

Rose, T. (1984). Current uses of corporal punishment in American public schools. *Journal of Educational Psychology, 76*(3), 427-441.

Slavin, R., & Madden, N. (1989). What works for students at risk: A research synthesis. *Educational Leadership, 46*(5), 4-13.

Zirkel, P., & Gluckman, I. (1988). A legal brief: Constitutionalizing corporal punishment. *NASSP Bulletin, 72*(506), 105-109.

case 13

The Stepping Stone

BACKGROUND INFORMATION

The topic of career patterns has received attention from researchers and other writers over the years. This issue is especially important in school administration, because frequent job changes have been common among practitioners. Executives in the private sector often relocate as a condition of receiving a promotion; however, they frequently remain with the same employer when they do so. Principals and other administrators are more likely to gain promotion by changing both location and employers.

In examining the career patterns of educational administrators, a number of practical and ethical questions evolve. For instance, is it proper to accept a superintendency knowing that they will remain in that job only until they can secure a better position? Does the rapid turnover of administrators have a deleterious effect on schools and school districts? If an administrator receives a multi-year contract, is fulfilling the commitment an obligation?

Although questions surrounding the mobility of administrators are not new, they have been illuminated by efforts to reform public education. Critics of upwardly mobile administrators argue that (1) personal ambitions often take precedence over the goals of the school district, and (2) when superintendents resign to accept a more lucrative position after only a year or two, they damage the school district's prospects for long-term change. Many administrators respond to these criticisms by pointing out that they often have little job-related security. They further argue that it is the political environment in general, and the school boards in particular, that often cause rapid changes in leadership.

In addition to ethical issues of career development, this case also spawns questions about organizational culture and administrator behavior. A young administrator in his first superintendency attempts to model the behavior of an admired large-city superintendent. By ignoring the cultures of the local community and the school district, the newly appointed superintendent creates conflict with employees and the school board. He resents being called by his first name, and he feels that his age and inexperience contribute to the problem.

As you read the case, think about the ways that career goals and past experiences serve to influence leadership behavior. Also consider how the cultures of the community and school district ought to enter into the decision making of a school administrator.

KEY AREAS FOR REFLECTION

1. Career patterns of school administrators
2. Ethical and moral dimensions of career development
3. Influences on leadership behavior
4. The importance of community and organizational contexts with regard to leadership behavior
5. Human relations within organizations
6. The use of legitimate power

THE CASE

The Community

Hallville is located in northern Iowa. It is a friendly town of about 2,500 residents, many of whom have never lived anywhere else. Besides the bank, the Sears outlet store, Dotty's restaurant, an IGA grocery store, two taverns, and Klink's Farm Implements, there is not much else downtown. Being only 17 miles from the county seat, a community of 65,000, Hallville's residents have become accustomed to traveling elsewhere to meet most of their special needs.

Most everyone in Hallville knows everyone else. The town picnics, one in early June and one in late August, are the social highlights of the year. Loretta Helmich is the mayor, a part-time job that she does when she's not working at the bank. The police department consists of one full-time and two part-time officers. There is very little crime in Hallville.

The largest employer here is the corn processing plant located on the edge of town. Although not a very big operation, it has been highly successful and provides jobs for about 175 local residents. The town is surrounded by farms, many of them rather large operations of 400 or more acres.

The Schools

Hallville Community School District encompasses the town of Hallville and two adjoining townships and has two attendance centers: Hallville Junior/Senior High School and Hallville Elementary School. The basic information for each school is as follows:

Hallville Junior/Senior High School

Grade levels: 7 through 12

Enrollment: 440

Principal: Oscar McCammick

Assistant principal: Judy Buschak

Number of teachers: 26

Number of counselors: 1

Number of secretaries: 2

Custodians: 3

Other personnel (e.g., cooks, aides): 9

Hallville Elementary School

Grade levels: kindergarten through 6

Enrollment: 407

Principal: Denise Fischer

Number of teachers: 18

Number of counselors: 1

Number of secretaries: 2

Custodians: 2

Other personnel (e.g., cooks, aides): 13

The junior/senior high school is a relatively new structure erected six years ago. The elementary school is a much older facility, built circa 1955. The elementary school is located in town; the junior/senior high school is located just outside of town on a state highway.

The Need for a New Superintendent

Last year Wilbur Stineman, the superintendent, was killed in an automobile accident on his way home from a meeting in Des Moines. He had spent his entire career in the Hallville school district. He was a teacher, coach, counselor, and eventually principal at the high school before being named superintendent. His death stunned the community. Eleven years in the superintendency did not erode his positive relationships with virtually everyone who knew him.

Most everyone took for granted that Oscar McCammick, the principal at the junior/senior high school, would become the next superintendent. But the veteran administrator surprised the five-member school board when he told them he was not interested in the job. He said he really wanted to continue as principal and noted that he would miss working with the students. No other employees in the school district expressed an interest in serving as superintendent. For the first time in more than 50 years, it appeared that Hallville would hire a super-intendent from outside the school district.

The school board allowed representatives of both the school district employees and the community to be present during interviews conducted with candidates for the superintendency. Eighteen persons filed applications, and four were selected for interviews. The unanimous choice of the school board was Rob Zelker. Although only 31 years old and possessing limited experience, he impressed virtually everyone who met him. His appointment was especially supported by the two principals in the school district who also had an opportunity to meet the final candidates.

The New Superintendent

Prior to coming to Hallville, Rob spent three years as a principal in an elementary school in one of the larger cities in Iowa. He recently completed his specialist's degree and obtained his certification as a superintendent. Interestingly, one of the considerations that influenced the board's decision to appoint him was the fact that Rob grew up in a community in western Iowa that was in many ways like Hallville. The board president pointed out that Rob was a "farm boy," and even if he was not from Hallville, he would understand the people and relate well to them.

Rob's wife, Alice, is a nurse and she was able to get a part-time position working for a physician after they relocated. Their daughter, Amy, is in first grade. When Rob applied for the job in Hallville, he discussed the situation with Alice. Neither of them wanted to live in a real small town, but they were both willing to do so for a brief period to enhance Rob's career. So they rented a house anticipating a relatively short stay. There was never any doubt in Rob's mind that the position in Hallville was just a stepping stone to a better job; he ultimately wanted to be a big-city superintendent. Another factor that influenced Rob's decision to move to Hallville was the town's proximity to a state university where he had been accepted into a doctoral program.

Rob's final consideration before accepting the superintendency was the recommendation of his friend and role model, Dr. Nolan Smythe. Dr. Smythe was superintendent in the district where Rob worked as a principal. During his tenure in that district, they developed a close relationship, which stemmed largely from their contact as members of the same church. Even though Rob did not report directly to Dr. Smythe (principals reported to assistant superintendents), it was common knowledge among the administrative staff in the district that he was the superintendent's "fair-haired boy."

Rob idolized Superintendent Smythe, meticulously observing his behavior, watching the way he handled meetings with the staff and the school board, studying his demeanor around the central office, and especially noticing his approach to conflict. Being in a city of about 100,000 residents, the superintendent had myriad opportunities for visibility and took advantage of most. Among other things, he was on the board of directors of a bank, secretary of the Chamber of Commerce, and president of the country club. Nolan Smythe dressed and acted like a corporate executive. On more than one occasion he told Rob that personal appearance was extremely important if one wanted to gain respect as a leader. "You have to look the part," he told his young friend.

The First Year

The central administrative offices for the Hallville Community School District are located in a wing of the junior/senior high school. The staff for this segment of the school district includes only three employees, a secretary, a bookkeeper, and the superintendent. The secretary, Bonnie Stutz, is the sister of one of the school board members. The bookkeeper, Norine Dawson, is the widow of a former teacher and coach at the high school. Both employees have lived in Hallville their entire lives, and each has worked for the school district for over 20 years.

One of Rob's first acts as superintendent was to order new furniture for his office. No one blamed him since the existing furniture was well over 15 years old. Even the school board president had encouraged him to improve the appearance of the superintendent's office.

During the first few days, Rob toured the schools and attempted to see both principals. Although he had met them when he interviewed for the position, he wanted to get to know them better before school opened in about six weeks.

Toward the end of his first week in Hallville, Rob shared several of his perceptions of the school district with his wife as they were eating dinner.

"You know, Alice, this is a sleepy little town and I expected things to be a bit informal. But you wouldn't believe just how informal they really are. A couple of days ago, I decided to walk across the building and visit with Oscar McCammick in his office. When I got there, his secretary wasn't around, so I peeked into his office. He was inside talking with several teachers. When he saw me, he yelled for me to come on in. He was leaning back in his chair with his feet on his desk. But the best part was that he had on a pair of shorts. He told me he was going to try to get away a little early so he could get in 18 holes of golf."

"Well," his wife answered, "it is July. I don't suppose he has to see many students or parents at this time. I bet when school starts, he'll look like any other principal."

Rob shrugged his shoulders as to indicate that his wife may be right. Then he told his wife about the visit to the elementary school.

"When I got to the elementary school, the secretary was sitting there listening to the radio and reading *People* magazine. When I asked to see Mrs. Fischer, she said the principal had an appointment to get her hair done and would be back in an hour or so. She didn't even bother to ask who I was. Can you believe this?"

During the next few months Rob realized that the casual manner he observed in school district operations during those first few days was not atypical. Even school board meetings were extremely informal, with everyone using first names and persons in the audience allowed to speak just about anytime they asked to be recognized. What particularly irked him was that all the employees, even custodians, called him by his first name. Rob became convinced that his youth had a great deal to do with the way he was being treated. He also concluded that the informal atmosphere was unprofessional and a terribly inefficient way to manage a school district. By late October, he decided that he had to change a few things.

Rob's first step to instituting change was to have separate meetings with his central office staff and principals. During these sessions, he tried to explain why he was concerned about the casual behavior of key school district employees. Although the employees looked a bit surprised when they heard his comments, none took issue with them. Toward the end of both meetings, he distributed a list of new rules and stressed that he expected them to be followed:

1. The principals and two employees of the central office were to set an example by addressing him as Mr. Zelker, especially in the presence of others.
2. The secretary was never to call him Rob when talking to a third party on the telephone.
3. Visitors should never be allowed to enter the offices of administrators without first making a request with a secretary.
4. Unless there were extenuating circumstances, communication among administrators and central office staff were best done through memoranda. This would provide a written record of communication exchanges.

All four of the employees asked why these new rules were necessary. They also explained that they intended no disrespect toward Rob by addressing him by his first name. Rob told them that he was not angry, and assured them that he was not directing the new rules toward any single individual. He explained that these directives would improve the image and efficiency of the school system.

After setting new directions for his staff, Rob turned his attention to the school board. He developed a lengthy memorandum recommending procedural changes for school board meetings. Included were the following recommendations: (1) formal voice votes should be taken on all motions, (2) men should wear coats and ties to board meetings, and (3) patrons should be allowed to speak at board meetings for no more than three minutes and only if they were addressing an item on the agenda. Within 24 hours after its distribution, the board president came to see Rob.

Dale Klink owns the farm implement store in Hallville, and he has been president of the school board for three consecutive years. Even though the district is small, Dale rarely became involved in the day-to-day operations of the schools. He supports the contention that administrators should be left alone to perform their duties unless there are serious problems. Likewise, he did not visit the superintendent's office unless there was an important issue that needed attention. The memorandum, he decided, constituted one of those issues.

The two men met on a dreary mid-November day in the superintendent's office. After getting a cup of coffee and saying hello to Bonnie Stutz and Norine Dawson, Dale Klink entered Rob's office and shut the door.

"Rob, what the hell possessed you to send this memo to the board? Don't you think that it would have been better to call me about your concerns before communicating with the entire board? You know, this is a little embarrassing for me."

The demeanor and tone of Mr. Klink put Rob on the defensive. He calculated that some board members might object to his recommendations, but he did not expect the board president to be one of them. He collected his thoughts before responding to the board president.

"Dale, I certainly didn't want to embarrass you. I'm just trying to improve things. I thought that was what you expected from me. If I was out of line sending the memorandum, I'm sorry. But even now, I don't think I was wrong in trying to communicate recommendations to the board."

"Rob, you've been here four months now. In that short time, you've managed to get the principals all concerned; the women here in the office aren't too happy about some of your ideas either. You made up some new rules and didn't bother to even inform the board," the board president said.

These comments made Rob even more defensive. "Sure, this is a good school district," he responded, "but it could become a lot better. There is a tremendous amount of inefficiency around here."

"What's efficiency got to do with calling you Mr.?" Dale asked.

"It's not the informality so much that bothers me. It's the attitudes associated with employee behavior. For example, some of the key staff go to the bank, buy groceries, or get their hair done on school time. And when the administrators and central office staff are doing these things, they are sending the message to other employees. I believe that good examples have to start with us—the superintendent and school board. That's one of the reasons why I suggested that we try make our board meetings more formal and businesslike."

The board president took a drink of his coffee and stood up. He looked out the window for a moment and then turned to face the young superintendent.

"Rob, I've got to get back to my store. But let me tell you before I leave that you've got a lot to learn. This is a nice community. We've never had trouble with superintendents, and we don't want to start now. But you have got to understand that you're not going to come in here and change everything in a few months. We're not going to change the board meetings—at least not now. You're the one who needs to consider changing. The best thing you can do is forget you ever wrote this memorandum to the board. I'm going to suggest to the rest of the board that we do the same. We all make mistakes. What causes real problems is our unwillingness to recognize them."

That said, Dale Klink walked out of the office. Rob's heart was beating and he had little beads of perspiration on the back of his neck. He knew he was in trouble, and he was not sure what he should do. He picked up the telephone and called his trusted advisor, Dr. Nolan Smythe, but his secretary indicated that he was on a trip to Russia with a group of educators for the next two weeks.

THE CHALLENGE

Analyze the behavior of Rob Zelker in this case. What do you believe he should do at this point?

KEY ISSUES/QUESTIONS

1. Consider Rob's reasons for taking the position in Hallville. Do you believe that these reasons influenced his behavior once he was in the job?

2. Assess the board's judgment that Rob would adjust well to Hallville because he grew up in a similar community. Can we make valid assessments of people's values and beliefs based on their previous experiences?

3. To what extent do you believe that the high school principal's behavior in this case is typical or atypical for small/rural school districts?

4. Do most school administrators attempt to emulate the behavior of someone they admire? What evidence do you have for your answer?

5. Rob expects employees to respond to his directives because he is the superintendent. Thus he relies on legitimate power. What is legitimate power, and what are its advantages and disadvantages?

6. Assess Rob's suggestion that communications be in writing. If you were a principal in this district, how would you interpret this rule?

7. Rob judges that informality breeds inefficiency. Do you agree? Why or why not?

8. Do you think the school board knows that Rob is only planning to stay in Hallville for three years? What leads you to your conclusion?

9. Discuss the ethical dimensions of a superintendent taking a position without any intention of staying very long.

10. Assume that Rob had no ambition to complete a doctoral degree or to be a superintendent in a large school district. Do you believe his behavior in Hallville would have been different?

11. If you were superintendent in this district, would you be concerned that the principals and the two women in the central office occasionally left work to take care of personal matters? If not, why? If so, what would you do about it?

12. Explain why Dr. Smythe is so successful in his job whereas Rob, trying to emulate his behavior, is having so much difficulty.

13. Based on information in the case, do you believe Rob was adequately prepared to accept the position in Hallville?

14. When Rob instituted new rules for his staff, should he have consulted with the board before doing so?

15. Do you believe that Rob's age and inexperience influenced the ways in which employees treated him?

SUGGESTED READINGS

Anderson, S. (1989). How to predict success in the superintendency. *The School Administrator, 46*(7), 22, 24, 26.

Black, J., & English, F. (1986). *What they don't tell you in schools of education about school administration* (pp. 293-307). Lancaster, PA: Technomic.

Burnham, J. (1989). Superintendents on the fast track. *The School Administrator, 46*(9), 18-19.

Campion, M., & Lord R. (1982). A control systems conceptualization of the goal-setting and changing process. *Organizational Behavior and Human Performance, 30,* 265-287.

Chance, E., & Capps, J. (1992). *Superintendent instability in small/rural schools: The school board perspective* (ERIC Document Reproduction Service No. ED 350 121).

Clark, D., & Astuto, T. (1988). Paradoxical choice options in organizations. In D. Griffiths, R. Stout, and P. Forsyth, (Eds.), *Leaders for America's schools* (pp. 112-130). Berkeley, CA: McCutchan.

Grady, M., & Bryant, M. (1991). School board presidents describe critical incidents with superintendents. *Journal of Research in Rural Schools, 7*(3), 51-58.

Guthrie, J., & Reed, R. (1986). *Educational administration and policy* (pp. 166-175). Englewood Cliffs, NJ: Prentice-Hall.

Hart, A. (1991). Leader succession and socialization: A synthesis. *Review of Educational Research, 61,* 451-474.

Immegart, G. (1988). Leadership and leader behavior. In N. Boyan (Ed.), *Handbook of research on educational administration* (pp. 259-277). New York: Longman.

Jacobson, S. (1988a). Effective superintendents of small, rural districts. *Journal of Rural and Small Schools, 2*(2), 17-21.

Jacobson, S. (1988b). The rural superintendency: Reconsidering the administrative farm system. *Research in Rural Education, 5*(2), 37-42.

Kowalski, T., & Reitzug, U. (1993). *Contemporary school administration: An introduction.* New York: Longman (see chapters 10, 15).

Oberg, T. (1986). The ecstasy and the agony: Administrative success on one level does not guarantee success on another. *Journal of Educational Public Relations, 9*(2), 28-31.

Sergiovanni, T., Burlingame, M., Coombs, F., & Thurston, P. (1987). *Educational governance and administration* (2nd ed., pp. 206-219, 384-416). Englewood Cliffs, NJ: Prentice-Hall.

Sharp, W., & Newman, I. (1990). *Boards of education: Trust, confidence, and communication: A study of first year superintendents.* (ERIC Document Reproduction Service No. ED 325 931).

Stephens, E. (1987). The rural small district superintendent: A position at risk. *Planning and Changing, 18*(3), 178–191.

Yukl, G. (1989). *Leadership in organizations* (2nd ed.). Englewood Cliffs, NJ: Prentice-Hall (see chapter 8).

case 14

The One-Skill Superintendent

BACKGROUND INFORMATION

One of the facets of the superintendency that makes it a difficult position is the diversity of skills required. In recent years, for example, school administrators have been criticized for failing to provide visionary leadership to restructure schools for an information-based society. Yet historically, local school boards have expected superintendents to be efficient managers of public resources and not necessarily change agents.

Perhaps the most widely used approach for classifying administrative skills is a three-skill taxonomy that includes technical skills, interpersonal skills, and conceptual skills (Yukl, 1989). Technical skills involve knowledge related to certain procedures and methods required in administering schools. Budget development and administration exemplify technical skills. Knowledge of human behavior, motivation, attitudes, communication, and other facets of organizational life is central to human relations skills. Human relations skills are necessary for one to represent the school district to the community in an effective manner. Conceptual skills entail analytical and problem-solving skills. Long-range, visionary planning typifies an administrative task that relies heavily on conceptual skills.

Each administrative assignment is somewhat unique with regard to expected competencies in technical, interpersonal, and conceptual skills. In situations where role expectations are largely managerial, a principal and superintendent may be able to succeed even though his or her interpersonal and conceptual skills are weak. By contrast, a school district wanting to institute radical changes may be intolerant of a superintendent who simply makes everyone happy.

In this case, a superintendent devotes much of his energy to community relations. It is a role consistent with the school board's expectations; however, his behavior causes conflict with his deputy superintendent. The deputy concludes that she is being forced to do much of the superintendent's work because (1) the superintendent is basically incompetent, and (2) he is a self-centered individual who uses staff to advance his own career. She also believes that the superintendent is especially manipulative and inconsiderate toward her because she is a woman.

As you read this case, try to put yourself in the position of the deputy superintendent as well as the superintendent. Try to gain an understanding of why they have such different perceptions about the superintendent's goals and their own relationship.

KEY AREAS FOR REFLECTION

1. Role of the superintendent
2. Differing perceptions of the superintendent's goals and behavior
3. Male and female administrator relationships
4. General perceptions about skills for the superintendency
5. Community and school district as determinants of required skills for the superintendency

THE CASE

The City

One of Peter Marini's earliest memories of Wellington involved a demolition project in the downtown area, a scene he observed on his first trip to this city when he interviewed for the job of school superintendent. As he drove his new Buick down Main Street searching for the school district's administrative office, he saw two large stores, each more than 100 years old, being flattened by a swinging steel ball.

Wellington is one of the larger cities in this New England state. It is an industrial community that fell on hard times during the 1970s and 1980s. Unlike many similar cities, Wellington has been able to turn things around. The upward trend in economics and politics started about the time that Dan Ferriter was elected mayor. An energetic attorney who served two terms in the state legislature, Mayor Ferriter set out to bring new business to the city. He developed an aggressive campaign to attract technology-based corporations to replace the manufacturing companies that either closed or relocated.

When Dan Ferriter became mayor, it was already known that the school district would have to hire a new superintendent. One of the mayor's partners in a local law firm, John O'Dell, was on the school board. Through O'Dell, Mayor Ferriter urged the school board to find an articulate, community-oriented superintendent who could be an asset in the plans to rebuild Wellington.

The Search for a New Superintendent

The school board, composed largely of professionals and business executives, agreed with the mayor's agenda of finding a superintendent who could enhance the city's image. With the assistance of a consulting firm, the board prepared impressive materials to recruit a new leader. Among the qualifications they listed were the following:

- The superintendent must possess outstanding skills in public relations. He or she is expected to represent the school district positively at the local, state, and national levels.
- The superintendent must be able to deal with all elements of the community and be willing to actively participate in community functions. Above all, the superintendent must exhibit a commitment to develop a close working relationship with local governmental agencies.
- The superintendent must relate well to staff and possess exceptional communication skills.
- The superintendent must know how to effectively delegate authority.

Of all of the stated qualifications, it was the public relations aspect that loomed as the greatest priority in the minds of the school board and Mayor Ferriter. When he was a state legislator, Dan Ferriter observed how school districts won recognition more on what people believed they did than on what they actually did. Thus, he urged the board to employ someone who would create a positive image of the school district—an image that would assist the city in convincing businesses that Wellington was a great place to work and live.

From the very first contact with a consultant, Peter was ambivalent about the job in Wellington. He knew about the city, but had never been there. The consultant insisted that this was a very unusual opportunity, and after several conversations, he persuaded Peter to file his application. Even when Peter received a telephone call notifying him that he had been selected for an interview, he continued to have mixed feelings. But at this point, he felt committed to at least meeting the school board and listening to what they had to say. He was pleasantly surprised to find that the seven board members were positive, well-educated, and sincere individuals—just as the consultant had told him. And despite his negative perceptions of the physical environment after his drive down Main Street, he agreed to a second interview.

The board concluded that Peter Marini was the person they needed. He was a handsome man about 50 years old who had a definite charm that caused people to react positively to him. As part of his second interview, Peter and his wife had dinner with Mayor Ferriter and his wife. The next morning, the mayor telephoned John O'Dell and said, "This is the guy we want. He's perfect. Do whatever it takes to get him, and if I can help, let me know." The board recognized that it would take a great deal to get Dr. Marini to leave his current position as superintendent of a suburban school district in eastern Pennsylvania. It took a salary of $125,000, lucrative fringe benefits, and a commitment to support him in his efforts to rebuild the reputation of the school district.

The School District and Central Office Staff

Wellington City Schools consists of 3 high schools, 7 middle schools, and 22 elementary schools. Overall, about 22,000 students are enrolled in the district. The central office has a professional staff of 24.

On accepting the job in Wellington, Dr. Marini reorganized duties and responsibilities in the central office. The most notable change was that he appointed Dr. Teresa Howard, one of the three associate superintendents, to the newly created position of deputy superintendent. She was a veteran administrator who was well respected by administrative staff and other employees. At age 53, she had spent over 20 years in the school system as a teacher and administrator. In structuring the position of deputy superintendent, Peter Marini was explicit that the person in this job would be responsible for managing day-to-day operations.

A second major element of restructuring was the creation of a division of public relations. Dr. Marini employed Tad Evans, a person who worked for him previously, to be the director. When the organizational changes were completed, Tad Evans and Dr. Howard were the only two administrators who reported directly to Dr. Marini.

The Superintendent's Behavior

The superintendent and mayor were effective associates in efforts to promote Wellington and the public schools. They also became personal friends. Both were adept at public relations, and both knew how to use information for image-building purposes. The two were frequently seen together in public, and their close relationship was common knowledge.

Central office staff learned quickly that Dr. Marini did not spend much time in his office. Rather, much of his work was devoted to community activities; he became an active member of the Chamber of Commerce board; he became an important part of the mayor's program to recruit new industry; and he accepted every invitation to speak before local, state, and national groups.

During the first two years of Dr. Marini's reign as superintendent, the district did very well. This was especially true in athletics; however, there also were a number of academic achievements. Even though the public schools in Wellington had always captured their fair share of honors, under Superintendent Marini, each accomplishment, with the help of Tad Evans, was turned into a major media event. Mr. Evans knew how to stage press conferences and how to keep accomplishments before the public's eye. And he always made sure there were plenty of photographers there to take Dr. Marini's picture shaking hands with students or staff.

The Problem

Dr. Marini and his deputy, Dr. Howard, met every Monday morning for about two hours to go over issues that she felt needed his attention. During these sessions, she tried to get him more interested in the day-to-day operations of the school district. But this was usually to little avail. Once when she asked him some critical questions about the budget, he responded by saying, "Teresa, you know a lot more about budgets than I do. And I have every confidence that you will make good decisions. You don't need me getting involved."

The superintendent displayed the same level of disinterest in other critical tasks such as strategic planning. He would read materials given to him, but he always deferred to his deputy's judgments.

About midway through his second year in Wellington, Dr. Marini detected a change in his deputy's behavior. She seemed to be increasingly irritated and began to complain about work overload. He considered Dr. Howard to be an excellent deputy, and he realized that he was quite dependent on her. He decided to ask her if there was a problem. She responded by telling him that she was uncertain if she could continue in her present role.

"Why? Are you ill? Is it something I have done?" he asked.

"It would take me several hours to say everything I have to say, and you don't seem to have the time," Dr. Howard responded.

"Look, I'll take time. There is no one who is more valuable to me than you. I'll take whatever time is needed."

The two agreed to have a long lunch the next day in the superintendent's office. Dr. Marini started the conversation by reiterating his positive feelings about his deputy. He reminded her that he recommended a 10 percent salary increase for her last year that was approved by the board. It was the highest salary increase given to any of his staff members.

Then he asked, "Teresa, you don't seem yourself these days. Is anything wrong?"

"Would it matter if there was something wrong?" she responded.

"Our working relationship," he said, "is extremely important if we are to keep this school district and city moving forward. Yes, I do care how you feel and I want to know precisely what is bothering you."

Dr. Howard sat there for a moment and then looked up at him and said, "I really don't know where to begin. But here goes. Staff members in the central office are concerned—no, let me rephrase that. I am concerned about the fact that you don't get involved in critical functions such as budgeting and planning. I have to give you detailed briefings so you can be prepared to present recommendations that I developed to the school board. People are speculating that maybe you don't know enough about budgets and planning—that's why you have me do everything you should be doing."

Dr. Marini asked, "Is this a concern for most of the central office staff?"

"Yes, I believe it is. They are not used to having a superintendent who doesn't get involved in running the district. They don't know what you do with your time, and as a result, they are forming their own conclusions."

"What else are they, or you, concerned about?" he asked.

"I don't want to speak for the staff, but I guess I might as well lay the cards on the table as far as I'm concerned," she said. "I feel I'm running this district and you're getting all the credit. Last week at the annual Chamber of Commerce meeting, Mayor Ferriter gave you a special plaque recognizing your leadership in the school district and the community. You never once acknowledged how much help you received from your staff. Then there's the matter of salary. You came here with a salary of $125,000, not to mention fringe benefits. Last year, they gave you an $8,000 raise. I'm making $40,000 less and managing the school district. Do you think that is fair?"

"Teresa, the board brought me to this community to do certain things. I believe I am doing them quite well. You knew when I named you deputy that you would be in charge of the day-to-day management of the district. I don't think anyone has tried to take advantage of you."

"I work darn hard, Peter, and you know it. I get here early and leave late every day. Who knows what you are doing? Some of the secretaries in the central office don't even know who you are. You rarely visit any of the schools except to collect awards and make speeches at events that have a public relations benefit."

At that point Dr. Howard paused, and Dr. Marini could see she was really upset. He remained quiet while she regained her composure.

"Look, Peter, let me be as blunt as I can. I don't think you would treat a male deputy this way. You know I applied for your job, and the board did not even extend the courtesy of giving me an interview. Yet, I seem very able to run this district. If you're not willing to pay me more money, and I don't just mean a couple of thousand dollars, and if you're not willing to see that my accomplishments receive ample recognition, I don't think I want to go on in this job. Now you think that over and let me know what you decide." Dr. Howard got up and left the office before he could respond.

The meeting left Dr. Marini wondering if he really knew his deputy. He tried to imagine being in her position. Would he react in the same way? He wondered if he should replace her; he wondered if this was just a ploy to get more money. On the other hand, he wondered if he was as self-centered as Dr. Howard suggested; he even wondered if he should leave Wellington.

THE CHALLENGE

Analyze the relationship between the superintendent and his deputy. Is he being fair with her? Is she being fair with him?

KEY ISSUES/QUESTIONS

1. What alternatives does Dr. Marini have in dealing with this problem? Which of the solutions do you believe he should pursue?

2. Based on your experiences, do you think administrators tend to believe that their work is not properly recognized or compensated?

3. Is Dr. Marini, in your opinion, doing a good job as superintendent? Why or why not?

4. Is there any evidence in this case that leads you to agree with the impression that Dr. Marini lacks technical and analytical skills?

5. Do you think that administrators should be expected to exhibit a balance among technical, interpersonal, and analytical skills? Why or why not?

6. To what extent do you blame Dr. Marini for the problem with his deputy superintendent? Does Dr. Howard deserve any of the blame?

7. In school districts of 20,000 to 30,000 students, is it common for the superintendent to spend time in the school buildings? What is the basis for your response?

8. Do you believe that Dr. Howard's being a woman has anything to do with the way she is treated by the superintendent? What is the basis for your response?

9. How do you think the school board would react if they knew that Dr. Howard had confronted Dr. Marini with a demand that she be paid substantially more money?

10. Is there any evidence provided in this case to suggest that Dr. Marini misled Dr. Howard about her duties and responsibilities as deputy superintendent?

11. Consider the fact that the school board did not give Dr. Howard an interview when she applied for the superintendency. Given all the circumstances presented in this case, was the board justified in not interviewing her? Defend your response.

12. Is it common for superintendents in larger school systems to concentrate on one or two responsibilities and to delegate other matters to staff? What are the advantages and disadvantages of such a leadership approach?

13. The "representing role" of the superintendency (i.e., representing the school districts to all publics) is considered critical in some school districts. What conditions lead school board members to give this responsibility such a high priority?

SUGGESTED READINGS

Black, J., & English, F. (1986). *What they don't tell you in schools of education about school administration.* Lancaster, PA: Technomic (see chapter 12).

Boyd, W. (Ed.) (1979). *Education and Urban Society, 11:* 275–431 (special theme issue: Declining school enrollments: Politics and management).

Danzberger, J., & Usdan, M. (1984). Building partnerships: The Atlanta experience. *Phi Delta Kappan, 65*(6), 393–396.

Estler, S. (1987). *Gender differences in the perceptions of administrative role demands.* (ERIC Document Reproduction Service No. ED 285 277).

Foster, W. (1986). *Paradigms and promises.* Buffalo, NY: Prometheus Books (see chapter 8).

Goldhammer, K. (1983). Evolution in the profession. *Educational Administration Quarterly, 19*(3), 249–272.

Hess, F. (1983). Evolution in practice. *Educational Administration Quarterly, 19*(3), 223–248.

Hirsh, S., & Sparks, D. (1991). A look at the new central office administrators. *School Administrator, 48*(7), 16–17, 19.

Hoy, W., & Miskel, C. (1987). *Educational administration: Theory, research, practice* (3rd ed., pp. 302–309). New York: Random House.

Kowalski, T., & Reitzug, U. (1993). *Contemporary school administration: An introduction.* New York: Longman (see chapters 10, 14).

Milstein, M. (1992). The overstated case of administrative stress. *School Administrator,* 49(9), 12-13.

Murphy, J. (1991). Superintendents as saviors: From the Terminator to Pogo. *Phi Delta Kappan, 72*(7), 507-513.

Pajak, E. (1989). *The central office supervisor of curriculum and instruction.* Boston: Allyn & Bacon (see chapter 4).

Rist, M. (1991). Opening your own doors. *Executive Educator, 13*(1), 14.

Sergiovanni, T., Burlingame, M., Coombs, F., & Thurston, P. (1987). *Educational governance and administration* (2nd ed.). Englewood Cliffs, NJ: Prentice-Hall (see chapter 7).

Shakeshaft, C. (1989). *Women in educational administration* (updated edition). Newbury Park, CA: Sage Publications (see chapter 6).

Worner, R. (1989). Thirteen ways to help your inherited staff keep you afloat. *Executive Educator, 11*(5), 19-21.

Yukl, G. (1989). *Leadership in organizations* (2nd ed., pp. 153-157). Englewood Cliffs, NJ: Prentice-Hall.

Who Will Censure This Board Member?

BACKGROUND INFORMATION

Owens (1991) points out that administration is typically studied in the department, school, or college that houses the academic discipline to which it is to be applied. In most instances, an individual is expected to possess knowledge and skills in that discipline; however, the degree to which these expectations exist varies from one discipline to another. For instance, school administrators are usually required to exhibit competency in teaching (e.g., holding a teacher's license) whereas hospital administrators are rarely medical practitioners.

In addition to discipline-specific expectations, studies conducted in different types of organizations have identified three general areas of knowledge and skill that are critical to all administrators. The first and most readily recognized entails management responsibilities. For example, a school superintendent is expected to know how to build and manage a budget. The second category includes analytical tasks such as problem solving, policy development, and long-range planning. The third includes the spectrum of human relations tasks such as communication, interpersonal relationships, and conflict resolution. Despite growing evidence that practitioners encounter serious problems in the human relations aspects of their work, this category of knowledge and skills often receives the least amount of attention in both preservice and in-service education.

School superintendents are expected to maintain positive relationships with many publics and groups, but perhaps none is more critical than the rapport they have with members of the school board. Many individuals who are elected and appointed to school boards are not professional educators, and even today, a good number are not even college graduates. Their judgments about the superintendent are often influenced largely by their impression stemming from personal contact. Is the superintendent honest? Caring? Considerate? Fair?

This case reveals a situation in which a school board member reacts to a personal situation by trying to create problems for the school district. His behavior is deemed unethical by the board president; however, he wants the superintendent to be the one who reprimands him. In this respect, the case also focuses on ethical, legal, social, and political dimensions of school board membership.

In determining how to respond in this case, the superintendent needs to assess human relations issues. How can the conflict be resolved with a minimum of damage to (1) the school district, (2) the school board, and (3) the personal relationship between the superintendent and this particular board member?

KEY AREAS FOR REFLECTION

1. Relationships between school boards and superintendents
2. Ethical, legal, social, and political dimensions of board membership
3. Conflict resolution
4. Scope of superintendent responsibilities
5. Knowledge and skills in interpersonal relationships

THE CASE

The School District and School Board

The Richmond County School District covers 420 square miles of predominantly rural land. There are 7,800 pupils enrolled in two high schools, five middle schools, and ten elementary schools. The area has been experiencing modest growth in the past decade largely because of the county's proximity to the state capital, which is only 35 miles away. Land costs and taxes in Richmond County have made it an attractive site for small manufacturing companies. Although there have been nearly 500 new homes built here in the last ten years, most have been in a rural subdivision. The county seat, Collins, with a stable population of about 20,000, is the only city or town of any size in the county.

The school board has seven members who are elected from designated geographic areas to assure balanced representation among the 12 townships. At one time, virtually all members of the school board resided on farms, but in the last 20 years, that condition has changed. The current board members are as follows:

John Mosure (president), a farmer
Iris Dembica, a housewife
Elizabeth Highland, a real estate broker
Elmer Hodson, a farmer
Norman Salliter, an accountant and state employee

Martin Schultz, an attorney

Alicia Waddell, a pharmacist

Mr. Hodson is serving his third three-year term in office; Mr. Mosure and Ms. Highland are serving their second three-year terms; and the remaining board members are serving their first terms.

Politically, the board really does not have factions; however, Mr. Hodson has often disagreed with the others on policy issues. Socially, the board members seem to have positive relationships with each other, but again Mr. Hodson is often the exception, preferring to keep to himself.

The Superintendent

Matthew Karman became superintendent in Richmond County three years ago. His prior job was as superintendent of a smaller district in the same state. He is a friendly, somewhat reserved person. Unlike his predecessor in Richmond County who had been dismissed largely because of poor relations with the school board, Mr. Karman worked well with school boards and employees.

Mr. Karman's efforts to create a positive relationship with individual school board members were planned. Among his initiatives for achieving this goal were the following:

1. He had lunch with the school board president twice each month.
2. He had at least two social events involving the school board at his house each year.
3. He tried to have lunch with each of the board members at least once each year.
4. He always made himself accessible to board members, and he instructed his staff to always put board member phone calls directly through to him.
5. He personally delivered materials for school board meetings to their homes or places of business.

Just a few months ago when his contract was renewed for another three years, all seven board members supported the action. Several board members commented in the public meeting that they were extremely pleased that Mr. Karman had kept them informed and that he had exhibited a sincere interest in their opinions on school matters. He felt he had succeeded in establishing a trusting and cooperative relationship with his board.

The Problem

Superintendent Karman was driving down a lonely country road as the winds swirled across barren cornfields partially covered by snow. He was completing his monthly task of personally delivering school board packets three days before a meeting. The packets included recommendations and background information for items on the agenda. Although it was only mid-November, the chilling temperatures made it feel more like January. The fields were dotted with corn stalks cut about two inches above the ground that looked like wooden spikes someone had arranged to discourage trespassers.

After about 20 minutes of driving, Mr. Karman pulled into the driveway beside a large three-story farmhouse. He was greeted by a German shepherd barking alongside his car. The dog's barking summoned John Mosure from his barn where he was working on one of his tractors. He emerged with oil and grease all over his bib-overalls and hands.

"Greetings, John. I brought your board packet for our next meeting," Mr. Karman said as the farmer walked toward him wiping his hands on a soiled rag.

"Come on in the house and we'll have a cup of coffee," Mr. Mosure said as he waved his hand indicating that the superintendent follow him.

Although John Mosure has been on the board for nearly five years, this was his first experience as president. The two men had become good friends in the last three years, and they worked well together. Their wives also had become friends, and about every two months, the four of them went out to dinner together.

"John, I hope you've got some time today. I want to discuss a sticky issue with you, and it may take a little while."

The board member responded, "Well, we'll just make time. I'm not sure I'm going to be able to fix that tractor anyway. There is something wrong with the transmission, and I may have to take it into the dealer."

The two sat back enjoying the warmth of the kitchen and their coffee as Mr. Karman began telling him about the special problem.

"Two days ago, one of our high school principals, Bob Dailey at North Richmond High, received a telephone call from a friend who is the assistant commissioner of the state high school athletic association. This friend asked Bob if he knew a person named Elmer Hodson."

There was a moment of silence as John looked at the superintendent. Then he said, "Oh, no!"

Although Mr. Karman got along with Mr. Hodson, he knew that other board members generally left him alone. And despite the fact that John Mosure and Elmer Hodson are both farmers, they rarely take the same position on important matters. John, who has three children still enrolled in the schools, has been supportive of program expansion and has voted for two building-related referenda since being on the board. By contrast, Elmer opposes almost any effort to raise taxes. He has become the darling of the county taxpayers' association.

The superintendent continued with his story. "So, Bob tells his friend that he knows Elmer and he tells him that Elmer's on our school board. This guy with the athletic association then tells Bob that Elmer's sitting in his outer office waiting to file a complaint against Bob and the football coach at North Richmond High."

"A complaint about what?" asked the board president.

"Well, Bob's friend didn't know at the time because he had not talked to Elmer yet. He just knew he was there to lodge a complaint against Bob and Coach

Yates [the head football coach at North Richmond High School]. So he told Bob he was going to talk to Elmer and then call back before he did anything. About an hour later, Bob got another call. His friend said Elmer was all upset about the fact that the quarterback at North Richmond no longer lived with his parents. It seems that this student, Jeb Boswell, is now living with Coach Yates's family. So Elmer wants the athletic association to take action against North Richmond High School because they are playing this student even though Elmer claims he is no longer a legal resident of our school system. At the very least, he wants the athletic association to ban the student from playing in any further games."

"Is there any merit to his charges?" John Mosure asked.

"First," the superintendent answered, "there is no question that the student is living at the coach's house. It seems that the boy's parents moved to Colorado this past June. The boy and Coach Yates are pretty close, so Jeb asked his parents if it was okay to stay with Coach Yates to finish his senior year. He wants to graduate from North Richmond, and besides, Coach Yates is trying to get him a college scholarship to play football. Coach Yates and his wife agreed to work something out with the boy's parents to cover his room and board. So, since about late June, Jeb has indeed been living in the Yates home."

"Can a student do that and still be eligible for athletics?"

"Apparently so," the superintendent answered. "Before the final decision was made to have the student stay here, Coach Yates asked the athletic director at North Richmond to write a letter to the athletic association asking if this would be a violation. He was told that students whose parents moved out of a district could remain to finish their senior year without jeopardizing their eligibility so long as the parents and the school officials agreed to the arrangement. Bob Dailey, the athletic director, and the parents told Coach Yates that they had no objections to the boy staying here and continuing to play football."

"So, Elmer doesn't have any complaint. What's the problem?"

"John, we have to put this in perspective. Here we are one week before the state tournament in football. North Richmond has a 9 and 1 record and is one of the favorites to win the championship in their division. Jeb Boswell, the student in question, is the star of the team—he may even end up being all-state. You know who the backup quarterback on the North Richmond team is?"

The board president said he had no idea. "You have to remember, Matt, that I don't live in the North Richmond area. I'm a South Richmond booster [the other high school in the district]."

"The second string quarterback is a senior named Ron Hodson."

The two looked at each other and John smiled. The superintendent continued, "You got it, John. The second string quarterback is none other than the grandson of Elmer Hodson. Get the picture? Elmer's got an axe to grind because he feels this other kid has deprived his grandson from playing quarterback. At the very least, Elmer selfishly wants to see his grandson play in the state tournament. Mr. Dailey tells me, however, that the grandson doesn't know anything about what Elmer is doing. He's supposedly a pretty good kid, and probably would be embarrassed if he knew."

"You know, I just remembered something," commented John. "You recall last summer when we were approving contracts for employing driver education teachers. Elmer opposed Coach Yates being hired to teach driver education. He said he had heard that he was not a good instructor. Do you think that was linked to his feelings about his grandson as well?"

"Who knows. With Elmer, it's hard to tell. He votes against a lot of things. But what's on my mind is what we do about Elmer. I think his going to the athletic association without informing the board or the administration was unethical and divisive. As a board member, he should have voiced his concerns to either you or me before running to the state athletic association. Had he done so, he would have found out that there is no merit to his complaint. Further, he would not have given the athletic association officials a negative impression of our school district."

"What did the fellow from the athletic association do about Elmer?"

"Nothing really. He explained that there was no violation and even told him that North Richmond's athletic director had asked for a clarification about Jeb playing football for North Richmond. Elmer responded by suggesting that the official might just be covering up the matter."

"So, why don't we just forget about this. Elmer is Elmer. He'll always be a pain. Why voters keep electing him is beyond me. Sometimes I think they enjoy all the trouble he stirs up."

The superintendent was not willing to let this matter slide. "John, we have to issue some type of reprimand or do something. What he did was unethical. I think you and the entire board should meet with him privately and issue a formal reprimand. Sometimes I think he believes he can get away with this stuff because people are amused by his behavior. Maybe it's time to say enough."

The board president got up to refill the coffee cups. He then returned to his chair. "I don't know. I'm not sure a reprimand will do any good. Elmer's pretty stubborn. We might just give him a lot of publicity, and you know how he loves to get his name in the paper. How about if you talk to him, Matt? You're experienced in dealing with people. I'm not. Maybe the best way to handle this is to have you give him the reprimand. We should get the support of the other board members, though, and then you can tell him you are speaking for all of us. What do you say? Will you do it?"

THE CHALLENGE

Analyze the superintendent's actions in this case. What would you advise him to do at this point?

KEY ISSUES/QUESTIONS

1. If you were the superintendent, would you be concerned that this incident would affect your personal relationship with Elmer or any of the other board members? How about your relationship with the principal and other staff at North Richmond High?

2. Is it common that individual school board members are reprimanded for their behavior?

3. Instead of reprimanding the board member, what other actions might be taken?

4. Do you believe that the superintendent is correct in his judgment that Elmer was acting unethically by going to the state athletic association with his complaint?

5. Who should set standards for school board member behavior?

6. Do you believe that the superintendent was correct in taking this problem directly to the board president? Would it have been better to talk to Elmer first to get his side of the story?

7. Is it ethical or legal for school board members to vote on matters that affect members of their immediate families?

8. If you were considering to accept a superintendency, what social and political behaviors might reveal the way the school board operates?

9. If you were superintendent, would you tell the media about Elmer's behavior? Why or why not?

10. Determine if your state has provisions for removing school board members from office. If so, what are these provisions?

11. What experiences and elements of academic study typically prepare an individual for the interpersonal requirements of educational administration?

12. What is your assessment of the school board president in this case? Is it typical for a board president not to want to shoulder the responsibility of regulating peer behavior?

13. Assess the suggestion made by the school board president that the situation should just be ignored. What are the advantages and disadvantages of doing so?

SUGGESTED READINGS

Alvey, D., & Underwood, K. (1985). When boards and superintendents clash, it's over the balance of power. *American School Board Journal, 172*(10), 21-25.

Banach, W. (1984). Communications and internal relations are problems for board members. *Journal of Educational Public Relations, 7*(3), 8-9.

Bolman, L., & Deal, T. (1992). Images of leadership. *American School Board Journal, 179*(4), 36-39.

Bryant, M., & Grady, M. (1990). Where boards cross the line. *American School Board Journal, 177*(10), 20-21.

Castallo, R. (1992). Clear signals. *American School Board Journal, 179*(2), 32-34.

Goldman, J. (1990). Who's calling the plays? *School Administrator, 47*(11), 8-16.

Grady, M., & Bryant, M. (1991). School board presidents describe critical incidents with superintendents. *Journal of Research in Rural Education, 7*(3), 51-58.

Hamilton, D. (1987). Healing power: How your board can overcome the heartbreak of disharmony. *American School Board Journal, 174*(9), 36-37.

Hayden, J. (1987). Superintendent-board conflict: Working it out. *Education Digest, 52*(8), 11-13.

Herman, J. (1991). Coping with conflict. *American School Board Journal, 178*(8), 39-41.

Institute for Educational Leadership (1986). *School boards: Strengthening grass roots leadership.* Washington, DC: The Institute for Educational Leadership (see chapters 8, 9).

Kowalski, T., & Reitzug, U. (1993). *Contemporary school administration: An introduc-*

tion (pp. 125-128, 368-373). New York: Longman.

McDaniel, T. (1986). Learn these rarely written rules of effective board service. *American School Board Journal, 173*(5), 31-32.

Menzies, J. (1986). Power base preferences for resolving conflict: An educational management team consideration. *Journal of Rural and Small Schools, 1*(1), 6-9.

Myer, R. (1983). How to handle a board member who wants to play his own game. *American School Board Journal, 170*(11), 27-29.

Natale, J. (1990). School board ethics: On thin ice? *American School Board Journal, 177*(10), 16-19.

Owens, R. (1991). *Organizational behavior in education* (4th ed.). Boston: Allyn & Bacon.

Tallerico, M. (1991). School board member development: Implications for policy and practice. *Planning and Changing, 22*(2), 94-107.

Yukl, G. (1989). *Leadership in organizations* (2nd ed.; pp. 177-180, 191-194). Englewood Cliffs, NJ: Prentice-Hall.

case 16

A New Superintendent—A New Leadership Style

BACKGROUND INFORMATION

Many writers have observed that collective bargaining emerged in public education as a means of giving teachers and other employees a voice in determining conditions of employment. Early encounters with the process, especially in the 1960s and 1970s, showed that many school districts were truly bureaucrat-like organizations. The reaction to union demands to establish master contracts often elicited harsh responses from superintendents and school board members. They ranged from outright refusals to bargain (in states where the process was not required) to condemnations of the teachers for behaving unprofessionally to complete accommodation (i.e., giving the teachers everything they requested simply to keep them satisfied). Collective bargaining is a common form of conflict, and in closed organizations, all conflict is viewed as counterproductive. The more bureaucratic the organization, the more likely that administrative reactions to employee demands will be designed to eradicate the conflict as quickly and effortlessly as possible.

Gradually, the attitudes and behaviors of administrators toward negotiating with employee groups have changed. In large measure three conditions are responsible. First, research and theory have provided added insights into the differences between professionally dominated, public-service organizations (such as schools) and private, manufacturing, profit-seeking organizations (such as automobile companies). For the most part, notions that schools could behave as private organizations and could anticipate similar outcomes have been attenuated. Second, experience with the process of collective bargaining has shown that neither ignoring nor accommodating employee disenchantment is a meaningful solution to the underlying cause of conflict. Third, theorists and practitioners alike have increasingly recognized that conflict is inevitable in all organizations. Thus, effective leadership entails the management of conflict toward a positive outcome, not merely the eradication of conflict.

An administrator's view of organizational life contributes to the behavior of that individual. In this case, a new superintendent views unionization, collective bargaining, and relationships with teachers differently than most of her senior staff. In the first weeks of her superintendency, she inherits a serious problem with negotiations. Unlike her predecessor, she is determined to take an active role in trying to resolve the matter. Her behavior is contrary to the norms of the school district, and as might be expected, administrative staff begin to question her motives and competence.

Beyond issues of organizational culture, leadership behavior, and collective bargaining, this case also raises issues of administrator succession. Newly appointed principals and superintendents face the challenge of integrating personal behavior with established norms. A practitioner's ability to understand the dynamics of this process and to make necessary adjustments is often critical to success.

KEY AREAS FOR REFLECTION

1. Organizational culture and leadership behavior
2. Careers for women in educational administration
3. Administrator succession
4. Collective bargaining
5. Conflict in public, professionally dominated organizations
6. Career patterns of school administrators

THE CASE

Janice's Entry into Administration

Two years ago Janice Melton achieved her primary professional goal. At age 42, she was named superintendent of the third largest school district in her state. It was quite an accomplishment, considering that she was the first female ever to be named superintendent in a district with more than 5,000 students in this western state.

Janice grew up in an "education" family. Her father was a teacher and middle school principal for 41 years. Her mother taught kindergarten in the public schools for 11 years and then became a professor of early childhood education at a local college. Janice had a close relationship with her parents, and as a child she listened to many dinner conversations that related to teaching. Ever since she could remember, she never doubted that she too would someday be a teacher.

After graduating from college, Janice taught English at a high school for five years. During that time, she completed her master's degree in English by attending night classes and summer school. One of the elective courses she took was called Introduction to School Administration. The instructor in that class encouraged her to consider a career in administration. Janice talked to her father about the suggestion, and he enthusiastically concurred. Since she had been a good student in college and graduate school, she was able to get a fellowship to pursue doctoral studies on a full-time basis. So after completing her master's degree and her fifth year of teaching, she became a full-time student.

Doctoral study was an exciting venture. Beyond the intellectual stimulation, she enjoyed becoming part of a cohort that included students from seven different states and two foreign countries. After 24 months, she completed her Ed.D. degree, and just four weeks after graduation, she married Bob, an adjunct professor of English, whom she met at a faculty party while in graduate school. He has since become a successful freelance writer whose work has appeared in many leading magazines, including *Reader's Digest*.

During the final months of graduate school, Janice applied for a number of positions, both in the public schools and in universities. Although she preferred to become a school administrator, she was uncertain how employers would respond to her lack of administrative experience. Therefore, she also pursued vacancies for teaching in higher education. To her surprise, she received invitations to interview for nine positions, two of which were in universities.

After having had interviews for four different jobs, Janice accepted a position as a high school principal in a school only seven miles from the university. Bob had encouraged her to accept a position as an assistant professor at a university in another state, but Janice really wanted to work in the public schools. The position she accepted represented somewhat of a compromise. She could be a principal, and they could continue to live in a university environment—a condition that was beneficial to Bob's career.

The principalship was demanding, but Janice never regretted her decision. She learned a great deal in a very short period. Her superintendent was extremely pleased with what she had done at the high school, and after only three years, he offered her a position as assistant superintendent for secondary education. The central office job included new challenges and learning opportunities, and those experiences convinced her that she ultimately wanted to become a superintendent.

The First Superintendency

Midway through the second year in her new position, Janice started to selectively apply for superintendencies. She was invited to interview for two jobs. One was in an affluent suburban community, and the other was in a relatively small town called Medburg. Medburg just happened to be Janice's hometown, and her parents still lived there. Her preference was the suburban community, but just one week after her interview, she was informed that she was no longer being considered for that position. Two weeks later, she was offered the job in Medburg.

Janice's parents were thrilled at the prospect of her moving back to Medburg. Although she was living only 150 miles from her parents, she only saw them two or three times a year. In deliberating whether to accept the superintendency in Medburg, she gave serious thought to two questions: (1) Was it really wise to become superintendent in your hometown? (2) How would Bob react if she accepted the job?

Despite not wanting to relocate, and despite apprehensions about his wife becoming a school superintendent, Bob knew how much this job meant to Janice. As they were having dinner the night before she had to make a decision, he told her, "Listen, Medburg College [a small liberal arts school] has a fine library. I can get by quite nicely there. My career won't suffer, so don't worry about that. We'll make new friends. And you know I like your parents, so that isn't an issue. As far as I'm concerned, you can decide either way and it's okay with me." The next morning, she telephoned the school board president and accepted the job.

Janice's appointment was greeted with enthusiasm by the professional staff in the school district. Most knew her parents, and they thought she would be a fine leader. And they were correct. Under her stewardship, the schools prospered. She was especially successful at establishing coalitions to get things done. She involved parents, students, and teachers in many key decisions. She established a number of partnerships with local businesses and Medburg College.

The Big Offer

One evening as Janice was relaxing and reading the newspaper, Bob called her from the kitchen,

"It's for you. Somebody named Anderson from Washington City."

Janice picked up the phone in the den and said hello. She discovered that Anderson was Neal Anderson, president of the school board in Washington City, one of the largest cities in the state.

After informing Janice of his identity, the caller said, "Dr. Melton, I got your name from Professor Berkowicz at the university. He told me you were a former student of his, and he went on to rave about your accomplishments as a school administrator. I called him to get names of possible superintendent candidates because our board voted to dismiss our superintendent last night. We want to replace him as soon as possible."

Janice listened intently and only responded by saying, "Yes."

"As you may know, Dr. Melton," he continued, "we are in the midst of a collective bargaining problem. In part, this situation led to the decision to reassign our superintendent to some other position in the district. We want to hire a replacement as soon as possible. We can't afford a year-long search or anything like that. That's why I called Henry Berkowicz, an old friend, and asked for several names of outstanding candidates. The board has already agreed to invite the three persons he recommended to us. Obviously, you're one of the three."

"Well, Mr. Anderson," Janice responded, "I'm flattered. I really am. But I've only been in my current position for two years. My husband and I are just getting situated here, and to tell you the truth, we plan to stay here for a while."

The school board president answered, "I know you have been in Medburg for a short time. But Dr. Melton, this is a rare opportunity. I don't know what your salary is in Medburg, but I can assure you it will be much higher here. This is a good school district. I have a great deal of faith in Henry's recommendations. So please, before you say no to talking to us, give it some thought. Talk to your husband. If you come and interview and things don't work out, we'll understand."

Janice discussed the telephone call with Bob. As usual, he indicated that it was her career and she should make the final decision. She also talked to her present school board president and told her about the invitation. In the final analysis, Janice thought she had nothing to lose by talking to the board in Washington City. At the very least, it would be a good experience.

The interview with the school board in Washington City went very well. Janice's intuition told her that they were impressed with her, and she left feeling that the job may actually be offered to her.

One week after the interview, Janice received a call asking her if she would agree to return for a second interview. She inquired if either of the other two candidates was being invited for a second interview, and she was told that the issue had not yet been decided. She learned, however, that presently she was the leading candidate.

The second interview went well. She had dinner with the board at one of the city's fine restaurants, and the following morning at a breakfast meeting, the board president offered the superintendency to her. When compared to her job in Medburg, the salary and fringe benefits constituted about a 40 percent increase. Uncharacteristically, she responded immediately, "Yes, I'll take the job."

The Problem

The Washington City School District has a total enrollment of 45,500 students. Dr. Melton found herself with more central office staff than she had teachers in Medburg. Collective bargaining was a perennial problem in this district, and this year was no exception. Three issues had become critical to settling a contract with the teachers' union: (1) an inflexible demand for a 6 percent salary increase, (2) a provision that would permit building representatives to have two hours of released time each week to conduct union-related business, and (3) a provision to allow a payroll deduction plan for union dues.

Dr. Melton quickly learned that about 75 percent of the administrators in the district differed from her in one basic way—they were promoted to their current positions from within the organization. In fact, many of them had never worked in another school district. This information was significant with regard to the dismissal of her predecessor, Dr. Arlen Bixler. For he too had worked his way up through the school system, and his dismissal was opposed by most of the administrative staff. Dr. Bixler spent 29 years in the Washington City system as a teacher, assistant principal, principal, assistant superintendent, and superintendent.

Janice speculated that there would be some resentment toward her as an "outsider," let alone a "female outsider." She was comforted, however, by the knowledge that the entire school board was supportive of her. On her first day as superintendent in the district, Neal Anderson, the board president, sent Janice flowers and a note of congratulations. It read:

Janice,

Our board is totally committed to supporting you as you provide needed leadership for our schools. We are especially optimistic that you have the leadership skills to get us beyond the constant bickering and name-calling that has evolved from collective bargaining. Never hesitate to call on us for help and encouragement. If you need to make changes, even at the highest levels of administration, don't feel that we will stand in your way. We recognize that you have to have freedom to do things your way. We are behind you 100 percent.

Neal

Dr. Melton decided that she first had to convince the staff that she could provide leadership. She adopted a strategy of trying to change attitudes rather than dismissing key officials—an act that she thought would merely complicate matters. In an effort to create a positive relationship with her administrative staff, she issued a prepared statement outlining her positions on key issues. Included were the following points:

1. Her administration is focused on the future. She was not interested in previous relationships, allegiances, and the like.
2. She expects the administrative staff to function as a team. In order to accomplish this goal, mutual respect is essential.
3. The first goal of her administration is to settle a contract with the teachers' union.

The statement was distributed at a meeting she held with the entire administrative staff in the school district on the first afternoon she was in office.

On the second day of her tenure in Washington City, Dr. Melton called the teachers' union president, Malcolm DuMont, and asked him to meet with her as soon as possible. When he received the call, Mr. DuMont was both stunned and suspicious. Never before had he received a call from the superintendent asking for a private meeting. Dr. Bixler went out of his way to avoid direct contact with the teachers' union leadership. After receiving assurances that the meeting would be purely informational, Mr. DuMont agreed to meet with the new superintendent.

In Washington City School District there are four assistant superintendents and a deputy superintendent. The person directing the collective bargaining process is David Zellers, assistant superintendent for personnel. He received a telephone call from Dr. Melton informing him of her intention to meet with Mr. DuMont. Zellers, one of the staunchest supporters of the former superintendent, reacted negatively to the news.

"Dr. Melton, I think you're making a big mistake," he warned. "These people play hardball. The first thing they will do is to try to drive a wedge between you and the board's negotiating team, especially since you are new and don't know all the circumstances. The rule—or at least the practice—around here has been that if they want to meet with someone from administration, they meet with me."

Dr. Melton responded calmly. "Well, there may have been good reasons for that practice, but I'm not sure it's the best way to establish mutual trust. I want to assure the union leadership that I care about teachers. I want them to know that I'm willing to work with them to build bridges. We simply cannot continue to exhaust our energy fighting each other."

"Am I going to be invited to this meeting?" Zellers asked.

"No," the superintendent responded, "I think it's best that this first meeting be a time for me to become acquainted with Mr. DuMont. I don't want to give any indication that this is a quasi-bargaining session."

The meeting with the union president was held in the superintendent's office and lasted about one hour. As per Dr. Melton's request, the two did not discuss any specifics related to the unresolved contract between the school board and the teachers' union. Rather, they talked about the general conditions and needs of the school district. At the end of the meeting, however, Malcolm DuMont strongly urged Dr. Melton to become personally involved in settling the contract.

He told her, "Just by the fact that you called me, I can see that you are different. If you really care about students and teachers, you won't allow business to be conducted as usual. Why, I believe that if they left us alone, you and I could settle the contract over a long lunch."

Dr. Melton thanked him for meeting with her, but she made no commitments about her future role in the bargaining process.

The next morning, when she arrived at her office, there was an envelope sitting in the middle of her desk marked "confidential." She opened it and read the contents:

Dear Dr. Melton:

Your recent meeting with Mr. DuMont from the teachers' union is a matter that we find very disturbing. Fully accepting your authority to meet with whomever you please, we respectfully urge you not to become prematurely involved in the district's bargaining dispute. We believe your predecessor, Dr. Bixley, was a scapegoat. He tried to convince our three relatively new board members that we must be firm with the union. They not only rejected his position, they also persuaded two of the four remaining board members that Dr. Bixley was a barrier to settling a contract.

The bitter feelings about collective bargaining are not new in Washington City. Most of us are former members of the teachers' union in this very district. We know how they operate.

We always have been able to bring collective bargaining to a successful conclusion; and given the opportunity, we will do so again. We cannot afford to have the union bosses running this school district. We urge you to direct your efforts to educating our novice board members rather than having direct discussions with the union's president. There is no room for compromise with this group.

Respectfully,
David Zellers, Assistant Superintendent for Personnel
Alice Bontrager, Assistant Superintendent for Pupil Personnel Services
Duane Ibenhouse, Assistant Superintendent for Finance
Clyde Willis, Deputy Superintendent

Tom Zibick, the assistant superintendent for instruction, was the only high-ranking administrator who did not sign the letter. Dr. Melton called him into her office and showed him the letter. She asked if he knew about it. He said he did. She then asked if he was requested to sign the letter, and he said he was.

Anticipating her next question, he said, "I really don't want to discuss the letter. I didn't sign it because I don't think such letters are appropriate and because I believe that a superintendent should be able to make critical decisions without being second-guessed by her staff."

Dr. Melton sat at her desk after the conversation. Her thoughts were like a roller coaster, ranging from anger to concern. Was she being treated fairly? Did she have the right to make decisions about meeting with the union president? Were her staff members correct in being critical of her behavior, or was their behavior proof that she must become personally involved if relations with the teachers were to become more positive?

THE CHALLENGE

Analyze what occurred in the case. What would you advise Dr. Melton to do at this point?

KEY ISSUES/QUESTIONS

1. Assess Dr. Melton's career. To what extent is her ascension to her current position typical or atypical?

2. Is it common for a new superintendent to receive conflicting views regarding needs, problems, and solutions? What evidence do you have to support your response?

3. Based on what you read, describe your impression of the Washington City School District with regard to being an open or closed organization.

4. Do you have any concerns relative to the search that was conducted by the school board in Washington City? Is there a symbolic dimension to their behavior in selecting a new superintendent?

5. Do you have sufficient information to judge whether Dr. Melton was really prepared to become superintendent of Washington City? Why or why not?

6. To what extent might personal values and beliefs affect a superintendent's disposition toward unions and collective bargaining? Explain your response.

7. What would be the advantages and disadvantages of Dr. Melton deciding to heed the advice of four of her five top assistants?

8. Evaluate the timing of Dr. Melton's behavior. Should she have met with the union president so soon after starting her new job?

9. Should Dr. Melton inform the board of the letter she received from her top aides? Why or why not?

10. Do you think Dr. Melton can be successful in this position if she does not replace all or some of her top assistants?

11. Do you believe that Dr. Melton's leadership style can be equally effective in small and large school districts? Why or why not?

12. Why do bureaucratic-like organizations resist conflict?

13. Do you think that Dr. Melton was impulsive in accepting the superintendency in Washington City?

14. Administrators often rely on behaviors that have proven successful in past experiences. Is this a good practice?

SUGGESTED READINGS

Blumberg, A. (1985). A superintendent must read the board's invisible job description. *American School Board Journal, 172*(9), 44-45.

Cuban, L. (1985). Conflict and leadership in the superintendency. *Phi Delta Kappan, 67*(1), 28-30.

Danzberger, J., Kirst, M., & Usdan, M. (1992). *Governing public schools: New times, new requirements.* Washington, DC: Institute for Educational Leadership.

Darling, J., & Ishler, R. (1989-90). Strategic conflict resolution: A problem-oriented approach. *National Forum of Educational Administration and Supervision Journal, 7*(1), 87-103.

Dopp, B., & Sloan, C. (1986). Career development and succession of women to the superintendency. *Clearing House, 60*(3), 120-126.

Forest, J. (1984). The leadership team: Is the strategy working? *Thrust, 14*(1), 29-31.

Gonder, P. (1981). *Collective bargaining: Problems and solutions.* Arlington, VA: American Association of School Administrators.

Hanson, E. (1991). *Educational administration and organizational behavior* (3rd ed.). Boston: Allyn & Bacon (see chapter 3).

Hoffman, R., & Granger, J. (1991). *Career-bound and place-bound superintendents' attitudes toward collective bargaining.* (ERIC Document Reproduction Service No. ED 340 132).

Johnson, S. (1987). Can schools be reformed at the bargaining table? *Teachers College Record, 89*(2), 269-280.

Johnson, S. (1988). Unionism and collective bargaining in the public schools. In N. Boyan (Ed.), *Handbook of research on educational administration* (pp. 603-622). New York: Longman.

Kowalski, T., & Reitzug, U. (1993). *Contemporary school administration: An introduction.* New York: Longman (see chapters 7, 11, 14).

Lieberman, M. (1984). Beware of these four fallacies of school system labor relations. *American School Board Journal, 171*(6), 33.

Lieberman, M. (1988). Professional ethics in public education: An autopsy. *Phi Delta Kappan, 70*(2), 159-160.

Owens, R. (1991). *Organizational behavior in education* (4th ed.). Boston: Allyn & Bacon (see chapter 9).

Trotter, A. (1993). Deep in the heart of Houston. *Executive Educator, 15*(4), 23-25.

Yukl, G. (1989). *Leadership in organizations* (2nd ed., pp. 134-135). Englewood Cliffs, N.J.: Prentice-Hall.

Site-Based Conflict

BACKGROUND INFORMATION

Dissatisfaction with the performance of public elementary and secondary schools coupled with the realization that schools are not likely to improve by simply doing more of what they are already doing has led to growing interest in concepts of decentralization. Even though most of these concepts have been labeled *site-based management* (SBM), they are in reality a variety of approaches to school governance.

Over the past 50 years, school systems have often restricted freedoms for individual schools to develop their own policies—even in the areas of curriculum and instruction. Interventions of the federal government and the courts are largely responsible for creating a compliance orientation that made superintendents and school boards fearful of not applying uniform policy across all units of the organization. Tyack (1990) described the resulting condition as *fragmented centralization.*

In large measure, the current interest in decentralization is sparked by several beliefs: (1) Teachers will become more effective if they are treated more like true professionals. (2) Decisions about student instruction will be improved if teachers are empowered to truly individualize their work. (3) The overall governance of schools will improve if individual schools are not shackled by school districts' policies and rules. (4) Schools will improve if all those who are part of the school community are allowed to participate in critical decisions. Clearly, giving individual schools more authority to chart their own courses increases flexibility. But will it result in increased accountability and productivity? Critics note, for example, that having more people involved in decisions does not necessarily result in better decisions. Many observers also realize that SBM is dependent on school boards, administrators, and communities being willing to treat teachers as true professionals—a condition that has not existed previously (Kowalski & Reitzug, 1993).

One area of special interest in school administration is the leadership role of principals in schools that have decentralized governance. On the one hand, the principal ought to be trusting of individuals—especially those who are given the power and authority to make critical decisions. On the other hand, principals are usually expected to maintain some degree of control to assure that decisions are made in a timely fashion, and they are typically expected to provide direction to assure that democratically derived decisions are not counterproductive to the goals of the school. In this regard, principals working with school councils must walk a fine line between allowing others to make key decisions and maintaining responsibility for those decisions.

This case is about an experienced principal who volunteers to participate in a first phase of implementing SBM. In creating a school council, he decides to permit council members to be elected by the groups they represent (teachers, parents, and staff), and although he also is a member of the council, he assumes neither leadership nor an active role. The situation is complicated by the fact that the school council includes representatives of two factions that are constantly vying for power. The laissez-faire response to this constant conflict angers the council chair, a parent who also is the president of the parent-teachers association.

KEY AREAS FOR REFLECTION

1. Problems associated with decentralized governance of schools
2. Social conflict among individuals and groups in schools
3. Dynamics of group decision making
4. Leadership role in group processes
5. Selection of group membership
6. Leadership role in conflict resolution

THE CASE

The Community and School District

Sunland is a prosperous city in a southern state. With a population of approximately 75,000, it has grown nearly 25 percent in the last 20 years. New industries and businesses continue to locate in the area, and it is projected that the population will reach 100,000 by the year 2010. Sunland also is the county seat for LaSalle County.

The public schools that serve the city of Sunland are part of the LaSalle County School District. Serving the entire county, the school system has 3 high schools, 6 middle schools, and 19 elementary schools. Although growth has taken place throughout the county, much of it is centered in Sunland; thus a new middle school and three new elementary schools have been built in the city in the past decade.

The Superintendent and Site-Based Management

Three years ago, the school board employed Dr. Ursula Jones as superintendent. The 42-year-old administrator had been associate superintendent for instruction in a large-city school system in an adjoining state. Dr. Jones had a reputation as a change agent—a reputation that was enhanced in her three years in LaSalle County. One of her primary projects was to install SBM.

During her first year in LaSalle County, Dr. Jones developed and shared a plan to move toward a decentralized system of governance. She announced that the adoption of SBM would be done initially on a voluntary basis in elementary schools where principals were most interested and supportive. In the second year, she interviewed principals who had expressed an interest in becoming involved in the first phase of the project. The following year, three elementary schools were selected for participation.

Incentives were provided for the three participating schools. First, the principals were sent to a two-week seminar during the summer to prepare them for the process. Second, each school received $20,000 for staff development to be used during the first year. There were no restrictions for these funds other than the requirement that they be used for activities related to preparing faculty, staff, and selected parents to function within this new governance structure. And third, each school was given budgetary control in two critical areas: (1) supplies and equipment and (2) travel.

Elm Street Elementary School and the Principal

One of the newest schools in the district is Elm Street Elementary. It opened just four years ago to accommodate expanding populations. Presently, the school has three sections per grade level in grades kindergarten through five, but there are plans to add a fourth section at each grade level when additional space becomes necessary. When the school was opened, teachers from across the district were invited to apply for the vacancies, and about 70 percent of those selected were current employees of the school system.

Albert Batz was a principal in a smaller elementary school when he was selected to become Elm Street's first principal. An outgoing, friendly individual, he relates well to students, staff, and parents. Prior to becoming an administrator he spent 12 years teaching fifth grade in the LaSalle County system.

Mr. Batz spends virtually all of his time walking around the building. He loves to interact with teachers, students, and the cooks and custodians. It is not uncommon for him to walk into a classroom and join whatever activities are taking place; he always makes two or three trips a day to the teachers' lounge to have coffee and engage in conversation; and one of his favorite midmorning hideaways is the kitchen, where he can get the latest gossip from the cooks and sample the daily dessert.

Some teachers speculate that Albert purposely spends most of his time away from the office to avoid management problems that tend to consume other principals. When he came to Elm Street, he brought his secretary, Mrs. Lumans, with him. She is one of those secretaries who appears quite capable of managing the school on her own. Rarely does she call Mr. Batz back to his office to handle a routine problem.

The Implementation of Site-Based Management

When Dr. Jones announced that three elementary schools would be selected for the first phase of SBM implementation, the first volunteer was Albert Batz. He had long been committed to shared governance, and unlike some other administrators, he was not concerned with maintaining power over teachers. He treated teachers as peers rather than subordinates. His attitude was exemplified by the fact that he allowed teachers to vote their approval before committing the school to the SBM project. Overwhelmingly, they concurred with his position.

In addition to being in philosophical agreement with the processes of shared governance, decentralization, and teacher empowerment, Albert had another motive for moving his school in this direction. When he came to Elm Street School, he encountered what was for him a novel problem. Some of the teachers, having come from various parts of the school district, did not get along with each other. In particular, there were two groups that seemed to be engaged in continuous conflict. One group, consisting of four teachers, came from Harrison Elementary School, an older school in Sunland. The spokesperson for this group was Jenny Bales. The other group, consisting of three teachers, came from Weakland Township Elementary School—one of the rural schools in the county district. The designated leader of this group was Leonard Teel. Both groups competed to gain the political support of other teachers in the school, but neither had been successful.

Over the course of several years, Albert learned that Mrs. Bales and Mr. Teel had similar traits and needs. In their previous schools, each had been the dominant teacher—that is, the teacher in the school who had the greatest power to influence others. In watching them fight over every little issue, Albert concluded that they were vying for this stature at Elm Street School. For the most part, teachers who were not part of their groups (and 15 teachers were not) preferred to stay out of their constant battles.

When Elm Street was selected for the SBM project, the principal was required to establish a governance committee. He created a school council consisting of six teachers, three parents, a representative of the nonprofessional staff, and himself. Rather than appointing the members, though, he allowed the faculty, the parent-teachers association, and the staff to elect their representatives. Mrs. Bales and the three other teachers in her group and Mr. Teel and the two other teachers in his group all became nominees. Two other faculty members were also nominated, creating a situation where nine teachers competed for the six positions on the council. Twenty-two teachers were eligible to vote, and each could vote for up to six candidates. The final tallies were as follows:

Amy Raddison (not aligned with either faction)	14 votes
Tim Paxton (not aligned with either faction)	14 votes
Jenny Bales	7 votes
Arlene McFadden (aligned with Jenny Bales)	7 votes
Leonard Teel	7 votes
Lucille Isacson (aligned with Leonard Teel)	6 votes
Janice Summers (aligned with Jenny Bales)	5 votes
Tammy James (aligned with Leonard Teel)	4 votes

Despite receiving few votes outside of their own factions, Bales and Teel, and one ally each, were elected to the council. Both Amy Raddison and Tim Paxton were relatively young and inexperienced teachers.

Initially, Mr. Batz hoped that service on the school council would bring recognition to both Mrs. Bales and Mr. Teel, and over time, he thought there was a good chance the two would become allies in working to improve the school. But after meeting with the council for four or five months, he realized that the adversarial relationship between the two teachers was becoming more intense. The council provided a formal arena where they could attack each other. An example occurred at an early December meeting. One of the agenda items involved a request to send a team of five teachers, including Mr. Teel and the two teachers loyal to him, to a mid-January conference in California. Mrs. Bales challenged the request.

"Just because we have a good budget for staff development doesn't mean that we should send people on vacations."

Leonard Teel shot back immediately, "Vacation! Who said anything about vacation? This is a conference on model SBM programs. Teachers from all over the United States will be there. We can learn a great deal by participating."

"We don't have to go to California to learn about SBM," Mrs. Bales answered. "There are plenty of good programs closer to home. And for that reason, I urge everyone to vote against this request."

Barbara Whitlow, president of the PTA, had been elected as a parent representative to the council and subsequently as the group's chair. It took three ballots before anyone received the simple majority that was required, and of course, Mrs. Bales and Mr. Teel were candidates. Although she did not particularly want another time-consuming assignment, Mrs. Whitlow agreed to accept the responsibility.

Now presiding over yet another conflict between Mrs. Bales and Mr. Teel, Mrs. Whitlow turned to Mr. Batz and asked if he would comment on the merits of the request. Unlike his demeanor at other times, the principal typically kept a very low profile in council meetings. When put on the spot by Mrs. Whitlow, though, he answered.

"You know that I don't like to take sides. As principal, I need to remain neutral. I have to work closely with all the teachers. There is merit to both positions. Is it a good conference? Probably. Are there good conferences and workshops closer to home? Probably. I'm afraid each of us will just have to use good judgment."

The principal's role on the council had been questioned on a number of occasions. Members wanted to know how the council interfaced with Mr. Batz's normal duties as principal. He always answered that he was just another member and wanted to be treated that way. He saw no conflict between the council's responsibilities and his duties as principal. Several members, especially Mrs. Whitlow, initially suggested that he chair the council, but he declined. Mrs. Bales and Mr. Teel, on the other hand, were content to have him play a passive role.

"The purpose of having this council is to avoid one individual having all the power to make decisions," Mr. Teel said. "I agree with Albert that he shouldn't be taking sides."

"Well, so do I," added Mrs. Bales. "So, I move that the request to send five teachers to the conference in California be denied."

"I second that motion," said Arlene McFadden, the teacher on the council loyal to Mrs. Bales.

Mr. Teel immediately requested a secret ballot. This was another trend that deeply disturbed Mrs. Whitlow. The council was increasingly taking secret votes, and she saw this as contrary to building a team spirit. Additionally, all the bickering in the weekly meetings consumed a great deal of energy and little time was left to deal with issues relating more directly to curriculum and instruction.

The next day, Mrs. Whitlow went to see the principal. With the door closed, she demanded to know why he refused to assume any form of leadership on the council.

"I just don't understand how you can sit back and allow Mrs. Bales and Mr. Teel to constantly be at each other's throat. Don't you see how destructive their behavior is to our mission?" she asked.

"Barbara, I still have some hope that those two will come together. Let's give this a little more time. Do you think they are suddenly going to love each other just because I tell them to do so?"

Mrs. Whitlow made it clear that unless he agreed to be more forceful on the council, she would resign. "You know, Albert, I have plenty to do besides spending 10 to 12 hours a week on school council matters. I am willing to put in time—but only if we are making progress. And quite frankly, I don't think that is the case. All I've done is sit and listen to those two argue. From what I have seen, I'm not sure we weren't better off without SBM. I think it is your responsibility to step in and do something to stop this negative behavior."

Mr. Batz pleaded with Mrs. Whitlow not to resign. He told her that her continued leadership was essential. He asked her to be more patient. But he would not make a commitment to change his own behavior. He merely said he would give some thought to becoming more vocal at council meetings.

Two days later, Mrs. Whitlow wrote a letter to Mr. Batz resigning from the council. In it, she very candidly stated her reasons, and copies of the letter were sent to the superintendent, Dr. Jones, and each member of the LaSalle County school board. In her letter, she also suggested that the whole idea of SBM ought to be examined more closely. She wrote:

> . . . If schools are going to be giving all of this leeway and added resources, we need to be certain that proper leadership is maintained. Simply going to shared decision making does not assure better education for our daughters and sons.

After finishing the letter, Mr. Batz put it in his top desk drawer and walked down the hall toward the kitchen. A smile came over his face as he got close enough to smell the freshly baked cookies.

THE CHALLENGE

Analyze the behavior of the principal in this case. Do you agree with Mrs. Whitlow that he has to take a more active role in the council? Is he exhibiting leadership?

KEY ISSUES/QUESTIONS

1. Describe the leadership style of Mr. Batz. Have you known principals who behave in a similar manner?
2. Is it common for schools to have a dominant teacher (i.e., one who is more influential than others)?
3. Should principals be required to chair school councils? Why or why not?
4. Do you agree with the principal's decision to permit council members to be elected? What other options could he have used to select council members?
5. Evaluate the structure of the committee. For a school this size, is the committee too large? Too small? Should other groups be represented?
6. Is there a possibility that the competing factions on the council will become allies over time? If so, what might cause this to occur?
7. Discuss this case from the perspective of decision-making theories.
8. How would you react to this situation if you were the school superintendent?
9. One possible solution to this situation would be to remove the four teachers who are members of the competing factions from the council. Would you support this action? Why or why not?
10. Why do you think that Mrs. Bales and Mr. Teel are content to have the principal play a passive role on the council?

11. Is it better for Mr. Batz to remain neutral than to side with either Mrs. Bales or Mr. Teel?

12. Principals involved in shared decision making vary in the degree of control they maintain over the process. Some permit participatory processes, yet they are able to manipulate or direct the outcome. How can they do this? Is such behavior ethical?

13. In general, are teachers adequately prepared to be members of school governance councils? Why or why not?

14. What is your position regarding SBM? What factors influence your position?

15. In general, do most teachers welcome the opportunity to have more freedom and responsibility in their practice?

SUGGESTED READINGS

Belli, G., & van Lingen, G. (1993). A view from the field after one year of site-based management. *ERS Spectrum, 11*(1), 31–38.

Bergman, A. (1992). Lessons for principals from site-based management. *Educational Leadership, 50*(1), 48–51.

Conley, S. (1989). "Who's on first?": School reform, teacher participation, and decision-making process. *Education and Urban Society, 21*(4), 366–379.

Conway, J. (1984). The myth, mystery, and mastery of participative decision making in education. *Educational Administration Quarterly, 21*(1), 11–40.

David, J. (1989). Synthesis of research on school-based management. *Educational Leadership, 46*(8), 45–47, 53.

Ferris, J. (1992). School-based decision making: A principal-agent perspective. *Educational Evaluation and Policy Analysis, 14*(4), 333–346.

Fraze, L., & Melton, G. (1992). Manager or participatory leader. *NASSP Bulletin, 76*(540), 17–24.

Golarz, R. (1992). School-based management pitfalls: How to avoid some and deal with others. *School Community Journal, 2*(1), 38–52.

Hallinger, P., & Richardson, D. (1988). Models of shared leadership: Evolving structure and relationships. *Urban Review, 20*(4), 229–245.

Herman, J. (1993). School-based management: Sharing the resource decisions. *NASSP Bulletin, 76*(545), 102–105.

Hoyle, J. (1991). The principal and the pear tree. *Journal of School Leadership, 1*(2), 106–118.

Kimbrough, R., & Burkett, C. (1990). *The principalship: Concepts and practices.* Englewood Cliffs, NJ: Prentice-Hall (see chapter 3).

Kohl, P. (1992). Sharing the power: Fact or fallacy? *Action in Teacher Education, 14*(3), 29–36.

Kowalski, T., & Reitzug, U. (1993). *Contemporary school administration: An introduction.* New York: Longman (see chapters 9, 12).

Kowalski, T., Reitzug, U., McDaniel, P., & Otto, D. (1992). Perceptions of desired skills for effective principals. *Journal of School Leadership, 2*(3), 299–309.

Kritek, W., & Schneider, G. (1993-94). Site-based management and decentralization. *National Forum of Educational Administration and Supervision Journal, 11*(1), 3–20.

Lange, J. (1993). Site-based, shared decision making: A resource for restructuring. *NASSP Bulletin, 76*(549), 98–107.

Lingquist, K., & Mauriel, J. (1989). School-based management: Doomed to failure? *Education and Urban Society, 21*(4), 406–416.

Michel, G. (1991). The principal's skills in site-based management. *Illinois Schools Journal, 71*(1), 33–38.

Midgley, C., & Wood, S. (1993). Beyond site-based management: Empowering teachers to reform schools. *Phi Delta Kappan, 75*(3), 245–252.

Miles, W. (1982). The school-site politics of education: A review of the literature. *Planning and Changing, 12*(4), 200–218.

Ogletree, E., & Schmidt, L. (1992). Faculty involvement in administration of schools. *Illinois Schools Journal, 71*(2), 40–46.

Sergiovanni, T. (1991). *The principalship: A reflective practice perspective* (2nd ed.). Boston: Allyn & Bacon (see chapter 3).

Smylie, M. (1992). Teacher participation in school decision making: Assessing willingness to participate. *Educational Evaluation and Policy Analysis, 14*(1), 53–67.

Tyack, D. (1990). Restructuring in historical perspective: Tinkering toward Utopia. *Teachers College Record, 92*(2), 170–191.

Watkins, P. (1990). Agenda, power and text: The formulation of policy in school councils. *Journal of Education Policy, 5*(4), 315–331.

Zerchykov, R. (1992). Tools for changing schools: School community councils. *Equity and Choice, 8*(3), 52–59.

Differing Perceptions of Effective Teaching

BACKGROUND INFORMATION

There are many compelling arguments for assuring teacher empowerment. Most relate to perceived benefits of making teaching a true profession. Some reformers argue that education cannot be improved unless individual schools are empowered, and schools cannot be empowered unless teachers are empowered. But despite such deductions, the concept of giving teachers greater authority generates questions in the minds of school board members, administrators, and even teachers. Perhaps the most recurring inquiries focus on future relationships between school principals and teachers. To what extent, for example, would principals continue to be responsible for teacher compliance with curricular policies? What legal and political problems might evolve for school districts if teachers could independently determine what and how they taught?

Moving away from the status quo toward teacher empowerment is likely to occur in evolutionary stages. Even in the long term, some school boards and superintendents may resist allowing teachers complete self-determination in instructional areas. It is more likely that the establishment of sociopolitical arrangements will occur in which principals and teachers engage in shared decision making—especially in areas that most directly relate to teaching. Kimbrough and Burkett (1990) described one such process that they labeled *participative supervision*—a process in which teachers and principals have a shared responsibility for instructional improvement.

Teacher empowerment and decentralization are threatening concepts for many administrators. Consider just three possible reasons. First, many administrators have not been academically or experientially prepared to engage in shared decision-making paradigms. Second, there are a myriad of unanswered questions about legal and political liabilities. And third, there simply are a number of principals and teachers who prefer to carry out policy and abide by rules rather than to be held responsible for creating their own.

Configuring new relationships between principals and teachers also generates concerns for role ambiguity. Role theory indicates that school administrators already face multiple and often conflicting role expectations from organizational superiors, faculty, students, parents, and the community at large. Will all of these groups understand and support new organizational formats for distributing power and authority?

The prospect of allowing greater freedoms for teachers also needs to be considered in light of the reality that there are varying beliefs about the purposes of public education. Kowalski and Reitzug (1993) wrote:

> In addition to being transitory, educational goals at any given time are less than universally embraced by the American public. This discord is visible in continuing debates in areas such as values clarification, prayer in the schools, and sex education. Americans generally acknowledge that the public schools should address the ever-changing needs of society and individual citizens, but there is significant disagreement with respect to how this should be accomplished, the parameters of curricular responsibility, and the focus of control of public education. (p. 110)

To a large extent, the diversity of perceived purposes for education flows from differing values and beliefs held by individuals. Whereas one parent may expect schools to concentrate exclusively on teaching the basics, another may anticipate that the public school will accommodate social, psychological, and emotional needs as well.

Conflict emerges in this case when a third-grade teacher's philosophy conflicts with the values and beliefs of some parents. The principal is placed in a situation where he must decide to support the teacher, support the parents, or seek a compromise. The principal's behavior is affected by the fact that he transferred the teacher to the third-grade assignment even though her previous experience had been at a lower grade level.

KEY AREAS FOR REFLECTION

1. The relationship of teacher empowerment and new relationships between principals and teachers
2. Differing role expectations for the principal
3. Differing philosophies for public education
4. Resolving conflict between parents and teachers
5. Balancing power and authority between administrators and teachers

THE CASE

The Community

In 1970, nearly 85 percent of the population in Ocean County resided in the city of Rio Del Mar—one of the Florida cities that had a remarkable growth rate after 1960. First retirees moved to the area, and they were quickly followed by commercial developments of all types. Housing, much of it rather modest, was built on the west side of the city to accommodate an unbelievable demand for residential property. The new developments were a radical contrast to the eastern part of the city that borders the ocean. Here there are luxurious mansions.

Although the rapid rise in population created a number of environmental concerns for local government, these problems have been overshadowed recently by growing crime rates. Trafficking of illegal drugs has reached crisis proportions. Since 1980, the increase of foreign immigrants into Rio Del Mar has quadrupled. Many immigrants came from poverty-stricken Caribbean countries, and most have located in the low-cost housing areas that were built in Rio Del Mar in the early 1960s.

Fear of growing crime and a lack of additional land for development have resulted in a middle-class migration to the rural parts of Ocean County. The mansions that dot the oceanfront remain, but many now have walls to protect them from unwanted intruders. The movement of families in this county is much like the demographic pattern that has been repeated in virtually all of America's great cities—those who can afford relocation seek refuge from the social ills of urban life. But those who relocate within Ocean County do not gain a new school system—they remain part of the Ocean County School District.

The School System

The Ocean County School District has doubled in enrollment since 1975. Until a few years ago, most of the system's schools were in Rio Del Mar, but because of demographic shifts, all 12 new schools built in the last five years have been located in outlying areas of the county.

The school district is governed by a seven-member school board. The board members represent various geographic sections of the county, and four of the seven are from Rio Del Mar. Board members are elected to four-year terms in nonpartisan elections.

With approximately 75,000 students, there are 83 attendance centers:

12 high schools

28 middle schools

42 elementary schools

 1 alternative high school

The central office staff consists of over 100 professionals.

Since 1982, the school system has implemented an in-district busing plan to achieve racial balance. Approximately 25 percent of the minority children in Rio Del Mar are bused to schools outside the city. No students are required to be bused to schools in Rio Del Mar; however, they may choose to attend any of these schools if room is available.

The Superintendent

Dr. Elizabeth Eddings is in her second year as the superintendent of the county school system. She came to her current position after having served as the superintendent of a parish (county) school system in Louisiana.

During the interview process, which was conducted under Florida's famous "sunshine law," Elizabeth impressed teachers and administrators with her candid opinions about the roles professionals should play in the educational program. She stated her support for teacher empowerment and site-based management. She was especially convinced that decentralization was an effective approach for dealing with the population diversity in this school system.

Elizabeth Eddings was born and raised in North Carolina. She is the oldest of five children. She started her teaching career after graduating from a state university in the western part of North Carolina in 1965; she completed her master's degree at another state university in 1968. After three years of teaching and one year of experience as an assistant principal, she moved to Florida, where she pursued her doctorate in educational leadership. Since completing her Ph.D., she has been an elementary school principal, assistant superintendent for instruction, and superintendent. She is active in several national organizations, and since accepting her current position, she has become active in national groups and has served on a number of special commissions.

The School

Seminole Elementary School is one of the newest schools in the district. It serves an unincorporated area about four miles north of Rio Del Mar. Three of the most expensive housing developments in the county are in this area. Most residents have annual family incomes over $100,000.

Nearly 40 professional staff are employed in the school. There are three kindergarten teachers (each teaches two half-day classes), six first-grade teachers, and five teachers in each grade level 2 through 5. The standard educational program is augmented by specialized teachers in art, music, physical education, and computers (there is a teacher who operates the computer laboratory and provides instruction in this area). Additionally, the school has a full-time guidance counselor, an assistant principal, and a half-time nurse. Both psychological services and social work services are provided through central office personnel. There are three special education programs housed in the school: two classes for the learning disabled and a class for the mildly mentally handicapped.

Compared to most elementary schools, the faculty here are quite young. Only a handful have more than ten years of teaching experience. Additionally, teachers at this school have very diverse backgrounds—only 6 of 37 attended college in Florida.

There are just over 800 students enrolled in this school. Approximately 100 are bused from neighborhoods on the northwest side of Rio Del Mar.

The Principal

Howard Carlsburg was employed as principal of Seminole Elementary School the year the school opened. He had 2 years of experience as an assistant principal and 11 years of experience as a fifth-grade teacher. His performance evaluations were always quite good and he developed a reputation for being innovative.

Mr. Carlsburg is viewed by the faculty as a "hands-on" leader who likes to spend time in the classrooms. He works with teachers on instructional problems and occasionally does some direct teaching (about once a month, he will actually serve as a substitute teacher). To create a schedule that permits interaction with teachers, he delegates much of what he calls "administrivia" to his assistant principal. These tasks are largely managerial and include such functions as attendance, lunch programs, transportation, discipline, and keeping necessary records.

On numerous occasions, Mr. Carlsburg has invited the superintendent to visit Seminole Elementary. He is overtly supportive of her, especially of her goals related to site-based management and teacher empowerment.

The Teacher

Alicia Comstock at age 29 is one of the relatively young teachers at Seminole Elementary School. She has been teaching at the school for two years. After graduating from a state university in West Virginia, she taught in Virginia for three years before her husband was transferred to Florida by his employer.

Currently, Alicia is teaching a third-grade class with 24 students. This is a new assignment for her since her previous teaching experience has been at the first-grade level.

Alicia has positive relationships with other teachers and with Mr. Carlsburg. She is an even-tempered, positive person. She is especially skillful in working with others because she is a good listener and has no need to be dominant in conversations. When you walk into her classroom, you feel welcome. Her room has a warm feeling; the walls are covered with the students' work and decorated bulletin boards. In watching her teach, you sense that she truly likes working with young children.

Performance Evaluation

School district policy requires that principals complete annual performance evaluations of professional staff under their supervision. This evaluation culminates with a formal conference between the principal and teacher sometime in mid- to late March. Principals are obligated to follow policy guidelines that set time parameters and to identify a standard instrument to be used, but beyond these uniform practices, principals often exhibit different styles in dealing with performance evaluations.

Mr. Carlsburg's approach to assessing teacher performance is to utilize the process in a formative manner. That is, he tries to make the performance evaluation a positive growth experience for the teacher, students, and himself. His style is not one of confrontation; rather, he attempts to gain the teacher's confidence.

The Change in Alicia's Assignment

Alicia Comstock was transferred to teach third grade prior to her second year at the school. Even though she accepted the assignment without complaining, she made it clear to Mr. Carlsburg that she preferred to continue in first grade. The principal explained that he had an opportunity to hire an exceptional young lady who had just graduated from a university in the midwest, but she would not accept the assignment at Seminole unless it was in the first grade. Not wanting to lose this candidate, the principal decided to transfer one of the current teachers from first to third grade.

Before deciding about the transfer, Mr. Carlsburg talked to each of the first-grade teachers. None volunteered to move to third grade. Mrs. Comstock, however, said she would do whatever was best for the school. Mr. Carlsburg decided that she would be cooperative and selected her for the third-grade assignment.

The Problem

In early October, Mr. Carlsburg received three complaints about Mrs. Comstock. First, a mother called to voice concern that her son was not being assigned homework.

"My daughter was in third grade last year and brought work home almost every day. Now my son is in Mrs. Comstock's class and he never has homework. Why?" she asked.

The principal asked the parent if she had talked to Mrs. Comstock and she said she had not. He said he would look into the matter. Before he had a chance to do so, he received two similar calls the next morning. He waited no longer and went directly to her classroom. In the hallway he told her about the calls. She explained that she did not believe that homework was appropriate for children in third grade.

"These children have a long school day, and they work very hard while at school. I just don't think you accomplish much by loading them down with additional work to do at home," she told the principal.

The principal asked her to see him after school so they could discuss the matter further. In the interim, he surveyed the other third-grade teachers and discovered that each was assigning homework. During his subsequent discussion with Mrs. Comstock, the principal suggested a compromise. He asked her to give homework assignments occasionally, explaining that she was the only third-grade teacher not doing so. Without emotion, she agreed to do so.

In late November, additional complaints about Mrs. Comstock were directed to the principal. This time, the concerns were broader than homework. The complaining parents were contending that the expectations for academic progress set by the teacher were too low. As one father put it, "My son has never been happier about school. But why shouldn't he be? He's never had a teacher who lets him decide what to do."

By December 1, the principal received complaints from the parents of nine students in Mrs. Comstock's class. Several indicated that they would direct their concerns to Dr. Eddings and the school board if they were not resolved. As a result of the complaints, Mr. Carlsburg visited Mrs. Comstock's class frequently, and he met with her on three different occasions to discuss his performance. His observations only served to convince him that she was a competent teacher.

Personally, Mr. Carlsburg felt some responsibility for the problem since he transferred her to third grade. Yet, he failed to share this fact with parents because he believed it had little bearing on their concerns. After weighing all of the circumstances, he concluded that the conflict stemmed from some parents having a very narrow perception of schooling—one that focused only on teaching basic skills. Because it was nearing a vacation period, the principal promised to meet with the complaining parents when school resumed in early January.

Mr. Carlsburg decided to invite all of the parents of students in Mrs. Comstock's class. He sent a letter to them explaining that there were concerns about the amount of student work required, and that a meeting would be held to discuss these concerns. Parents representing only 11 of the students attended the meeting, about a third of whom were supportive of Mrs. Comstock.

The principal began by saying that he hoped the meeting would be a springboard to positive improvements. He explained that he had not asked Mrs. Comstock to attend this meeting, because he did not want it to appear that her performance was on trial. He then went on to describe his classroom visitations and explain the elements of the formal evaluation system. He concluded by saying that he believed Mrs. Comstock to be a competent, sensitive, and caring teacher. He told the parents, "She views education as a process that addresses all the needs of a child. Thus, she has equal concerns for social adjustment, self-image, and educational progress. I don't think this means she is not teaching her students the basics." His comments were not well received by the complaining parents.

Benton Rodius, a stockbroker, emerged as the spokesperson for the group of parents who were objecting to Mrs. Comstock.

"Mr. Carlsburg, let me first say that I took a half day off from work to be here today with my wife. We obviously see this as a serious problem. Two years ago when we moved here from Vermont, I put my children in the public schools because I was told they were very good. My daughter, Betsy, who is now in Mrs. Comstock's class, started going to a private preschool program when she was three years old. She could read by the time she entered kindergarten. I don't think it's Mrs. Comstock's job to see that Betsy is happy. My wife and I take care of that. It is her job to challenge our child—to see that Betsy develops her skills. One of the things that is very wrong with public education is that we have this notion that schools can solve all of society's problems. I pay taxes so my daughter can receive a fundamental education, not to have someone tinker with social values and decide whether my child is happy."

The principal reacted that he thought it was unfair to characterize Mrs. Comstock as someone who did not care about learning. He also noted that children come to a public school with a variety of needs and that the school had to be concerned with the total child. He pointed out that some children in her class came from families living below the poverty level, and he explained that academic, personal, and social needs could not be cleanly separated as distinct tasks.

After listening to the principal's explanation, Mr. Rodius asked the principal, "Do you think it is excessive to want a teacher to challenge students to achieve as much as they can?" Before the principal could answer, he asked another question, "Well, forget that. Just tell us what your evaluation is of this teacher. Do you really believe she is doing a good job?"

"It would be inappropriate for me to discuss my formal evaluation of Mrs. Comstock. And besides, the process will not be completed until March. If you are asking me whether I think she is doing a good job given what I know now, my answer is yes."

One parent stood to defend Mrs. Comstock at this point. She said that her son had never shown as much interest in school as he has this year.

The complaining parents were not dissuaded by either the principal or the parental supporters of the teacher. Mr. Rodius said he would take the matter to Dr. Eddings.

THE CHALLENGE

Analyze the behavior of the principal in this case. What would you advise him to do at this point?

KEY ISSUES/QUESTIONS

1. Based on your personal experiences, do parents exhibit differing perceptions of what schools should accomplish?
2. What influences our values and beliefs regarding the purposes of public education?
3. Is the principal correct in concluding that the issue of transferring Mrs. Comstock to the third grade is inconsequential to the problem in this case?
4. If you were Alicia Comstock, would you have wanted to be at the meetings with the parents? Why or why not?

5. To what extent do you believe that the superintendent's goals are an issue in this case?
6. If you were the principal, what would you have done differently after receiving the first complaints from parents?
7. What are the differences between formative and summative evaluation? Which does the principal seem to favor?
8. What are some techniques that a principal can use to deal with differing parental goals for public education?
9. What judgments do you make about parental attendance at the two meetings?
10. How might community environment affect the behavior of parents, teachers, and administrators in this case?
11. The principal suggests that the conflict between parents and Mrs. Comstock could lead to some positive outcomes. Is he being realistic?
12. Is it possible to truly empower teachers and maintain administrative control? If so, how can this be done?
13. Analyze the leadership style of this principal. What are his strengths and weaknesses?

SUGGESTED READINGS

Beckham, J. (1985). Legally sound criteria, processes, and procedures for the evaluation of public school professional employees. *Journal of Law and Education, 14*(4), 529-551.

Bullock, W., & Davis, J. (1985). Interpersonal factors that influence principals' ratings of teacher performance. *Planning and Changing, 16*(1), 3-11.

Campbell-Evans, G. (1991). Nature and influence of values in principal decision making. *Alberta Journal of Educational Research, 37*(2), 167-168.

Deutsch, M. (1992). Typical responses to conflict. *Educational Leadership, 50*(1), 16.

Epstein, J. (1988). Parents and schools: How do we improve programs for parent involvement? *Educational Horizons, 66*(3), 59-95.

Goldring, E. (1990). Elementary school principals as boundary spanners: Their engagement with parents. *Journal of Educational Administration, 28*(1), 53-62.

Haughey, M., & MacElwain, L. (1992). Principals as instructional supervisors. *Alberta Journal of Educational Research, 38*(2), 105-119.

Howe, H. (1993). Thinking about kids and education. *Educational Leadership, 75*(3), 226-228.

Hoy, W., Tarter, C., & Witkoskie, L. (1992). Faculty trust in colleagues: Linking the principal with school effectiveness. *Journal of Research and Development in Education, 26*(1), 38-45.

Kowalski, T., & Reitzug, U. (1993). *Contemporary school administration: An introduction.* New York: Longman (see chapters 5, 8, 11).

Maehr, M., & Parker, S. (1993). A tale of two schools—And the primary task of leadership. *Educational Leadership, 75*(3), 233-236.

Margolis, H., & Tewel, K. (1988). Resolving conflict with parents: A guide for administrators. *NASSP Bulletin, 72*(506), 26-28.

Medley, D., Coker, H., & Soar, R. (1984). *Measurement-based evaluation of teacher performance* (pp. 14-23). New York: Longman.

Medley, D., & Coker, H. (1987). The accuracy of principals' judgments of teacher performance. *Journal of Educational Research, 80*(4), 242-247.

Moo, G. (1987). Communicating with the school publics. *NASSP Bulletin, 71*(501), 142-144.

Peterson, D. (1983). Legal and ethical issues of teacher evaluation: A research-based approach. *Educational Research Quarterly, 7*(4), 6-16.

Polardy, J. (1988). The effect of homework policies on student achievement. *NASSP Bulletin, 72*(507), 14-17.

Reetz, L. (1990-91). Parental perceptions of homework. *Rural Educator, 12*(2), 14-19.

Sapone, C. (1982). Appraisal and evaluation systems: What are the perceptions of educators, board members? *NASSP Bulletin, 66*(458), 46-51.

Snyder, K., & Anderson, R. (1986). *Managing productive schools: Toward an ecology.* Orlando, FL: Academic Press College Division (see chapter 8).

Spillane, R. (1989). The changing principalship: A superintendent's perspective. *Principal, 68*(3), 19-20.

Turner-Egner, J. (1989). Teacher discretion in selecting instructional materials and methods. *West's Education Law Reporter, 53*(2), 365-379.

Watkins, D. (1993). Five strategies for managing angry parents. *Principal, 72*(4), 29-30.

Yatvin, J. (1992). Memoir of a team player. *Educational Leadership, 49*(5), 50-52.

Zirkel, P. (1985). Defamation for educator evaluation. *NASSP Bulletin, 69*(477), 90-92.

The Clinic Controversy

BACKGROUND INFORMATION

Many secondary schools are confronted with growing problems related to teen-age pregnancies and sexually transmitted diseases. One response has been the establishment of school-based health clinics. Especially in urban schools serving large numbers of low-income students, these clinics provide a range of services from counseling on substance abuse to the distribution of contraceptives. Because of varying community values, such programs have spawned a great deal of controversy.

Increasingly, school administrators find they are caught between conflicting expectations. Society is demanding that educators reduce drop-out rates, increase student achievement, and accomplish these goals with no additional resources. At the same time, however, there is growing criticism that schools are infringing on responsibilities that should remain with families, churches, and other social agencies. As society becomes more diverse, the gap between these goals becomes even wider.

One dimension of this case involves the political nature of decision making. A superintendent attempts to address a growing drop-out rate in his school system by appointing a special committee to examine the problem. Although their conclusions are accurate, their recommendations are vague. He also turns to community leaders for advice, but they too fail to offer specific solutions. Thus, the superintendent decides to move forward knowing that he personally is taking a big risk. How does this behavior interface with theories on shared decision making?

Another focal point of the case is communication. How does the superintendent communicate with his staff? To what degree does the school district interact with the community? Are there established channels of communication that can be used when problems emerge?

One facet of organizational theory is the relationship between organizations and their environment. Both the nature of the community (the environment) and the culture and climate of the educational institutions (the organizations) affect such relationships. In this case, the diversity of the local community almost assures divergent views with regard to matters that have moral and religious implications.

KEY AREAS FOR REFLECTION

1. Changing demography and implications for public education
2. Curtailing drop-out problems in high schools
3. Conflict generated by problems having religious and moral implications
4. Communication between public schools and their communities
5. Shared decision making
6. Political dimensions of the superintendency
7. School-based health clinics

THE CASE

The Community

Shelton is a city in the East with just under 100,000 residents. In many ways, it is an exemplar of the American "melting pot"—an industrial city that attracted immigrants of varying races, cultures, and religions. Unlike other cities with economies that are highly dependent on manufacturing, Shelton has retained much of its population. In large measure, this had been attributable to the presence of several truck and recreational vehicle companies. Demand for their products has remained relatively high, and there has been little erosion of jobs to foreign markets.

The primary industries in Shelton include the following:

Truck trailer factory, 950 employees
Two recreational vehicle companies, 840 employees
Automobile ignition plant, 560 employees
Lawnmower assembly plant, 400 employees

Official census data indicate that the population in Shelton actually increased during the 1980s by about 8 percent.

Although the nature of the community has changed over the past two decades, a number of ethnic neighborhoods still are evident. For example, there are two relatively large Italian-American neighborhoods. Residents of German and Polish ancestry also remained clustered in separate parts of the city. Since the mid-1960s, the fastest-growing population groups have been African Americans and Hispanics. The most recent census provided the following demographic data:

White—59 percent

African American—31 percent

Hispanic—8 percent

Native American—1 percent

Other—1 percent

The city has its own hospital and a relatively new shopping center. The downtown area, however, is slowly dying. Most stores have relocated or have gone out of business. Several strip malls have been built on the fringes of the city, and many residents now shop at a large mall built in an adjoining county. Railroad tracks seem to be everywhere in Shelton. Being stopped by freight trains is a common occurrence as you drive through the city.

The School District

The Shelton City School District is one of four school systems in Parma County. Statistics for the district are as follows:

High schools: 4

Middle schools: 9

Elementary schools: 26

Current enrollment: 24,900

The superintendent is Dr. Fredrick Ochman, a veteran administrator in his sixth year as chief executive of this district. Prior to coming to Shelton, Dr. Ochman served as superintendent in two smaller districts. He is perceived by his staff to be a "hands-on" leader who likes to get involved personally with key issues.

The central office staff includes 14 professional employees, three of whom are assistant superintendents reporting directly to Dr. Ochman:

James Effrin, assistant superintendent for business

Lucy Natali, assistant superintendent for pupil personnel services

Richard King, assistant superintendent for instruction

The school district is governed by a seven-member board. Just three years ago, voters passed a referendum altering the method for selecting board members. Members had been appointed by the mayor to three-year terms. Now they were elected in nonpartisan elections. As a result, the school board has become more heterogeneous with regard to race and socioeconomic status. Only two members who were in office when Dr. Ochman was appointed superintendent remain on the school board.

Dr. Ochman's Accomplishments

Before Fred Ochman accepted the job of superintendent in Shelton, he knew it would be a challenge to continue the rich traditions of the four high schools. They had won many awards over the years, especially in athletics.

The changing demographic nature of Shelton provided a complex challenge for Dr. Ochman. On the one hand, he wanted to maintain racial balance in the schools, and this required flexibility in setting school-attendance boundaries. On the other hand, many long-term residents had fierce loyalties to "their" high schools, and forcing students to transfer could become a political nightmare. The superintendent, with the assistance of an ad hoc committee of administrators, teachers, and parents, devised a plan that has been able to retain acceptable racial balances while not unduly changing attendance boundaries. The core of the plan is a magnet school-within-a-school concept in each of the high schools. These are specialized programs that emphasize an area of study (one high school has a math-science magnet, another has a social studies magnet, another has a fine arts magnet; and the last one emphasizes technology). Students in the district may opt to attend any of the high schools as long as their enrollment does not result in unfavorable racial balances.

Dr. Ochman also has received high praise from his school board for maintaining community support for schools. He is active in the community and has encouraged the schools to reach out to their immediate neighborhoods. This has resulted in school advisory councils composed of teachers and parents and in a number of community-service programs such as adult education and recreation.

The New Challenge

Last year as the central office staff was reviewing data as part of the strategic planning process, they discovered some alarming figures about high school graduation rates. Data indicated that approximately 25 percent of all students in the district did not complete the twelfth grade. Further investigation revealed two dimensions of this problem that were especially cogent. First, the drop-out rate had increased most markedly among female students. Whereas 10 years ago boys were twice as likely not to complete high school as girls, the current figures indicated virtually no difference in graduation rates. Second, the drop-out rate was increasing most rapidly among those students who came from lower socioeconomic families (as identified by free-lunch data).

When these data were shared with Dr. Ochman, he moved forward immediately to study the issue. His first act was to establish an ad hoc committee consisting of three administrators, six teachers, four parents, and four students.

Dr. Natali was appointed chair of the committee. The superintendent gave the group three major tasks: (1) find out why the drop-out rate is increasing, (2) find out why the drop-out rate is accelerating so rapidly among girls from low-income families, and (3) recommend positive actions to ameliorate the situation. The committee was given a budget of $7,000, much of which was to be used to retain a consultant to assist the committee.

After studying the data for nearly six months, Dr. Natali issued a written report on behalf of the committee. Included were the following conclusions:

1. The relatively stable drop-out rate for male students is largely explained by the continued existence of low-skill jobs in the community and surrounding areas. Such employment opportunities tempt some students to leave school prematurely. This is especially true of male students who are not performing well academically.
2. The socioeconomic status of the family seems to influence student decisions about staying in school. Those from low-income families often are given little encouragement to do well academically. In some instances, these students may even be encouraged to quit school so that they can supplement family incomes. In many low-income families, there is only one parent, and not infrequently, this parent has not graduated from high school.
3. In investigating the accelerating drop-out rate among female students, one fact stands out. Many who leave school have become pregnant. Students involved in a pregnancy are five times more likely to drop out than those who are not. If the pregnant student is from a low-income family, she is four times more likely never to graduate from high school.
4. The overall rate of pregnancies among high school students has increased 45 percent in the last 10 years. Nearly 65 percent of the students who become pregnant qualify for free lunches.
5. Most students involved in a pregnancy have had virtually no consultation, sex education, or health care. Again, this is especially true of students from low-income families.

The report was less specific about recommendations. The committee was somewhat divided over possible actions; hence, the suggested actions were rather general. Included were the following three:

1. The school district should implement a sex awareness program.
2. Consideration should be given to establishing an alternative school for students who cannot function in the regular high schools. Such an option may attract more students to stay in school.
3. The school district should work with the council of churches in the community to address the moral nature of this problem.

The report was distributed to administrative staff and the school board. Dr. Ochman asked the secondary school principals to share the report with their staffs and to seek reactions. After about six weeks, Dr. Ochman held a series of meetings with administrative staff. He was especially interested in hearing their reactions to the report. The administrators challenged neither the data nor the conclusions, but they had mixed reactions to the recommendations. A few expressed uneasiness about becoming more involved in sex education programs; others stated concerns that an alternative school would encourage an even higher percentage of students to withdraw from the high schools. In general, the meeting failed to provide a clear course of action.

Following discussions with administrative staff, Dr. Ochman invited nine community leaders to meet with him to review the problem and the report. They included the mayor, the administrator of the hospital, the director of the mental health clinic, a priest, a minister, a rabbi, a physician, the director of the local family planning agency, and the president of the school board. He gave each a copy of the report and asked them to read it before their meeting. Again, data and conclusions were not challenged, but there was disagreement over a course of action. Perhaps the most positive outcome was that all present then realized how little coordination of community resources existed in Shelton.

Three months after the report was written, Superintendent Ochman concluded that any solution to the drop-out problem would contain an element of risk. More importantly, he understood that he would be the primary risk taker. After weighing all of the input he received, one outcome was clearly evident. He decided that if the drop-out rate was to be curtailed, the issue of pregnancies would have to be confronted. Ignoring it just because it was controversial would not be a sufficient response.

A Course of Action

As he pondered potential actions, the idea of creating student clinics in middle schools and high schools captured Dr. Ochman's attention. Such clinics had been established in other schools, especially in urban areas, and a growing number of educators was accepting the notion that these clinics constituted a realistic approach to dealing with controversial issues such as premarital sex, birth control, and abortion. They also have received more attention because the rate of sexually transmitted diseases among teenagers was increasing in many parts of the country. In addition to dealing with matters of sexual behavior, these clinics also provided counseling in areas such as substance abuse, prenatal care, and child care.

Dr. Ochman and Dr. Natali decided to visit two high schools in different cities that had implemented health clinics. Both were located in major metropolitan areas and served large numbers of students from low-income families.

During their visits Drs. Ochman and Natali heard a number of positive comments from the principals who have supervisory responsibility for the clinics. These assessments focused largely on ways that students used and benefited from the service. Dr. Ochman was especially interested in learning about faculty and community reactions to the clinics. The principals had far less information about this topic, but both indicated that there had been few complaints from either teachers or taxpayers.

On returning to Shelton, Dr. Ochman arranged another meeting with the group of nine community leaders who previously met with him to discuss the report. At this session, he described his visits to the two high schools and explained the objectives of their health clinics. Some concern about such clinics was voiced by two of the clergy present; however, most seemed mildly supportive. But when he asked if they would publicly support the idea, only the president of the school board stepped forward. Several indicated that they knew too little about the concept to make a commitment. The agency directors, however, pledged to cooperate if the clinics were established.

Dr. Ochman was concerned that a decision had to be made soon if action was to be taken the following school year. He decided that school clinics constituted the most reasonable alternative, and he presented the concept to the school board in the executive session prior to the regularly scheduled May meeting. The board president, Mr. Potter, also contributed several comments based on his presence in the meetings with the community leaders. Dr. Ochman then informed the board of his intention to present a recommendation at the June board meeting to establish health clinics in the high schools at the start of the next school year. There were no questions or discussions.

The day after the board meeting, Dr. Ochman met with the four high school principals and two assistant superintendents, Dr. King and Dr. Natali. He informed them of his intention to move forward to establish clinics, but only at the high schools. He added that the clinics would operate under agreements with the county mental health agency, the city hospital, and the welfare department. These agencies would provide support services when necessary.

The principals were not surprised at the announcement—it was commonly known among the staff that Dr. Ochman was leaning in this direction. Two of the principals reacted immediately by saying that this course of action was a mistake. They warned that many in the community would resist any attempt by the schools to become involved in birth control. One of the other principals present told the superintendent that he supported the move, and the fourth principal indicated that he was undecided but open-minded. Despite these mixed reactions, Dr. Ochman remained determined to move forward, and he asked each administrator to help make the program a success.

The following recommendation was prepared for the June board meeting:

Superintendent's Recommendation: That a student health clinic be established to provide assistance for students with a variety of health and emotional problems at each of the four high schools. Such problems will include drug and alcohol abuse and teenage pregnancies. A full-time director is to be employed for each of the clinics.

Dr. Ochman purposefully avoided terms such as "birth control" and "sex education." He also prepared background information for the school board that outlined the proposed linkages with community agencies. A $257,000 budget for operating the clinics for the upcoming year was also recommended.

Given that there was no response when he discussed his intentions in an executive session in May, Dr. Ochman was caught off guard when three board members voiced opposition to his recommendation. Board member Tony Copamagi was perhaps the most adamant.

He said, "I don't have problems helping kids who have trouble with drugs. But no way am I going to sanction our schools getting in the business of running a birth control clinic. This proposal is just too vague about what is going to be done. How do I know that we're not going to be giving out free condoms to kids?"

Dr. Ochman tried to respond personally to the concerns. He acknowledged that the clinics probably could not survive if they offended community standards, but he argued that the public's stance on this matter could only be determined if the clinics were tried. He suggested that a community advisory council be appointed by the school board to assure that functions remained in line with community standards.

Following this meeting, Velma Jackson, a board member and supporter of the recommendation, called Dr. Ochman and suggested that he delay action on this matter. She felt there was a good chance it would be defeated if it was presented in June. Dr. Ochman said he had already told his staff he was moving forward, and he expressed his concern that a delay might mean that the clinics could not become operational for another year.

When the recommendation was made in the June meeting, Mrs. Jackson moved to table it. She argued that more time was needed to answer questions about the proposal. The three board members who opposed the clinics spoke against her motion. They wanted the matter settled immediately. It was clear that a number of persons in the audience also opposed the superintendent's recommendation, because they cheered when these board members noted their concerns. The motion to table passed, however, by a vote of four to three.

The morning after the June board meeting, the *Shelton Daily Examiner,* the local newspaper, carried an editorial urging the school board to defeat the superintendent's recommendation. It was the first official act of opposition to come from an organization in the community, but it was to be followed by many others.

During the three weeks after the June board meeting, Dr. Ochman was inundated with letters opposing the clinics. A fourth board member came forward and indicated publicly that he probably could not support the idea. The newspaper also reported that a confidential source had revealed that at least two high school principals were opposed to the clinics.

Two board members who opposed the clinics visited Dr. Ochman and pleaded with him to withdraw the recommendation. They generally supported him, and they did not want to see him destroyed by this one issue. Even his three top assistants suggested to him privately that he retreat.

There was little public support for Dr. Ochman's recommendation. He received some telephone calls and letters from individuals who said they admired his fortitude, but they were unwilling to get involved in the dispute.

As the July board meeting drew near, Dr. Ochman arranged to have lunch with David Potter, the board president. He asked the board member for advice. Mr. Potter, a juvenile judge in Shelton, told Dr. Ochman that he would support his recommendation.

But Mr. Potter warned, "It has little chance of being approved. There may be as many as five votes against it. Listen, everyone will understand if you pull back from this thing. It may be the prudent thing to do."

THE CHALLENGE

Place yourself in Dr. Ochman's position. What would you do with the recommendation for the health clinics?

KEY ISSUES/QUESTIONS

1. Relate the community to the problem in this case. Does the nature of the community have any special influence?

2. Identify the issues that make student health clinics controversial. What motivates some citizens to oppose them?

3. Evaluate the procedures employed by Dr. Ochman in reaching his recommendation in this matter. Do you think they were appropriate?

4. To what extent might an administrator's personal values and beliefs affect decisions in controversial areas such as health clinics?

5. Describe Dr. Ochman's leadership style. Would you like to work with him?

6. Are data concerning the relationship between pregnancies and drop-out rates in Shelton typical for the United States? What are the figures in your school district?

7. Information in the case suggests that visits to the two high schools helped the superintendent make up his mind to move forward with the recommendation. Were these visits a good idea?

8. Discuss the legal and ethical dimensions of school board members stating publicly how they will vote on matters before there has been an opportunity to fully study the matter.

9. Is it prudent for a superintendent to withdraw a recommendation that has no chance of passing? Is it ethical?

10. Do you think that linkages with community agencies are a good idea for the health clinics? Why or why not?

11. Dr. Ochman decided that ignoring the pregnancy problem was not a feasible alternative. Is his behavior consistent with the way managers in highly bureaucratic organizations approach conflict? Why or why not?

12. If you were Dr. Ochman, would you have insisted that your staff provide greater direction in dealing with this problem?

13. Can you identify any alternative actions that may have produced public support for the recommendation to establish the health clinics?

14. Do you think the clinics would have been more acceptable to the public if they were called something else? Would they have been more acceptable if there had been assurances that they would not deal with contraception and abortion counseling?

SUGGESTED READINGS

Albert, K. (1989). *School-based adolescent health programs: The Oregon approach* (ERIC Document Reproduction Service No. ED 323 272).

Berger, M. (1982). The public schools can't do it all. *Contemporary Education, 54*(1), 6–8.

Bonjean, L., & Rittenmeyer, D. (1987). *Teenage parenthood: The school's response.* Bloomington, IN: Phi Delta Kappa Foundation (Fastback No. 264).

Buie, J. (1987a). Schools must act on teen pregnancy. *The School Administrator, 44*(8), 12–15.

Buie, J. (1987b). Teen pregnancy: It's time for schools to tackle the problem. *Phi Delta Kappan, 68*(10), 737–739.

Cook, L. (1987). This proposed health clinic triggered a rhetorical meltdown. *American School Board Journal, 174*(5), 27–28.

Cuban, L. (1988). A fundamental puzzle of school reform. *Phi Delta Kappan, 70*(5), 341–344.

Dryfoos, J. (1991). School-based social and health services for at-risk students. *Urban Education, 26*(1), 118–137.

Edwards, L., & Brent, N. (1987). Grapple with those tough issues before giving that clinic the go-ahead. *American School Board Journal, 174*(5), 25–27.

Ennis, T. (1987). Prevention of pregnancy among adolescents. Part I. The school's role. *School Law Bulletin, 18*(2), 1–15.

Evans, R., & Evans, H. (1988–89). The African-American adolescent male and school-based health clinics: A preventive perspective. *Urban League Review, 12*(1–2), 111–117 (see entire issue related to alleviating teenage pregnancies).

Forste, R., & Tienda, M. (1992). Race and ethnic variation in the schooling consequences of female adolescent sexual activity. *Social Science Quarterly, 73*(1), 12–30.

Frymier, J., & Gansneder, B. (1989). The Phi Delta Kappa study of students at risk. *Phi Delta Kappan, 71*(2), 142–146.

Hahn, A. (1987). Reaching out to America's dropouts: What to do? *Phi Delta Kappan, 69*(4), 256–263.

Harold, R., & Harold, N. (1993). School-based clinics: A response to the physical and mental health needs of adolescents. *Health and Social Work, 18*(1), 65–75.

Harrington-Lueker, D. (1991). Kids and condoms. *American School Board Journal, 178*(5), 18–22.

Kirby, D., & Lovick, S. (1987). School-based health clinics. *Educational Horizons, 65*(3), 139–143.

Kowalski, T., & Reitzug, U. (1993). *Contemporary school administration: An introduction.* New York: Longman (see chapters 11, 12).

Naughton, S., & Edwards, L. (1991). AIDS/HIV risk assessment and risk reduction counseling in a school-based clinic. *Journal of School Health, 61*(10), 443–447.

Nelsen, F. (1988). What evangelical parents expect from public school administrators. *Educational Leadership, 45*(8), 40–43.

Norris, B. (1985). High school pregnancy clinic survives storm. *Times Educational Supplement, 3617* (October 25), 17.

Nudel, M. (1992). Health for hire. *American School Board Journal, 179*(10), 36–38.

Owens, R. (1991). *Organizational behavior in education* (4th ed.). Boston: Allyn & Bacon (see chapter 10).

Patterson, H. (1993). Don't exclude the stakeholders. *School Administrator, 50*(2), 13–14.

Peng, S. (1987). Effective high schools: What are the attributes? In J. Land & H. Waldberg (Eds.), *Effective school leadership* (pp. 89–108). Berkeley, CA: McCutchan.

Ravitch, D. (1982). The new right and the schools: Why mainstream America is listening to our critics. *American Teacher, 6*(3), 8–13, 46.

Rienzo, B., & Button, J. (1993). The politics of school-based clinics: A community-level analysis. *Journal of School Health, 63*(6), 266–273.

Schwartz, D., & Darabi, K. (1986). Motivations for adolescents' first visit to a family planning clinic. *Adolescents, 21,* 535–545.

Scott-Jones, D. (1993). Adolescent childbearing: Whose problem? What can we do? *Phi Delta Kappan, 75*(3), K1–K12.

Vandermolen, J., & Nolan, R. (1993). Agenda for at-risk kids. *American School Board Journal, 180*(1), 40–41.

Will, S., & Brown, L. (1988). School-based health clinics: What role? *American Teacher, 72*(3), 4.

case *20*

"Narc" or Social Worker? or Maybe, Educational Leader?

BACKGROUND INFORMATION

Administrators face many pressures as they attempt to balance their personal and professional lives. Many spend as much as 60 to 75 hours a week on work-related activities. High school principals, for instance, often find it necessary to devote three to four nights a week to their work. Research on job demands of school administrators has shown that time requirements are one of the least satisfying aspects of employment for principals (Kowalski & Reitzug, 1993).

Stress caused by conflict is also an inevitable aspect of organizational leadership. Owens (1991) stated that there are two essential components of conflict: (1) divergent (or apparently divergent) views and (2) incompatibility of those views. Administrators increasingly find that they are expected to address competing wants and needs—and to do so with less than adequate resources. It is precisely these circumstances that cause political activity to become a part of public education.

However, pressure and stress are not always dysfunctional. Several studies have shown that individual personality differences play a critical role in stress management. Thus, some principals may find conflict, work expectations, deadlines, and the like to be devastating. As the pressures accumulate, they eventually reach a point where they can no longer cope. By contrast, other principals have productive mechanisms to counteract the pressures of work. Some even look forward to conflict as a catalyst for positive change.

Since the mid-1970s, changes in the world and in American society have fueled cries that elementary and secondary schools should be restructured. These demands have increased expectations that school leaders should be bold innovators willing to take risks. Yet, the public does not always respond positively when change is actually attempted nor do the cultures and climates of most schools encourage administrators to be adventurous.

In this case, a new principal attempts to curtail the number of expulsions in her school caused by substance abuse. Based on the recommendation of an ad hoc committee, she develops an in-school suspension program. Some parents object, saying that students caught using drugs should not be permitted to remain in school. These criticisms become much more intense when two students who are part of the in-school suspension program are arrested for selling cocaine in the school's parking lot.

KEY AREAS FOR REFLECTION

1. Career decisions
2. Readiness for the principalship
3. Job satisfaction
4. Control of pupil conduct
5. Job-related stress
6. Principal and staff relationships
7. Political dimensions of controversial decisions

THE CASE

"Are you crazy?" Lowell Tatum asked his wife as the two were having dinner at their favorite restaurant in San Francisco. "Now let me get this straight. You want to leave your nice job as coordinator of English Education to become a high school principal? You ought to think about this—maybe for two or three years!"

Patricia Tatum has faced challenges all of her life, and with very few exceptions, she usually comes out the winner. Born in Los Angeles in a low-income family, she is the oldest of six children. Neither of her parents graduated from high school, but they provided a warm, caring family environment. They also set high expectations for their children.

All through school, Patricia was a good student and a leader. Her interests were diversified. She was an athlete (track), a cheerleader, and president of the student council. When she graduated from high school, she ranked sixth in a class of 389. She received an academic scholarship to attend a private university, which was only about 20 miles from her home. Even though she maintained two part-time jobs, she finished her degree in four years and graduated cum laude.

One of Pat's part-time jobs during college was as a teacher's aide in a parochial elementary school. It was there that she first developed thoughts of becoming a teacher. She found it tremendously satisfying to work with the students. However, she was not majoring in education, and she still had some desire to fulfill her original career goal—to become a lawyer. Pat had been accepted by both law schools to which she applied. As the end of her undergraduate experience drew near, she became increasingly undecided about her future. Six weeks after receiving her B.A. degree in English, she made her choice.

Forgoing law school, Pat accepted a position as a copy editor with a small publishing firm and enrolled in a master's program that would qualify her to be licensed as a high school English teacher. Over the two years it took to complete the degree, she occasionally thought about law school, but when she did her student teaching, she once again experienced the joy of being with students. Her doubts disappeared.

While pursuing her master's degree, Pat met Lowell Tatum. He too was a graduate student completing a master's in business administration. Lowell was a stockbroker in Los Angeles. When they completed their degrees, they got married.

Although their intention was to stay in the Los Angeles area, Lowell's employer offered him a promotion that necessitated a transfer to San Francisco. Pat encouraged him to take the job. Within weeks after relocating, Pat secured a teaching position at a suburban high school.

Four years after moving to San Francisco, Pat and Lowell had their first child. Lowell convinced her to take a leave of absence from teaching for one year so she could spend time with the child. The one-year absence stretched into six years, and Pat gave birth to a second child. All during this period, she had been taking courses at a local university. By the time the second child was one year old, she had accumulated quite a few graduate credits. Encouraged by several of her professors, she enrolled in a doctoral program.

At age 34, Pat found herself with two children, a successful husband, a doctorate in school administration, and intense desire to return to work. Her husband's career had prospered, and from a financial perspective, there certainly was no need for her to get a job. But her desire to develop her own career was rather strong.

Dr. Tatum's first attempts at returning to education involved applying for assistant principalships. She was stunned one afternoon when she received a telephone call from the school district where she had been previously employed asking her if she was interested in the position of coordinator of English for the entire system. She had not even thought about working in a central office, and she was flattered by the inquiry. She agreed to become an applicant and was even more surprised when she got the job.

At first her new position was exciting; it certainly was a change from what she had been doing for the last five or six years. But each time she visited one of the schools, Dr. Tatum realized how much she missed the excitement and action related to working with students. Toward the end of her first year as a coordinator, she talked to her supervisor, Dr. Ernesto Javier, about her future. The two had developed a positive relationship, and she was comfortable being candid with him.

"I don't want you to think I'm unhappy, because I'm not," she told him. "It's just that I miss being with students. I can't explain it."

Dr. Javier was an experienced administrator, having been a principal for 14 years prior to accepting his present position as associate superintendent for instruction.

"What are you trying to say? Do you want to go back into the classroom?"

"I think what I would really like is to work as a building-level administrator," she answered. "That's what I intended to do when I finished my doctorate, but when this opportunity came along, I didn't want to pass it up."

Dr. Javier shook his head indicating that he understood. He looked at Dr. Tatum and said, "I don't think we will have any assistant principalships open for next year. I will help you move to another district if that is what you really want. Personally, I hope you stay here and continue the fine job you are doing."

Dr. Tatum left the meeting feeling good about the fact that Dr. Javier was supportive. She did not tell her husband about the conversation and decided to wait until school was out in about three weeks before deciding whether to look for a new position.

About two weeks after their meeting, Dr. Javier called Dr. Tatum and asked to continue their discussion. They agreed to get together that afternoon.

"Pat, Mr. Malovidge at Western Valley High School just submitted his resignation. He is moving to Seattle," Dr. Javier told her. "I talked to the superintendent about this matter just this morning, and we have decided to name an interim principal. It's pretty late in the year to be conducting a search. To get right to the point, I am offering the job to you."

Dr. Tatum was caught off guard. She struggled to respond.

"Why me?" she finally asked. "Aren't there assistant principals there that are willing to take the job?"

"That's the problem. Two of them want the job very badly. I think picking one over the other would be a mistake. And besides, I don't think either one could do as good a job as you."

Dr. Tatum indicated that she wanted two or three days to think it over. He told her she had 48 hours to give him an answer.

"Before I leave, would you explain the implications of this being an interim position," she requested.

"Certainly. If the person does well, there is a good chance he or she could stay on as the regular principal. In any event, we will conduct a search around December or January, but obviously if you take the job and all goes well, you have the inside track."

After leaving Dr. Javier's office, Dr. Tatum called her husband and suggested that they have dinner at their favorite restaurant. She told him to be prepared for a surprise.

The prospect of his wife becoming a high school principal was disconcerting to Lowell Tatum. Although he supported her career, he worried that this particular position would be too stressful. Yet, he knew that he could never dissuade her if she already had made her decision. And she had.

Western Valley High School has 2,308 students in grades 9 through 12. The school's population is diverse, both from a standpoint of economics as well as race. Most students come from middle-class homes and about 40 percent of the graduates enroll in four-year institutions of higher education.

As the district's coordinator of English, Dr. Tatum had been to Western Valley High School about a dozen times in the previous year. She was most acquainted with the teachers in the English department. Mr. Malovidge, the principal, delegated instructional matters to one of his assistants so she had only met him once or twice.

Of the three assistant principals at the school, two, Joe Howard and Bill Fine, were not especially pleased that Dr. Tatum had been named interim principal. Both had substantially more experience than she, and neither had ever worked under the direct supervision of a female. The third assistant principal, Sally Farmer, was approximately Dr. Tatum's age, and she had been in her position for just two years. She made no comments about Dr. Tatum's appointment, but she actually was relieved that neither of the other two assistants had been selected.

In her first meetings with the assistant principals, Dr. Tatum outlined her aspirations and expectations. She stressed that she wanted the four of them to function as a team and asked for their input as to how the administrative assignments should be divided. Toward the end of July, the four reached agreement that Dr. Tatum and Ms. Farmer would devote much of their time to instructional programs. Mr. Howard would be responsible for many of the management functions, such as food services, scheduling, budgets, and the like. Mr. Fine agreed to supervise extracurricular programs, including athletics. No one wanted to assume the task of overseeing student discipline; hence, Dr. Tatum decided that all four of them would share responsibility in this area.

Over the course of the first four months, it became abundantly clear that Dr. Tatum was not going to be able to devote most of her time to instructional programs. The magnitude of unexpected problems overwhelmed her when school started in the fall. It seemed that regardless of how well she scheduled her time, there were always emergencies that required attention.

The most perplexing problem facing Dr. Tatum was student use of illegal drugs and alcohol. Based on visits to the school last year, she knew that the problem existed but underestimated its level. Even with four administrators attending to discipline problems, Dr. Tatum was devoting an inordinate amount of her time to this one task. All the serious problems ended up on her doorstep.

Dr. Tatum's predecessor had taken a hard line toward substance abuse. As a result, Western Valley had one of the highest expulsion rates among the 11 high schools in the district. The assistant principals were mildly supportive of expelling students caught using illegal drugs because their responsibilities were lessened by not keeping the students in school. Dr. Tatum, by contrast, was more inclined to weigh the consequences for the students.

Over the objections of the assistant principals, Dr. Tatum established a committee to review the school's policies for adjudicating substance abuse infractions. She invited a parent who is a social worker and another who is a psychologist to join four teachers and Mr. Fine on the committee. From mid-November to mid-January, this group mulled over mounds of data. After extensive discussion, the committee voted four to three to recommend the establishment of an in-school suspension program. They argued that first offenders ought not be expelled—staying in school was seen as their best hope for overcoming their problems. Among those not supporting this recommendation was Bill Fine. He contended that without maintaining a hard-line policy the incidence of drug use would actually increase.

Dr. Tatum, however, thought the recommendation had merit, and she decided to discuss the issue with Dr. Javier. He too viewed the recommendation positively, but he told her that it was her decision.

He did offer a caveat, though. "You know we just advertised the vacancy for your job two weeks ago. The superintendent and I think you are doing a good job. Do you really want to stick your neck out and try something like this? Especially at this time?"

Dr. Tatum spent much of the following week weighing the positives and negatives relative to creating an in-school suspension program. She decided to do what she believed was in the best interests of students. She announced her approval of the committee's recommendation.

The program was initiated on March 1. There was little overt opposition. Several teachers commented that it was a good idea, but most said nothing about it—at least to Dr. Tatum. On March 20, Dr. Tatum learned that she had been selected as the school's regular principal.

Through the remainder of that school year, there were few problems with the in-school suspension program. Even Bill Fine was beginning to think that it might work. In early June, Dr. Tatum made the program a permanent part of Western Valley High School.

As the next school year got under way, there was an unusually high number of drug-related discipline cases. By late October, the in-school suspension program was bulging at the seams. For the first time since starting the program, Pat received complaints. One of them came in a letter from a parent:

Dear Dr. Tatum:

It has come to my attention that students who are caught using drugs are being allowed to stay in school. As a parent, I think this sends the wrong message. My wife and I tell our children that using illegal drugs is a serious offense. I'm not sure that your approach to dealing with the problem reinforces our contention. I urge you to discontinue the in-school suspension program.

The in-school suspension program suddenly became a bigger part of Dr. Tatum's life. Not only was she still spending much of her time with discipline-related problems, but also she was having to respond to critics. Bill Fine, who just a few months ago was saying that the concept might work, was now telling everyone that he opposed the in-school suspension program from the start. Joe Howard and Sally Farmer did everything they could to distance themselves from the program. Dr. Tatum's mounting frustration became apparent to her husband.

"Pat, why don't you get out of this job. You don't need the grief. You are a good educator. You're not a social worker or a narcotics detective. At least in your old job you could work in education. As I listen to you now, you sound more like a policewoman than an educator."

Dr. Tatum did not run away from problems. She continued to believe that the in-school suspension program was a good idea. And besides, the other elements of her job were very satisfying. So despite her frustration, she decided to neither leave her job nor do away with the program.

Just days after the students returned in early January from the holiday break, two who were in the in-school suspension program were arrested by undercover police for selling cocaine in the school's parking lot. Dr. Tatum did not even know the police were working near Western Valley High School.

The arrest made the evening news on all of the San Francisco television and radio stations. The next morning the story was carried in the newspaper. In almost all instances, the media coverage included comments about the in-school suspension program.

A reporter on the local television show gave the following lead for his focused story on the student arrests:

In-school suspension at Western Valley. A solution or a part of the problem? Parents and teachers at Western Valley are up in arms over the continued use of an in-school suspension program instituted by Dr. Patricia Tatum, the school's principal. The concerns were heightened by the recent arrests of two students who were placed in this program and were later caught selling drugs in the school's parking lot. Officials in central administration said they are looking into the problem and did not want to comment at this time. Dr. Tatum said she felt that it was critically important to keep these students in school and to offer them assistance and that throwing them out into the streets was not the answer.

The morning after the arrests, Dr. Tatum received a call from the superintendent's secretary requesting her to meet with the superintendent at 3:00 PM that afternoon. Dr. Nicolas Constantine does not meet regularly with principals, and she surmised that this special occasion was probably related to the arrests. During their meeting, the superintendent encouraged Dr. Tatum to set firmer guidelines for allowing students to remain in school. He also pointed out that the school district had an alternative school for high school students.

"There is a way to keep these kids in school without having them stay at Western Valley," he told her.

"But many of them will not go to the alternative school when they are expelled. This issue was examined in detail when we studied the expulsion problem over a year ago," Dr. Tatum explained.

The meeting ended with Dr. Constantine advising her to meet with Dr. Javier as soon as possible. He pointed out that she either had to assure more supervision for the in-school suspension program or she would have to discontinue it.

When Dr. Tatum returned to her office, she met with the assistant principals. They encouraged her to discontinue the program. She was not surprised, but she was disappointed. Beyond the bad publicity and parental complaints, she knew that the program had helped some students. No one seemed willing to talk about the successes. Following the meeting with her administrative team, she called Dr. Javier to arrange an appointment with him.

Dr. Tatum expected Dr. Javier to echo the sentiments previously voiced by the superintendent. He did not. His comments reflected a political orientation toward the problem.

"Listen Pat, these things happen. Most people overreact. This isn't the first time students will get busted for selling drugs in the parking lot, and it certainly won't be the last. But I have to tell you, I don't think you ought to continue the suspension program. You're taking too much heat over this."

Dr. Tatum and her supervisor agreed that she would make a decision about the program in one week. She called the media to report that the program was being reconsidered and that a decision about its future would be made shortly. Two days later, Dr. Tatum received an anonymous letter that was more stinging than any of the previous complaints. The letter con-tended that she was incompetent and being protected because she was an African-American female. The letter was written on Western Valley High School stationery.

For the first time in her brief career as an administrator, Dr. Tatum was doubting whether she had what it took to survive in this difficult job. She knew that other high schools had successful in-school suspension programs. She asked herself if this was attributable to more competent principals. She thought that her detractors might be correct. Maybe she was incompetent.

Dr. Tatum decided to have yet another meeting with Dr. Javier. He thought she was seeing him to announce her decision on the suspension program. Rather, she shared her self-doubts and requested his counsel. Dr. Javier carefully weighed his response.

"Pat, I probably am to blame for getting you into this job. If you are unhappy, maybe you should get out. But if you're considering leaving just because of the in-school suspension issue, I think you're making a mistake. If it's not drug problems, it will be something else. That's the life of a high school principal. If you decide you want out of Western Hills, I'll find you a job back here in our division. I sort of got you into this, and I'll get you out. But only if you look me in the eye and tell me this is what you really want. Don't let all your dreams and your goals go just because of one problem."

THE CHALLENGE

Place yourself in Dr. Tatum's position. What would you do?

KEY ISSUES/QUESTIONS

1. Do you think Dr. Tatum was prepared to become principal of this school? Why or why not?

2. Was it a good idea to appoint a committee to recommend what should be done about substance abuse problems?

3. What is your impression of the behavior of the three assistant principals in this case? Would you have taken any action with regard to their behavior in this case?

4. Do you think that Dr. Tatum's family situation has any bearing on this case? If so, in what respect?

5. What are the advantages and disadvantages of in-school suspension programs? To what extent do they involve risk?

6. Is the size of the school an important consideration in this case? If so, why?

7. What is your impression of Dr. Javier? Do you think his attitude is too casual?

8. What alternatives could Dr. Tatum have pursued instead of the in-school suspension program?

9. Do you think school administrators receive adequate academic preparation to deal with problems such as the one in this case?

10. When Dr. Tatum was working as a subject coordinator in the central office, she was neither satisfied nor dissatisfied. Is this really possible? What evidence do you have to support your response?

11. Do you think that women face special problems in the secondary principalship? Would this problem have been as great if the principal had been a man?

12. Analyze the assignments of the principal and the four assistants. Was it a good idea to divide responsibilities the way they did? Was it advisable to have all four share responsibility for student discipline?

13. Dr. Tatum perceived her administrative staff as a "team." Do you think the four constituted an administrative team? Why or why not?

14. Do you believe that Dr. Tatum had an accurate picture of how her teaching staff felt about the in-school suspension program?

SUGGESTED READINGS

Buscemi, M. (1985). What schools are doing to prevent alcohol and drug abuse. *The School Administrator, 4*(9), 11–14.

Chen, M., & Addi, A. (1992). *Principals' gender and work orientations of male and female teachers.* (ERIC Document Reproduction Service No. ED 346 071).

Daria, R. (1987). Remedy for drug abuse: Honesty, discipline, help for troubled students. *American School Board Journal, 174*(8), 37, 54.

Dryfoos, J. (1991). School-based social and health services for at-risk students. *Urban Education, 26*(1), 118–137.

Erickson, H. (1985). Conflict and the female principal. *Phi Delta Kappan, 67*(4), 288–291.

Farrar, E., & Hampel, R. (1987). Social services in American high schools. *Phi Delta Kappan, 69*(4), 297-303.

Fertman, C., & Toca, O. (1989). A drug and alcohol aftercare service: Linking adolescents, families, and schools. *Journal of Alcohol and Drug Education, 34*(2), 46-53.

Gardner, D., & Buechler, M. (1989). *School based health clinics: Policy memo series no. 4.* (ERIC Document Reproduction Service No. ED 304 750).

Hawley, R. (1987). Schoolchildren and drugs: The fancy that has not passed. *Phi Delta Kappan, 68*(9), K1-K8.

Johnston, J. (1989). High school completion of in-school suspension students. *NASSP Bulletin, 73*(521), 89-95.

Knoff, H. (1983). Solving school discipline problems: Look before you leap. *Clearing House, 57*(4), 155-157.

Knopf, C. (1991). Middle school/junior high in-school suspension programs: Do we have what we need? *NCA Quarterly, 65*(3), 457-459.

Kowalski, T., & Reitzug, U. (1993). *Contemporary school administration: An introduction* (pp. 88-94). New York: Longman (see chapters 11, 14).

Lohrmann, D., & Fors, S. (1988). Can school-based educational programs really be expected to solve the adolescent drug abuse problem? *Journal of Drug Education, 16*(4), 327-339.

Owens, R. (1991). *Organizational behavior in education* (4th ed., pp. 114-122). Boston: Allyn & Bacon.

Raebeck, B. (1993). Beyond the dunce cap. *Executive Educator, 15*(4), 26-28.

Roberts, C., & Schoenlein, J. (1988). A positive student attendance program that works. *American Secondary Education, 17*(2), 28-30.

Rosiak, J. (1987). Effective learning demands drug-free schools. *NASSP Bulletin, 71*(497), 128-133.

Sheppard, M. (1984). Drug abuse prevention education: What is realistic for schools? *Journal of Drug Education, 14*(4), 323-329.

Sullivan, J. (1989). Elements of a successful in-school suspension program. *NASSP Bulletin, 73*(516), 32-38.

Tewell, K. (1989). Collaborative supervision—theory into practice. *NASSP Bulletin, 73*(516), 74-83.

Watson, D., & Bright, A. (1988). So you caught them using drugs: Now what? *Thrust, 17*(3), 34-36.

Zorn, R. (1988). New alternatives to student suspensions for substance abuse. *American Secondary Education, 17*(2), 30-32.

case 21

Let's Not Rap

BACKGROUND INFORMATION

In an ideal world, public school districts and their communities maintain a symbiotic association—a close working relationship that is mutually beneficial. Achievement of this goal is made more difficult, however, when the educational system serves a heterogeneous population. Imagine a school district attempting to build a new high school. Affluent taxpayers may be supportive because the increased taxes will have a minimal effect on their life-style; these individuals may also be inclined to see modern facilities as an important aspect of education. By contrast, other citizens object to higher taxes regardless of the reason.

But strife is not related solely to financial issues. Cultural differences too have been an especially powerful source of conflict in public education. This is becoming increasingly evident as America becomes a more diverse country. In some large school systems, students may speak as many as 50 or 60 different languages. These students also bring unique values and beliefs with them to school each day.

This case focuses on a situation in which two cultural groups articulate different expectations with regard to a decision a high school principal must make. The principal becomes embroiled in controversy when a "rap" group is invited to give a convocation at her school. The purpose of the program is to have the celebrities deliver an antidrug message, but the group's appearance infuriates members of the school's Jewish community who contend that several in the group are anti-Semites. The principal has to decide whether or not to permit the convocation.

In addition to focusing on the relationship between a school and its community, this case shows that serious conflict can emerge for school administrators at almost any time. Here the principal learns of the controversy by listening to a radio talk show—a condition that raises questions about communications.

According to Owens (1991), conflict is a product of incompatible goals. The result usually is "the classic, zero-sum, win-lose situation that is potentially so dysfunctional to organizational life" (p. 244). In the real world of practice, people do not agree on the purposes of education, nor do they show consensus as to how these purposes should be achieved.

Many theorists conclude that conflict within organizations, including schools, is inevitable. Therefore, they feel the challenge for administrators is not to simply eradicate institutional stress; rather, effective management entails trying to use such situations to improve organizational life. That is to say, administrators attempt to use conflict as a catalyst for positive change.

KEY AREAS FOR REFLECTION

1. Conflict in organizations
2. Race relations
3. Relationship of schools and their communities
4. Communication among administrative staff
5. Free speech and public schools

THE CASE

The Principal

Barb Doran is principal of Roosevelt High School, a well-known secondary school located in a major city in Virginia. She has been at Roosevelt for less than two years, but she has already convinced many students, parents, and staff that she is a competent administrator.

After teaching English for 12 years, Ms. Doran became an assistant principal in a middle school. She remained in that position only two years before being promoted to high school principal. Serving five years in that assignment, she decided to seek an even more challenging position. That is when she accepted the post at Roosevelt—a school four times as large as the one in which she previously worked.

The Surprise

Barb Doran was driving home from the airport listening to a radio talk show. She had just returned from a meeting in Orlando, Florida, and it took less than a minute of listening to realize that the topic of that day's program had a great deal to do with her. As she departed the airport parking lot and headed for the interstate she increased the volume. The show's host had just accepted another call.

"I think the principal should have the courage to cancel this program. What good does it do to send an antidrug message if the group sending the message also preaches hate? Our children don't need more mixed messages."

The next caller took a totally different position, "We all know there has been some racial trouble at Roosevelt High. African-American students just don't get treated the same as white students. If a white kid gets caught smoking in the rest room, he gets a slap on the wrist. If a black kid gets caught smoking, he gets a three-day suspension. Now, I think this principal will cancel the "rap" group. And it will be just another indication of how they don't care about minority students at Roosevelt."

Preparing to take a commercial break, the host commented, "For those of you who just tuned in, tonight's topic deals with a new controversy at Roosevelt High. Should the school allow a "rap" group to deliver an antidrug program? Some parents say no because the group has been accused of being anti-Jewish. African-American students and parents say that some are trying to cancel the program just because the entertainers are black. What do you think? Give us a call at 555-1500. I'll be back in a moment to take your calls."

Barb Doran stared at the road ahead. She was aware of the scheduled convocation, but the news of the controversy was a surprise. She whispered to herself, "Why me, Lord?"

The School

Roosevelt is a rather large high school enrolling 2,750 pupils. Most come from middle-class families; however, students from families at all levels of the economic continuum are represented. The student population is also mixed racially, ethnically, and religiously. Nearly 40 percent of the student body is classified as minorities (31 percent African American, 4 percent Asian, 3 percent Hispanic). About 10 percent of the students identify their religion as Judaism, and another 5 percent indicate that they are Muslims.

Many of the minority students attending Roosevelt come from middle- or upper-middle-class families. Over the years, the school has been recognized as a positive model of racial integration. About 60 percent of the graduates enroll in four-year institutions of higher education.

PARA

Since coming to Roosevelt, Ms. Doran has faced several challenges. Perhaps the greatest has been related to growing criticisms about the treatment of African-American students at the school. A group of about 25 parents formed an organization last year called PARA (Parents Advocating Racial Awareness). Leaders told the media that their organization was formed in response to what they believed to be an inadequate awareness of African-American culture by Roosevelt staff. Their specific concerns included the following:

1. The school's curriculum did not adequately address issues of cultural diversity.
2. African-American students were treated more harshly by teachers and administrators imposing disciplinary measures.
3. The school officials had made little effort to allow the African-American community to have input into the operations of the school.

In response to these concerns, Barb attended PARA meetings whenever she could. Over the last year, she felt she was winning their confidence and making strides in reducing their concerns. For example, when she appointed a school advisory council composed of ten parents, ten staff members, and ten students, she gave PARA the option to select two of the parents.

The Problem

Several weeks ago, Reginald Colter, a senior student, made an appointment to see the principal. Reggie is the only African-American student on Roosevelt's Student Council. Reggie's father, an attorney, is one of the leaders of PARA.

"Ms. Doran, I have a great opportunity for our school, and I wanted to see how you felt about it. My cousin is a technician for a "rap" group called The Inner City. They're on a concert tour and scheduled to appear in this city in the near future. One of the things they do while on tour is to present shows at high schools. They do this to discourage students from using drugs. My cousin said he would see if they can do a show here at Roosevelt when they are in town. What do you think?"

"Well, I don't know, Reggie. I've never heard of this group. What type of show do they do?" Ms. Doran asked.

"They do some numbers and talk to the students about how drugs can really mess up their life. These guys know about the streets, and kids listen to them. They won't be doing anything nasty."

Reggie showed her a promotional brochure about the group.

"And the best thing, Ms. Doran, is that the show is free. It won't cost the school a single penny. What do you think? They would need to know as soon as possible."

Ms. Doran indicated that the program might be worthwhile. She thought that it might be a program that would bring positive responses from PARA—and she was always looking for ways to make the group's members feel better about the school. She told Reggie to see Wallace Slater, one of the assistant principals. Mr. Slater was in charge of extracurricular activities and he was the only African-American administrator at the school.

Mr. Slater called two schools where the group had performed, and in both instances, he received positive responses from the administrators. Both schools were in more urban settings, but he figured their program would produce the same results. He told Reggie to contact his cousin to confirm the program. He then wrote a note to Ms. Doran.

Barb,

I talked to Reggie this morning about the convocation idea. I checked this group out with two principals. They said there was no problem. The group is popular and all students should react positively. I've placed it on the schedule for the 23rd of this month. I'll keep you informed.

Wallace

The very day that Ms. Doran left for her committee meeting in Orlando, concerns about the impending appearance of The Inner City at Roosevelt High started to surface. The convocation was announced in the student paper, and the news was greeted enthusiastically by students. Most parents who saw the announcement had never heard of the group. Several, however, had.

About three months ago, a national tabloid did a story on The Inner City, and in the article, several group members were accused of anti-Semitism. The group had recorded a record that had questionable lyrics. While being interviewed by a local television newscaster in New York, two group members stated that the lyrics related to Jews unfairly treating African Americans.

"Hey, all you have to do is look into the ghettos of this city. See who suffers and see who created the situations that exist. These Jewish landlords and business owners have taken from the black community, and they give nothing back," a group member told the reporter.

Another commented, "African Americans have to help themselves. The Jews in this city are not going to solve the problems they created."

Several leaders in the Jewish community had read the article. Thus, the announcement that this group would be appearing at their high school caused alarm. Almost overnight, the issue of the convocation ballooned into a major controversy. The Jewish community was mobilized to stop the convocation. On the other side was PARA. They were demanding that the program be held.

Wallace Slater knew that Barb Doran would be back in several days. He did not want to spoil her trip by calling her. He decided that things could wait until she returned.

Reaching a Decision

As Ms. Doran reached her subdivision, she turned her car around and drove toward the high school. When she entered her office, she immediately focused on the stack of mail on her desk. At the top was a folder containing information about the "rap" group controversy. Among the items in it was a copy of an article from yesterday's newspaper.

Another Controversy Erupts at Roosevelt High

Some parents of Roosevelt High School students are objecting to a scheduled appearance at a school convocation of a rap group called "The Inner

City" next week. The parents contend that at least two members of the group have made anti-Semitic statements to the press and that lyrics in some of their songs are distasteful and not in the best interests of racial harmony. Principal Barb Doran is out of town and not available for comment. Assistant principal Wallace Slater said the group was scheduled to deliver an antidrug message to the student body. He said he was unaware of any controversy surrounding the group before yesterday. Superintendent Paul Tolliver indicated he is looking into the matter and plans to talk with the principal when she returns to her office tomorrow.

She sat at her desk reading the other items in the folder. There were over two dozen phone messages—most relating to the convocation. The one that was most pressing was from the superintendent, Dr. Tolliver. She called him at home.

"Barb, I'm glad you're back," he told the principal after answering the phone. "I suppose by now you know what is going on. What do you know about this 'rap' group?"

"Well, I have to tell you that I was caught by surprise. I know about the convocation, but the controversy has emerged just in the last few days while I was gone. I'm a little surprised that Wallace Slater didn't call me to let me know what was going on."

"I tried to reach you in Orlando this afternoon, but you had already checked out of the hotel. Listen, we really need to make a decision on this. And the sooner, the better. The Jewish community is up in arms, demanding that we cancel the program. This PARA group is all over the media saying that the program better not be canceled. How did we get into this, anyway?"

"Dr. Tolliver, I have to accept responsibility. I had Wallace check the group out, and he got nothing but positive feedback. We have been trying to work with PARA, and just when I think we're making progress, something like this has to come along. I will get to this issue in the morning. You can be assured of that. But let me ask you, do you have any strong feelings one way or the other?"

There was a pause before the superintendent answered. "Barb, let's say this situation were reversed. Let's say it was a Jewish group that had been accused of putting out an anti–African-American message. Would we bring them into the school—even if they were delivering an antidrug message?"

"Are you saying, Dr. Tolliver," asked Ms. Doran, "that I should cancel the program?"

"No, I'm not necessarily saying that. I'm just trying to point out all sides of this issue. I know you just got into town and you may want to talk to some of your staff before making a decision. Whatever you decide, I'll stand with you. I know it's not an easy decision, but it's one that is best made by you and your staff. Try to tell me what you are going to do by midafternoon tomorrow."

Ms. Doran sat at her desk and thought about possible options to resolve the controversy. On the one hand, she believed that schools should be a forum for free speech. She also thought about the potential good that might come from having the group deliver its antidrug message, and she contemplated the positive effects of the convocation with respect to PARA. But on the other hand, she thought of what she would do if she were a Jewish parent. Would she want this group coming into the school? What would happen if they used lyrics or made comments that further infuriated the Jewish community?

The next morning Ms. Doran met with the three assistant principals to discuss the issue. She asked for their input. Mr. Slater suggested that the convocation be held but that part of it should be devoted to a discussion between the group's members and leaders of the Jewish community.

"If this controversy exists, why not discuss it? Shouldn't students hear both sides?" he told the other administrators.

The other two assistant principals held different views. One suggested that the convocation be canceled; the other suggested two convocations—one with the "rap" group and another on racial prejudice. He argued that students could then select which one they would attend.

The meeting ended without a decision. Ms. Doran looked at the clock on the wall in her office. In less than two hours, she had to call Dr. Tolliver.

THE CHALLENGE

Put yourself in Ms. Doran's place. What would you do to resolve this conflict?

KEY ISSUES/QUESTIONS

1. Develop a list of alternatives from which the principal can choose to resolve the conflict. Identify the advantages and disadvantages of each.
2. If you were the principal, what would be your reaction to learning about this problem by listening to a talk radio show?
3. Should schools be a place for free speech? What restriction, if any, would you recommend as a principal?
4. What are the advantages and disadvantages of canceling the program?
5. What do you anticipate will be the repercussions if the program is canceled?
6. What do you anticipate will be the repercussions if the program is not canceled?
7. What are your impressions of Dr. Tolliver, the superintendent? Do you approve of his behavior in this case? What would you have done if you were the superintendent?
8. Can you think of any ways that this conflict can be used to produce positive outcomes?
9. Some administrators contend that the best problems they encounter are those that they create. Do you believe there is ever merit in creating conflict?
10. Why do highly bureaucratic organizations attempt to avoid conflict? Can they ever be successful?
11. What weight would you give to PARA in deciding on a course of action?

12. What might have been done differently to check out the reputation and past record of the "rap" group?

13. Can you develop a policy that might prevent this type of conflict from occurring in the future?

SUGGESTED READINGS

Drake, T. & Roe, W. (1994). *The principalship* (4th ed.). New York: Macmillan (see chapter 7).

Harrington-Lueker, D. (1993). Practicing tolerance. *Executive Educator, 15*(5), 14–19.

Hollen, G. (1984). School assemblies as supplements to classroom learning. *NASSP Bulletin, 68,* 134–135.

Hoy, W., & Forsyth, P. (1986). *Effective supervision: Theory into practice.* New York: Random House (see chapter 7).

Kowalczewski, P. (1982). Race and education: Racism, diversity, and inequality implications for multicultural education. *Oxford Review of Education, 8*(2), 145–161.

Kowalski, T., & Reitzug, U. (1993). *Contemporary school administration: An introduction.* New York: Longman (see chapters 8, 9).

Margolis, H., & Tewel, K. (1988). Resolving conflict with parents: A guide for administrators. *NASSP Bulletin, 72*(506), 26–28.

McLeer, J. (1983). Understanding anti-Semitism. *Curriculum Review, 22,* 99.

Owens, R. (1991). *Organizational behavior in education* (4th ed.). Boston: Allyn & Bacon (see chapter 9).

Pate, G. (1988). Research on reducing prejudice. *Social Education, 52,* 287–289.

Sherman, R. (1990). Intergroup conflict on high school campuses. *Journal of Multicultural Counseling and Development, 18*(1), 11–18.

Stover, D. (1990). The new racism. *American School Board Journal, 177*(6), 14–18.

Stover, D. (1991). Racism redux. *Executive Educator, 13*(12), 35–36.

Valverde, L. (1988a). Principals creating better schools in minority communities. *Education and Urban Society, 2*(4), 319–326.

Valverde, L. (1988b). Principals embracing cultural reality. *Teacher Education & Practice, 4*(1), 47–51.

Zirkel, P., & Gluckman, I. (1983). Stop, don't raise that curtain. *Principal, 62,* 45–46.

We Don't Want the Devil Teaching Spelling

BACKGROUND INFORMATION

Two contemporary issues surface in this case. The first involves teacher autonomy, especially as it relates to professionalism and the corresponding authority to select instructional materials. The second pertains to religiously related objections to curricular content and instruction.

Participatory decision making has emerged from the school-reform debate as a primary consideration for administrators. Principals, for instance, are faced with the dilemma of maintaining control while allowing teachers greater latitude to function as true professionals. As schools become more decentralized, issues that create tensions regarding control versus latitude will become increasingly common. Such conditions also make demarcations between school district and school responsibility more indeterminate. Corwin and Borman (1988) wrote:

> . . . district administrators are held accountable for things they cannot always control. This condition is a product of decentralization processes within formally centralized school districts. School districts are organized officially as hierarchies. Implementing educational policy is legally and politically the responsibility of high-level district administrators. However, in practice only certain decisions are centralized. Many others have been decentralized, and administrators can never fully control such responsibilities. (p. 212)

Thus, when teachers are given freedom to make certain decisions, their actions may spawn questions of responsibility not only between principal and teachers but also between the principal and the central office administrators.

Writing about participative decision making, Owens (1991) described three tests that could serve as a rule of thumb for deciding whether teachers should be participants in certain decisions. These included a test of relevance (i.e., is the decision to be made germane to the teacher's formal role), the test of expertise (i.e., are the teachers competent to make the decisions), and the test of jurisdiction (i.e., does the principal/school have jurisdiction and thus the power to delegate the decision to the teachers). A fourth test is suggested here. It is a test of resources. That is, do the participants have sufficient resources to complete their assignment? Resources may include materials, fiscal support, or even the necessary time required to meet and reach consensus.

One of the central questions in this case relates to the leadership of principals. Even though there are many valid arguments for giving teachers greater control over their work lives, administrators must face the reality that they will likely be held accountable by the school board and general public for organizational decisions. In this particular case, elementary school principals allow a group of teachers, who work in the gifted and talented program, to make recommendations on material purchases directly to an assistant superintendent. Is this going too far in the direction of teacher autonomy? Should a principal remain responsible for materials selection and curriculum? And what responsibility do the assistant superintendent and superintendent have for teacher decisions?

KEY AREAS FOR REFLECTION

1. Teacher professionalism and autonomy in decision making
2. Principal responsibility for controlling instructional decisions
3. Tensions between hierarchical structure and decentralization of decisions
4. Censorship and the schools
5. Public relations and reactions to parental dissatisfaction

THE CASE

"I really like these materials. They would fit in so nicely with what we are trying to accomplish in this program. And besides, these are exactly the type of materials that students today get excited about."

The judgment came from Sandy Oberfeld, a second-grade teacher. She was addressing about 20 of her colleagues in a meeting at Samuels Elementary School. The teachers were evaluating potential materials for a supplemental program provided to meet the needs of gifted and talented elementary students.

"I agree," said Beatrice Sachs. "My children like something different. They have so many toys and gadgets at home, it's hard to motivate them. I think Sorcerer is a novel way to get these children to work independently on their spelling. Unfortunately, we are dealing with a new generation of students—boys and girls who have learned to think and process information by watching television and playing video games."

The elementary school gifted and talented program in Maple Creek School District is clustered in three of the system's 10 elementary schools. The district is located in one of the most affluent communities in suburban Chicago. Per-pupil expenditures are among the highest for any school district in Illinois.

The 21 teachers who work with students enrolled in the gifted and talented program meet after school once every two months to discuss materials, share ideas, and coordinate programming. At this particular meeting, they were discussing a new piece of software called Sorcerer—an instructional game designed to help elementary age children develop spelling skills. Sandy Oberfeld, coordinator of the group, was demonstrating the product. She had seen it at a conference she recently attended, and being quite impressed, she requested a review copy.

The reactions of the teachers were generally positive. Only one in the group, Lucy McNeil, raised a question about possible reactions in the community.

"You know in this day and age," she said, "one is never sure what parents are going to complain about. I'm just concerned that some might find fault with the characters in the software."

None of the others reacted to her comments and Lucy concluded that she was being overly sensitive. The teachers agreed to purchase 63 copies of the product so that each of them would have three copies to use.

Long before teacher empowerment was a popular phrase, administrators in Maple Creek School District gave teachers a great deal of autonomy in selecting instructional materials. When the elementary gifted and talented program was started in the elementary schools in the early 1970s, teachers were given a budget and the freedom to select materials. Initially, the principals in the three schools housing the programs met with the teachers and were members of the decision-making group (i.e., they also voted on purchases, key decisions). But in 1983, the principals stopped meeting with the group. Their schedules and confidence in the teachers led to this decision.

The requisition for the purchase of 63 sets of Sorcerer was transmitted through Sandy directly to the assistant superintendent for instruction, Dr. Wilbur Youngman. This was normal procedure since he had the supervisory responsibility over the budget category from which the materials were purchased and he had general supervisory responsibility for coordinating gifted and talented programs in the district. Neither Dr. Youngman nor any other administrator questioned the request when it was routinely processed.

After the programs were delivered, all 21 teachers used them especially with regard to independent study; they became a popular choice for both in-school and homework assignments. The game is constructed around a system of rewards and punishments given to students based on their spelling performance. Within two months, the program had become one of the most popular in the gifted and talented program.

However, one month after Sorcerer was introduced in the school system, the first complaint against the product was registered. Nancy Tannin, principal at Lakeside Elementary School, received a telephone call from a parent, Mrs. Baker. It was one of those calls that catches a principal completely off guard.

"Miss Tannin, this is Mrs. Baker, Sally's mother. How are you today?"

"Just fine," answered the principal. She vaguely remembered Mrs. Baker whom she met at an open house earlier in the school year. "What can I do for you, Mrs. Baker?"

"Well, I'm calling about a computer program my daughter brought home the other day. She is in the gifted and talented program, and as you know, students who are involved regularly bring home books and other materials provided by the teachers. I became inquisitive because Sally brought home this computer game that she just couldn't leave alone. She was spending hours after school playing the game, and she was so intense. I asked her what it was, and she said Sorcerer. Do you know what I'm talking about?"

The principal had never heard of Sorcerer, and she admitted that fact to Mrs. Baker. She went on to explain that the gifted and talented teachers had their own budget to purchase materials, and since this was a supplemental activity, it was not unusual that principals would not know about it. She then asked Mrs. Baker, "Is there a particular problem with this game?"

"Absolutely. At least there is as I see it. The theme deals with witchcraft and magic. Now I realize that its purpose is to improve spelling skills, but why is it necessary to do so in the context of controversial material? You may think I am overreacting—and maybe I am. But in this day and age, parents have to be especially sensitive about the values and beliefs that others attempt to impose on their children."

Miss Tannin told Mrs. Baker that she would look into the matter and thanked her for calling the issue to her attention. She thought that Mrs. Baker was being overly cautious. Additionally, she had a great deal of confidence that the teachers would not use offensive products. Hence, she did not make Mrs. Baker's complaint a high priority. She would simply inquire about Sorcerer the next time she saw one of the teachers working in the gifted and talented program.

Two days after Mrs. Baker's telephone call, Miss Tannin discussed the complaint with one of the teachers. The teacher reacted with surprise and commented that this program had been highly successful—at least in terms of student usage. Miss Tannin was satisfied and did not pursue the issue further.

Miss Tannin telephoned Mrs. Baker and told her that she had investigated her concern. She then told her that the teachers assured her there was nothing evil or offensive about Sorcerer. Mrs. Baker asked, "Did you look at it?"

"Well, no I did not," Miss Tannin answered. "To be honest, I didn't think it was necessary. Our teachers are competent professionals. I trust them to make good decisions."

Mrs. Baker reacted with a degree of anger. "I don't think it is asking too much of you to look at this product personally. Maybe the teachers are wrong this one time. I don't want to be a nuisance, but I must tell you that you probably have not heard the last of this. So be prepared."

Shortly after this conversation with Mrs. Baker, Miss Tannin telephoned the other two principals in the schools housing the gifted and talented programs, Deloris Gragolis and Mitch Sancheck. She asked them if they had received complaints about Sorcerer. Both affirmed that they had received calls in the past few days, and they added that teachers in their buildings assured them that the program was not offensive. The three principals agreed not to restrict the use of Sorcerer. Additionally, they decided to communicate in writing with the concerned parents, pointing out that the teachers found the material totally suitable and that their children were not required to use the program.

The three principals alerted Dr. Youngman to the situation at their next principals' meeting. This occurred approximately one week after their conference telephone call. Since Dr. Youngman had officially authorized the purchase of the software, they felt he should be apprised of the parental complaints. He simply instructed the principals to monitor the situation.

True to the warning that Mrs. Baker issued to Miss Tannin, the parental objections to Sorcerer did not subside. Rather, they multiplied and became increasingly critical of the principals for not taking action. Just over two weeks after Miss Tannin received the first complaint, a letter to the editor appeared in the local newspaper condemning the use of Sorcerer.

We are parents of elementary school children who participate in the gifted and talented program in the Maple Creek School District. Recently, our children have been exposed to a distasteful and evil set of materials called Sorcerer. These materials are supposed to assist our children with their spelling skills, but in reality, they expose our children to witchcraft and other evil concepts.

The adoption of Sorcerer is yet another example of how our public schools have become a pawn for those who wish to drag our society into the mud. Parents who support our public schools with hard-earned tax dollars should not have to be concerned that positive values taught at home are being eroded by tasteless games in school.

Perhaps the most discouraging element of our complaint is that the school administration appears unwilling to do anything about this situation. Our calls to principals have either been ignored or they have been answered with suggestions that we don't understand the value of such material. As taxpayers and as parents, we urge others to join our protest. Let's keep our schools free of witchcraft, devil worship, and other evil concepts. Call your school board member now!

(The letter to the editor was signed by 46 parents.)

Within the first day after the letter was in the newspaper, superintendent Philip Montgomery received calls from four of the seven school board members. Each wanted to know what this was all about. Since he also was uninformed, Dr. Montgomery told them he would look into the situation and respond later.

Dr. Montgomery summoned Dr. Youngman to his office hoping to get the answers he needed. His assistant shared his limited information on the issue of Sorcerer and assured the superintendent that the principals were carefully monitoring the situation. Not satisfied, Dr. Montgomery asked him to arrange a meeting with the three principals. When contacted, the principals suggested that Mrs. Oberfeld, the coordinating teacher in the gifted and talented program, also attend the meeting.

The next day, the six educators met in the superintendent's conference room. Dr. Montgomery indicated that the school board members wanted to know what this was all about. What are the parents' objections? Why are these materials being used if they are objectionable? Who made the decision to buy the materials in the first place?

"Sorcerer is similar to a popular video game that got some negative publicity recently," explained Mrs. Oberfeld. "At the time we decided to purchase it, we were not aware of this. And even if we were, I'm not sure it would have made a difference. These right-wing groups are always objecting to something. Now that they no longer think that communists are hiding under every desk, they think the devil is running the public schools. The fact of the matter is that this program is highly successful in motivating children to work on their spelling. It is a resource material, so if parents find it objectionable, they should direct their children not to use it. Why should all students be deprived because a group of fundamentalist parents find the software objectionable?"

Dr. Montgomery, who had moved to Maple Creek from another school district just two years ago, turned to the principals and asked them to comment.

Miss Tannin spoke first. "We have a great deal of confidence in Mrs. Oberfeld and all the other teachers who work in the gifted and talented program. Every one of them supported the use of this material. When complaints were registered, we asked the teachers to reexamine Sorcerer. They did, and their support was not shaken."

"But did you look at the material?" the superintendent asked.

The three principals and Dr. Youngman responded that they had not viewed the program. That prompted the superintendent to ask another question.

"Who authorized this purchase?"

Miss Tannin answered, "The teachers recommended buying Sorcerer, and Dr. Youngman has supervisory responsibility over the budget account that was used."

Dr. Youngman reacted. "Well, I approved the purchase, but I think principals are responsible for the materials that are being used in their schools. I'm not the one who decided that principals would no longer meet with the teachers to select materials for the gifted and talented program. My job, quite frankly, is simply to see that there is money in the budget and that the requisition has been processed properly. I don't think any of you want me to be deciding what you are going to use for instructional programs in your schools."

Mrs. Oberfeld was disturbed by what she was hearing. "Before we start blaming each other, we ought to step back and think about what is at issue here. Are we going to allow a group of parents, a small group at that, to dictate what we use in our schools? I think these individuals would like to control every major decision. If they get their way on this, their behavior will be reinforced and they'll be back with some other ridiculous demand. These are persons who promote censorship. They want to control what people read and how they think."

Dr. Montgomery asked for further clarification about the procedure for purchasing materials in the gifted and talented program.

After listening further, he said, "It seems to me that if I were a principal, I would want to have some authority over what was being used in my school. You three seem to have no problem letting others select instructional materials."

Mitch Sancheck responded, "We have a great deal of faith in our teachers. Our system has worked well for ten years, and I think it would be a mistake to change it because of this complaint."

"Well, maybe you are correct. But how do we resolve this issue?" the superintendent asked.

Miss Tannin said, "We're here to carry out policy. Whatever you decide, we'll go along. We're not inflexible."

After about a minute of silence, Dr. Montgomery said to Dr. Youngman, "The four of you continue meeting. I have to leave to attend a luncheon. I'll be back about 3:00 PM. I expect a recommendation to be on my desk. This is not something that will just go away. We have to respond to the complaints more fully."

THE CHALLENGE

Place yourself in Dr. Youngman's position. What would you do? Then place yourself in the position of one of the principals. Do you now have a different perspective of the problem?

KEY ISSUES/QUESTIONS

1. To what degree do issues of teacher autonomy and empowerment presented in this case typify those that are emerging with regard to site-based management?

2. Evaluate the process for purchasing materials for the gifted and talented program in this school district.

3. Do you think that the principals acted responsibly in this case? Evaluate their behavior from the following perspectives: (a) professional responsibility, (b) moral and ethical leadership, and (c) effective management.

4. If you were Dr. Montgomery, whom would you hold responsible for this situation?

5. Assess the argument that the materials should not be removed because students are not required to use them. Is this an adequate response? Why or why not?

6. To what extent do you think the nature of the community is a factor in (a) the problem arising and (b) the type of solution that should be pursued?

7. Do you agree with the superintendent's comment that if he were a principal he would want to control the purchase of instructional materials in his school? Why or why not?

8. If you were Dr. Youngman, what actions would you initiate to prevent problems like this from arising in the future?

9. Do you think most communities will support concepts of teacher empowerment that permit teachers to make most decisions about instruction and the selection of instructional materials? Why or why not?

10. Identify potential legal issues that relate to this case.

11. Assume that the administrators decide to remove Sorcerer from the schools as the parents are demanding. What reaction would you anticipate from the teachers?

12. Assess the teachers' decision making on instructional materials from three perspectives: (a) the relevance of roles to the decisions being made, (b) their knowledge base to make such decisions, and (c) their authority to make such decisions.

13. Assume that the administrators decided to support Mrs. Oberfeld and leave Sorcerer in the schools. What reaction would you anticipate from the school board?

SUGGESTED READINGS

Agee, H. (1993). Preserving intellectual freedom: The principal's role. *ALAN Review, 20*(2), 7-9.

Bailey, G. (1988). Guidelines for improving the textbook/material selection process. *NASSP Bulletin, 72*(515), 87-92.

Corwin, R., & Borman, K. (1988). School as workplace: Structural constraints on administration. In N. Boyan (Ed.), *Handbook of research on educational administration* (pp. 209-237). New York: Longman.

DeRoche, E. (1985). *How administrators solve problems.* Englewood Cliffs, NJ: Prentice-Hall (see chapter 9).

Donelson, K. (1987a). Censorship: Heading off the attack. *Educational Horizons, 65*(4), 167-170.

Donelson, K. (1987b). Six statements/questions from the censors. *Phi Delta Kappan, 69*(3) 208-214.

Fege, A. F. (1993). The tug of war over tolerance. *Educational Leadership, 51*(4), 22-24.

Georgiady, N., & Romano, L. (1987). Censorship—Back to the front burner. *Middle School Journal, 18,* 12-13.

Glen, C. L. (1992). Who should own the schools? *Equity and Choice, 9*(1), 59-63.

Guthrie, J., & Reed, R. (1986). *Educational administration and policy* (pp. 333-343). Englewood Cliffs, NJ: Prentice-Hall.

Jones, J. L. (1993). Targets of the right. *American School Board Journal, 180*(4), 22-29.

Kowalski, T. J., & Reitzug, U. C. (1993). *Contemporary school administration: An introduction.* New York: Longman (see chapter 10).

McCarthy, M. (1988). Curriculum censorship: Values in conflict. *Educational Horizons, 67*(1), 26-34.

McCarthy, M. (1985). Curriculum controversies and the law. *Educational Horizons, 64*(3), 53-55.

Meadows, B. J. (1990). The rewards and risks of shared leadership. *Phi Delta Kappan, 71*(7), 545-548.

Molnar, A. (1993). Fundamental differences? *Educational Leadership, 51*(4), 4-5.

Owens, R. G. (1991). *Organizational behavior in education* (4th ed.). Boston: Allyn & Bacon (see chapter 10).

Pajak, E. (1989). *The central office supervisor of curriculum and instruction.* Boston: Allyn & Bacon (see chapter 11).

Pajak, E., & McAfee, L. (1992). The principal as school leader, curriculum leader. *NASSP Bulletin, 76*(547), 21-30.

Pierard, R. (1987). The new religious right and censorship. *Contemporary Education, 58*(3), 131-137.

Pierard, R. (1983). What's new about the new right. *Contemporary Education, 54*(3), 194-200.

Rowell, C. (1986). Allowing parents to screen textbooks would lead to anarchy in the schools. *Chronicle of Higher Education, 33*(26), 34.

Snyder, K., & Anderson, R. (1986). *Managing productive schools: Toward an ecology* (pp. 333-341). Orlando, FL: Academic Press College Division.

Weil, J. (1988). Dealing with censorship: Policy and procedures. *Education Digest, 53*(5), 23-25.

Zirkel, P., & Gluckman, I. (1986). Objections to curricular material on religious grounds. *NASSP Bulletin, 70*(488), 99-100.

Does Decentralization Lead to Inequities?

BACKGROUND INFORMATION

Although in the early parts of the twentieth century the centralization of authority in public school districts was encouraged by superintendents and school board members infatuated with scientific management, it became even more pervasive during the 1960s and 1970s. During these two decades, schools were required to respond to a multitude of social, political, and legal forces produced in their ecosystems. Consolidation, for example, created fewer but larger school districts; teachers, frustrated by a lack of power, turned to unionization; civil rights legislation resulted in new regulations for schools; and the courts increasingly became the arbiter for disputes in areas such as desegregation and student rights (Kowalski & Reitzug, 1993).

Observing how these environmental demands were affecting public education in the 1960s and 1970s, Tyack (1990) judged that administrators were pushed toward a compliance mentality to protect the interests of their organizations. Fundamental issues such as employing teachers and making placement decisions for special education students took on added importance, and centralized control and an increasing number of district policies emerged as safeguards against litigation. But failing to comprehend this complex situation, many critics continue to assume that superintendents use districtwide policies and rules to protect their own power. If their assumption were true, movement to decentralization would be far less complicated than it really is. In fact, many issues influence school governance, especially in the legal realm, and most encourage a compliance mentality.

In recent years, school reformers have advocated massive transformations in school governance as one means for achieving improvement. Concepts of decentralization, in particular, have been advocated on the basis that they (1) result in a greater sensitivity to specific educational needs within a given community, (2) encourage greater parental participation in governance decisions, and (3) allow teachers greater authority (and thus parameters to function more as true professionals). But in considering ideas such as site-based management, many administrators have had to weigh the potential benefits against the risks associated with lessening central office control over functions where compliance with law is essential. In essence, autonomy and empowerment constitute an approach-avoidance situation for superintendents and school boards.

In this case, a superintendent decentralizes budgets and requires schools to establish school councils. In less than two years, some parents judge that the policy is contributing to disparities in resources and programs among the district's elementary schools. A parent, who happens to be an attorney, questions the legality of the policy on the grounds that it is treating children unequally. In this context, questions are raised about "equality of educational opportunity" and the responsibilities of board members and the superintendent to assure that those opportunities are protected.

KEY AREAS FOR REFLECTION

1. Tensions between centralization and decentralization
2. Legal interpretations of "equal opportunity"
3. Central office interventions in site-based management
4. Revolutionary versus evolutionary change
5. The use of school councils to make important decisions
6. The decentralization of budgets and effects on school spending and programs

THE CASE

The Community

Haver Ridge is the seat of government for Marvin County in central Illinois. With a population of approximately 16,000, the community has experienced moderate growth since the mid-1950s. An industrial park on the edge of town has attracted several new businesses in the past 15 years, the net result being the creation of about 400 new jobs.

Marvin County is predominately rural, with grain farms consuming about 80 percent of all the acreage. Haver Ridge and Fellington are the only two cities in the county, the latter having a population of approximately 10,000. In the past ten years, a new hospital and a municipal airport were built midway between the two cities on the highway that connects them. There are several small towns scattered around the county, but they consist of little more than a grain elevator and a gas station.

Among the largest employers in Haver Ridge are Marvin County Community College and the East Marvin Community School District. Collectively, these institutions employ approximately 850 individuals. The college basically serves residents in three counties, and the enrollment has remained relatively stable since the early 1970s.

The School District

A number of years ago, the elementary and secondary public schools in Marvin County were reorganized into two districts. Their boundaries were established by drawing a line down the center of the county from north to south; and as a result, both districts are quite large geographically. The West Marvin County School District, based in Fellington, has about 1,000 fewer students than the East Marvin County School District. The latter district's central office, high school, middle school, and three of five elementary schools are located in the city of Haver Ridge.

The east district includes seven schools:

School	Grades	Enrollment	Building Description
Haver Ridge High School	9-12	1,275	Modern one-story built in 1978, located on large site with Middle School
Haver Ridge Middle School	7-8	788	Modified open-space, modern one-story built in 1988
Adams Elementary	K-6	675	Modern one-story built in 1982, located adjacent to city park
Clark Elementary	K-6	280	Two-story built in 1950, located in downtown area
Lincoln Elementary	K-6	580	Modern one-story built in 1984, located in large subdivision
Wild Creek Elementary	K-6	256	Two-story built in 1962, located in rural setting
Milltown Elementary	K-6	302	One-story built in 1956, located in rural setting

Although three of the elementary schools, Adams, Clark, and Lincoln are located in Haver Ridge, Clark has many features that set it apart from the other two. Three are especially cogent. First, because Clark is housed in an older facility, the classrooms and special-use areas (e.g., media center) are smaller than those at Lincoln and Adams. Second, Clark is located in the downtown area on a relatively small site; Adams and Lincoln are located on large sites in residential areas. And third, Clark has a stable, experienced staff with the average age being 51; Adams and Lincoln have many younger, less experienced teachers.

The School Board

Twenty years ago, the school board in the East Marvin County School District was dominated by farmers. That condition has changed considerably. Of the seven current board members, only one lives on a farm. The present members are as follows:

Board Member	Occupation	Years on the Board
Delbert Daniels	Loan officer at a local bank	3
Sheila Edell	Housewife (married to a farmer)	10
George Grogan	Dean of instruction, Marvin County Community College	3
Bill Lucas	Owner of the local McDonald's restaurant	7
Victoria Price	English instructor, Marvin County Community College	1
Ned Sustanit	Plant manager, truck trailer factory	5
Joe Wildman	Counselor, West Marvin Community School District.	1

Mr. Lucas is president of the school board.

Unlike many school boards, the members in this district are not divided into factions. Occasionally, votes are not unanimous, but such outcomes are issue-related, not manifestations of philosophical differences. Members respect and like each other. Also somewhat unusual, the board members have been vigorously supported by the teachers' union in their bids for election or reelection. Accordingly, relationships between the school board and the teachers have been quite positive.

The Administration

When a long-term superintendent retired three years ago, the board employed Burton Packard as their new chief executive. Dr. Packard had been working as an assistant superintendent for instruction in a district just 20 miles from Chicago. A mid-career administrator who had acquired a reputation as a strong instructional leader, both as a principal and central office administrator, he impressed the school board members with his enthusiasm and ideas. During his interview, he told the board that he was totally dedicated to creating democratic schools—places where teachers and parents would be equal partners in making critical decisions. Dr. Packard was the unanimous choice of the board.

There are two assistant superintendents in the district. Both have been in their current positions for a number of years. Ryan Fulton, the assistant for instruction, moved to his present position six years ago after having served as principal of Haver Ridge High School for eight years. Jane Westman, the assistant for business, moved to her present position four years ago after having served as principal at Lincoln Elementary for 13 years.

Of the seven principals in the district, two have been employed during Dr. Packard's tenure. Historically, most principals were promoted from within the district. Essential data concerning the principals are as follows:

School	Principal	Age	Years in Position	Prior Position
High School	Mel Hammond	52	18	Asst. principal—same school
Middle School	Dr. Elain Byers	37	2	Asst. principal—another district
Adams	Norene Vidduci	34	2	Asst. principal—another district
Clark	Mary Simpson	58	21	Teacher—same school
Lincoln	Bart Jennings	45	4	Teacher—same school
Milltown	Alex Brown	50	17	Principal—another district
Wild Creek	Betty Stinemyer	41	9	Teacher—same school

The only elementary schools having assistant principals are Adams and Lincoln.

Implementation of Site-Based Management

On his arrival in Haver Ridge, Dr. Packard gave each of the elementary schools one year to plan implementation of site-based management. He made it clear that his primary concerns were that (1) elementary schools have greater freedom in determining instructional priorities, (2) decisions about instructional priorities should be made by school-based councils composed of administrators, teachers, and parents, and (3) instructional priorities reflect the specific needs of students attending each school. He argued that one of the major problems with public education was that teaching in far too many schools continued to be geared toward an imaginary "average" student. He viewed decentralization as a necessary structure to assure that curriculum and instruction would become more targeted to individual student and specific community needs.

To provide necessary resources to achieve the stated goals, the district's instructional budgets were decentralized. Each principal was given nearly complete control over a school budget. Provided that neither laws nor policies were violated, principals were given the authority to allocate funds as they saw fit. This included decisions about personnel as well as supplies and equipment.

The two rural schools, Milltown and Wild Creek, had long-standing traditions of parental involvement. Each had a very active parent-teacher association; therefore, transition to site-based management was viewed by the principals as the next logical step to democratic governance. The principals at Adams and Lincoln were enthusiastic about Dr. Packard's agenda for change because they were both strong advocates of teacher empowerment. At Clark, however, the principal and teachers were rather passive about moving to site-based management. Mrs. Simpson was candid with the superintendent about sentiments in her building, but she assured him that they would work hard to see the program was implemented.

Perhaps the most avid supporters of Dr. Packard's plan were the members of the school board. They praised his efforts publicly and enlisted support from prominent community leaders.

As Dr. Packard completed his first year as superintendent, he required each principal to submit a decentralization plan. Included were (1) information about the composition of the school's council, (2) information about the methods for selecting members, and (3) details about fiscal control of the decentralized budget. The superintendent believed that school principals had to be given a great deal of latitude if decentralization was to be successful. His greatest concern was that principals would judge the initiative to be a public relations ploy. So despite the fact that he did not agree with some elements of the proposals, he decided not to alter them.

The First Two Years of the Program

The decentralization process has been in place for nearly two full school years. But even in that short period of time, there have been noticeable differences in the directions pursued by the schools. For example, Adams Elementary has made cooperative learning a centerpiece of their instructional program. Many of their resources have been used for teacher staff development and the purchase of microcomputers and materials to facilitate implementation.

A summary of the decentralization process in the elementary schools is provided below:

School	Council Membership	Primary Foci
Adams	6 teachers, 6 parents, principal	Cooperative learning; investment in computers, staff development, and instructional materials
Clark	6 teachers, 4 parents, principal	Traditional programming; emphasis on remedial programs; investment in materials, supplemental texts
Lincoln	4 teachers, 8 parents, principal	High technology environment; emphasis on increasing time on task and high levels of individualized instruction; investment largely in technology and revamping of media center
Milltown	4 teachers, 4 parents, principal	Traditional programming; investment in computers and instructional materials

Wild Creek   4 teachers, 4 parents,   Mastery of learning; investment in
                  principal   computers, staff development and
                                       consultants

The functions of the school councils varied across the seven schools. At Adams
and Lincoln, the councils met at least twice each month. Frequently, teachers
and parents made recommendations. This was also true, but to a lesser degree,
at Milltown and Wild Creek. At Clark, Mrs. Simpson had encouraged others to
make recommendations, but none of the teachers or parents ever did. She found
herself having to make all of the recommendations. Over the two years, the
council meetings (which were held once each month) had become routine. The
principal would make a recommendation, and everyone present would vote to
support it. Clark Elementary also had the poorest record of parental attendance.
Mrs. Simpson felt fortunate if two of the four attended a given meeting. Expanding resources for remedial work had become the highest priority at Clark.

The Problem

Each year, students in grades 2, 4, and 6 are required to take standardized achievement tests. Students receive individual results and schools receive an average score
for each grade level. For at least the last seven years, Lincoln has had the highest average test scores in the district—Clark has had the lowest. Listed below
are the results for sixth-grade students for the past three years. Years two and
three are years under the decentralization plan.

School	*Average Test Scores*			*Rank in District*		
	Yr 1	*Yr 2*	*Yr 3*	*Yr 1*	*Yr 2*	*Yr 3*
Adams	57.3	58.2	58.3	2	2	2
Clark	48.7	48.3	48.1	5	5	5
Lincoln	59.2	60.1	61.2	1	1	1
Milltown	55.2	55.3	55.3	3	4	4
Wild Creek	54.6	55.4	55.7	4	3	3

In past years, the local newspaper paid little attention to these scores. But
given the interest in Dr. Packard's decentralization program, the editor decided
to do a story linking test scores with site-based management. The reporter who
wrote the story suggested that increases at Lincoln may be the result of the
school's investment in technology. Additionally, her articles hinted that the poor
performance of Clark's students may be affected by the fact that so much attention is being given to remedial work.

Dr. Packard reacted immediately to the articles. He argued that it was far
too early to draw conclusions about decisions being made in the schools or about
student performance on statewide achievement tests. He also expressed confidence that Principal Simpson was doing a good job of implementing site-based

management. Perhaps most importantly, he explained that many factors affected student performance on standardized tests, including a student's family life and economic status.

The newspaper accurately reported Dr. Packard's comments. The reporter also interviewed several school board members, and noted that they uniformly agreed with the superintendent's explanation. Mr. Lucas, board president, was quoted as saying that he was generally pleased with the test results. He also expressed optimism that the scores would improve even more once the benefits of site-based management were realized.

Several parents of Clark students, however, expressed different opinions. The most vocal was Anthony Bacon, an attorney and director of employee relations at the community college. Although he was concerned that students at Clark were scoring lower than their peers in the district, he was far more troubled by what he learned in the newspaper articles about site-based management. In particular, he disagreed that individual elementary schools ought to be given so much discretion in making programmatic and budgetary decisions. He decided to attend a school board meeting and voice his misgivings personally. He called Dr. Packard's secretary and asked to speak at the April meeting, which was scheduled approximately one week after the series of articles appeared.

Mr. Bacon knew only two of the school board members, who were fellow employees at the community college, Dr. Grogan and Mrs. Price. He had never met Dr. Packard. At the meeting, he read a prepared statement:

Ladies and gentlemen, Dr. Packard, and members of the school staff, I appear here today as a concerned parent. I have two children who attend Clark Elementary School. When we moved to this community four years ago, my wife and I chose to buy an older home in the downtown area. We did so primarily because we enjoy the challenge of remodeling. I must admit we were concerned at first about our children attending Clark Elementary. Our concern was based solely on the fact that the other elementary schools in the district were newer facilities. I called the superintendent before we made a final decision about purchasing the house, and he assured me that programmatically, all the elementary schools offered the same opportunities to students. And as far as I know, that information was correct; however, the condition changed two years ago when this decentralization plan was put into effect. And that is essentially why I am here today. I realize that there may be many benefits related to decentralizing governance—but I also know that there are potential pitfalls. I have not objected previously because I did not realize the magnitude to which critical decisions have been delegated to school committees. In reading the recent series of newspaper articles, I was shocked to discover that elementary schools had been given so much freedom. Those articles led me to ask additional questions. This evening I am here to share several specific concerns. First, it is obvious to me that the school councils do not function the same across the five elementary schools. In checking with one of the parents on the Clark Council, I was told that their role was essentially to approve decisions already made by the principal. But at Lincoln, the parents and teachers assume a broader role—one that permits them to suggest initiatives and the like. For example, one of the parents on the Lincoln Council is Mary Burgess, the director of instructional technology at our college. She played a pivotal role in getting the school to invest in technology. Second and more importantly, I argue that the level of decentralization put in place will not only fail to narrow gaps in resources and student performance, it will actually serve to widen them. Each school receives essentially the same amount of resources per student. But the needs of students across the elementary schools are not the same. And this reality is the circumstance that drives inequities in the program. The principal at Clark feels obligated to devote more resources to remedial activities than would be true at other schools. But should this result in the students there having less in the way of technology? And if Mrs. Burgess can share her expertise to improve Lincoln, shouldn't other schools also have access to her knowledge? At what point do board members and central office administration intervene when local leadership places students in a given school at a disadvantage? Are you really meeting your responsibilities by delegating so much authority to school principals and councils? Where would we be today if the federal government in the 1960s refused to intervene when some southern states were still segregating their universities? In essence, the school board and superintendent are like the federal government. You have the duty to see that all students receive equal access to a quality education. If schools are allowed to pursue their own course, we are likely to see even more dramatic disparities in future years. I respectfully request that you reexamine your decentralization plan.

The board members were all taking notes, and after Mr. Bacon finished reading his statement, the president thanked him for being candid. He then turned to Dr. Packard and asked if he had a response to Mr. Bacon's comments. The superintendent indicated that he would look into the matter and provide a reply in the next two weeks.

Several of the school board members were affected by the queries raised by Mr. Bacon. They telephoned Dr. Packard in the days following the meeting and suggested that he not take this matter lightly. They prompted him to be especially thorough in preparing a response.

One week after the April board meeting, the board president requested a special executive session and asked Dr. Packard and the school district's attorney to be present. The purpose was to have Dr. Packard share his reply to Mr. Bacon before it was issued. At the meeting, the superintendent outlined the following points:

1. Mr. Bacon's contention about the operations of the councils was partially correct. However, differences in procedures and roles were not by design. Mrs. Simpson, the principal at Clark, had tried repeatedly to get stronger parental involvement in her school's council. The parents and teachers are not prevented from making recommendations—to date, they have chosen not to do so.

2. When the council was first formed at Clark, Mr. Bacon was issued an invitation to be a parental representative, but he declined. He said that his schedule would not permit him to participate at an appropriate level.

3. It was true that the other schools had invested more heavily in computers and other technology over the past two years than had Clark. It was also true that each school receives the same per-pupil amount for instructional supplies and equipment.

4. The decision to invest heavily in remedial materials at Clark was supported by all the members of the school's council. Mrs. Simpson had made the recommendation, but she explained that she talked to most of her teachers before she did so.

5. There is evidence that the number of students enrolled at Clark who are from low-income families is increasing. For example, the number of free and reduced lunches increased by approximately 7 percent over the past two years. This factor, more than any other, may be responsible for slight declines in test scores. And even if this is not the reason, it is most unlikely that decisions related to decentralization are responsible.

6. All students in the school district are receiving the same basic education that is prescribed by the state department of education. If Mr. Bacon's arguments were taken at face value, virtually every school district with more than one elementary school would have some inequities.

In conclusion, Dr. Packard recommended that the board not alter its policies on decentralization, including its policy on budgetary allocations. He did say, however, that Mrs. Simpson would be directed to allocate at least 25 percent of next year's equipment and supply funds to purchase additional computers and/or software for her school. The board's attorney indicated that, in his opinion, Dr. Packard had prepared an appropriate response. The board directed Dr. Packard to put these points in a letter and send it to Mr. Bacon.

After receiving the official response from the superintendent, Mr. Bacon said the following in a telephone call to Dr. Grogan, one of the school board members.

"I don't think the superintendent's perception of equal opportunity is correct. To assume that your only responsibility is to see that all schools provide the minimum curriculum prescribed by the state is myopic. If students at Lincoln spend eight hours a week working with computers, and students at Clark spend only two, is that equity? Just for a moment, George, forget about the legal dimensions of this issue. Answer the question as a professional. You are an educator and administrator. Is it ethical or moral to provide these opportunities to some students solely because they are from higher-income families and attend certain schools?"

Dr. Grogan responded, "Our attorney has looked at Dr. Packard's response, and he feels the superintendent is correct about the equity issue. Schools across this country are going to site-based management. If there were serious legal problems, do you think this would be occurring?"

Dr. Grogan urged Mr. Bacon to contact the superintendent directly. He suggested that their conversation could produce some adjustments to the way decentralization was being handled.

Mr. Bacon met with the superintendent the following day and told him he was still concerned about the issues of equity he raised at the school board meeting.

Dr. Packard responded, "The differences among our schools are not that great. For example, the number of computers at Milltown is essentially the same as it is at Clark. There are many ways to educate children. Computers are not the only answer, nor are they the only measure of educational opportunity. I argue that our program is successful. If schools did not have the opportunity to make decisions based on specific school needs, Clark may not have been appropriately responsive to the need for more remedial work. Schools can never be totally equal—nor should they be. I believe schools are most effective when they are responsive to the real needs of their clients."

The conversation went on for about an hour, but it did little to diminish the differences between the two men. Over the course of the next few weeks, Mr. Bacon enlisted the support of five other families in the Clark community to support his position. In mid-May, this group retained an attorney from a prominent law firm in the state capital, and they prepared to officially challenge the school district's decentralization plan. Via letter, Dr. Packard and the school board president were notified that unless corrective actions were taken to resolve the complaints outlined by Mr. Bacon prior to the next school year, a suit would be filed claiming that the current governance system has, de facto, exacerbated conditions of inequality among the district's elementary schools.

The board members became even more concerned, but they did not want to draw back from their commitment just because a few families were unhappy. The day after receiving the letter, the board president, Mr. Lucas, again summoned the board, Dr. Packard, and the school attorney to an executive session. The attorney was asked what he thought would happen if this matter was litigated.

He responded, "As I told you before, I think that Dr. Packard's response is reasonable. I cannot predict how a lawsuit would turn out. If you are asking me if we can mount a reasonable defense, my answer is yes. But as you know, litigation can be expensive, time consuming, and there is never any guarantee."

After deliberating, the board members asked Dr. Packard to again reconsider the matter. At least two of them indicated that they thought Mr. Bacon was raising some very good points. They directed the superintendent to check with the state school boards' association and other agencies to see if there were similar problems in other districts. Dr. Packard was told to prepare a written report by the June board meeting.

THE CHALLENGE

Assume the role of Dr. Packard. What would you do at this point?

KEY ISSUES/QUESTIONS

1. What are the advantages and disadvantages of Dr. Packard deciding to stand firm and not alter the decentralization program?

2. Do you think that the superintendent's decision to require Clark Elementary to allocate at least 25 percent of next year's equipment and supply budget to technology is a sufficient response?

3. Assess the superintendent's position regarding intervention in decisions made by school councils.

4. Based on what you read, do you think the superintendent provided sufficient information regarding goals of the decentralization program?

5. Do you agree that achievement test scores over the past two years probably do not reflect the effects of decentralization?

6. Discuss the legal dimensions of Mr. Bacon's contention that a school district does not meet its obligations to provide equal educational opportunity by simply assuring that all students receive the minimum education prescribed by the state.

7. What is your assessment of Mrs. Simpson? Can you judge whether she is an effective principal?

8. Is it typically more difficult to get parental involvement in low-income communities? Why or why not?

9. Dr. Packard pointed out that Milltown Elementary had about the same number of computers as Clark Elementary. Is this point cogent? Why or why not?

10. Reflect on the decision the superintendent must make from the following perspectives: (a) legal, (b) economic, (c) educational, (d) moral, (e) ethical, and (f) political.

11. The community context, the administrative staff, and school board members are described in the case. To what extent do these factors influence your thinking with regard to what the superintendent should do?

12. Assume that Dr. Packard had taken a different approach to decentralization—one in which (a) all schools are required to have uniform councils (size and representation), (b) budgets are not to be totally decentralized, and (c) the change process is designed to be gradual and evolutionary. Do you think the outcomes would have been better? Worse?

13. Would the problem addressed by Mr. Bacon be alleviated if the school district had an "in-district choice" program (i.e., a program allowing parents to select any elementary school in the district)?

14. Do inequities exist among elementary schools in most public school districts, as suggested by Dr. Packard?

15. The decentralization plan in this district was approved by the board and made official policy. To what extent is this fact relevant to the challenge being presented by Mr. Bacon?

16. Assess the importance of the following two factors in this case: (a) the nature of the teaching staff at Clark Elementary; (b) the nature of the school facility and site at Clark Elementary.

17. Mr. Bacon was invited to serve on the Clark council but declined. Does this fact have any bearing on his challenge?

SUGGESTED READINGS

Baldwin, G. H. (1990). Collective negotiations and school site management. *West's Education Law Reporter, 58*(4), 1075-1083.

Baldwin, G. H. (1993). *School site management and school restructuring.* (ERIC Reproduction Services Document No. ED 355 633).

Bray, M. (1991). Centralization versus decentralization in educational administration: Regional issues. *Educational Policy, 5*(4), 371-385.

Brick, B. H. (1993). Changing concepts of equal educational opportunity: A comparison of the views of Thomas Jefferson, Horace Mann, and John Dewey. *Thresholds in Education, 19*(1-2), 2-8.

Burrup, P. E., Brimley, V., & Garfield, R. R. (1993). *Financing education in a climate of change* (5th ed., pp 8-16). Boston: Allyn & Bacon (see chapter 3).

Doyle, D. P. (1984). American schools and the future of local control. *Public Interest,* (77), 77-95.

Dunklee, D. R. (1990). Site-based management: Implications for risk management. *School Business Affairs, 56*(6), 24-27.

Hughes, L. W. (1993). School-based management, decentralization, and citizen control—A perspective. *Journal of School Leadership, 3*(1), 40-44.

Jewell, R. W. (1993). *The case against equal spending in the Missouri Public Schools.* (ERIC Reproduction Services Document No. ED 358 524).

Knab, D. (1991-92). Steps on the way to a democratic school constitution. *European Education, 23*(4), 74-84.

Kowalski, T. J., & Reitzug, U. C. (1993). *Contemporary school administration: An introduction.* New York: Longman (see chapters 12, 13, 16).

Lifton, F. B. (1992). The legal tangle of shared governance. *School Administrator, 49*(1), 16-19.

Mitchell, J. K., & Poston, W. K. (1992). The equity audit in school reform: Three case studies of educational disparity and incongruity. *International Journal of Educational Reform, 1*(3), 242-247.

Romanish, B. (1991). Teacher empowerment: The litmus test of school restructuring. *Social Science Record, 28*(1), 55-69.

Sharp, W. L. (1993). *School spending: Is there a relationship between spending and student achievement? A correlation study of Illinois schools.* (ERIC Reproduction Services Document No. ED 357 503).

Thomas, R. (1991). *An analysis of site-based management of a large urban school district.* (ERIC Reproduction Services Document No. ED 323 325).

Thompson, D. C., Wood, R. C., & Honeyman, D. S. (1994). *Fiscal leadership for schools: Concepts and practices* (pp. 56–60). New York: Longman.

Tyack, D. (1990). Restructuring in historical perspective: Tinkering towards utopia. *Teachers College Record, 92*(2), 170–191.

Wohlstetter, P. (1990). *Experimenting with decentralization: The politics of change.* (ERIC Reproduction Services Document No. ED 337 861).

Subject Index

This index is designed to assist you in locating subject areas in the cases. The subjects listed here include both major and minor topics included in the cases.

Topic	Relevant Cases
Administrator-Teacher Relationships	2, 4, 6, 7, 9, 10, 12, 16, 17, 18
Assistant Principals	5, 9, 12, 20, 21
Assistant Superintendents/Central Office	1, 2, 5, 6, 7, 9, 11, 14, 16, 20, 22, 23
Budgeting, Fiscal Issues	6, 17, 23
Business Manager	6, 11, 17
Career Development	5, 7, 11, 13, 14, 16, 20
Change Process	1, 6, 7, 8, 9, 16, 19, 20, 23
Communication Problems	1, 4, 5, 7, 8, 9, 11, 13, 14, 15, 16, 18, 19, 20, 22, 23
Community Relations (see Public Relations)	
Curriculum and Instruction	1, 3, 6, 7, 8, 10, 17, 18, 21, 22, 23
Decision-Making Procedures	5, 6, 7, 8, 9, 11, 17, 18, 19, 20, 21, 22, 23
Educational Outcomes	1, 10, 18, 19, 20, 21, 22
Elementary Schools	1, 7, 8, 17, 18, 22, 23